The WoodenBoat Series

PAINTING & VARNISHING

The WoodenBoat Series

PAINTING & VARNISHING

Series Editor, Peter H. Spectre

Text design by Richard Gorski and Nina Kennedy; cover design
by Richard Gorski; cover photograph by Benjamin Mendlowitz

Published by WoodenBoat Publications
P.O. Box 78, Naskeag Road
Brooklin, ME 04616-0078

Library of Congress Cataloging-in-Publication Data
Painting & Varnishing / editor, Peter H. Spectre.
    p.   cm. — (The WoodenBoat series)
    Articles from WoodenBoat magazine.
    ISBN 0–937822–33–7 (alk. paper)
    1. Wooden boats—Maintenance and repair.
        2. Boats and boating—Painting.
        3. Varnish and varnishing.
        I. Spectre, Peter H. II. WoodenBoat. III. Series.
VM322.P35 1995   95–39890
623.8'44—dc20

Introduction

The all-encompassing word for the final coats of sealers, oils, paints, and varnishes on a wooden boat is "finish," and it isn't called that for nothing. Coating the various surfaces, inside and out, is the last act, the culmination, of a long process of construction, repair, or maintenance. The wood- and metalworking has been done. The surfaces are prepared. The finish is applied. The job is finished.

It seems simple enough — what could it take? A brush, a bucket of paint or varnish, a happy Saturday afternoon slapping it on while in the background on the radio, the one with the bent shirt hanger for an antenna, the Red Sox duke it out with the Yankees.

Dry in the morning, congratulations at noon, sailing in the afternoon, nothing to worry about for a long, long time.

Right. And Scrooge McDuck is buried in Grant's Tomb.

The truth of the matter is that such a seemingly simple act — spreading a fluid on a surface — can be quite complicated, especially in the modern era with so many chemical concoctions to choose from and so many ways to apply them. This is a complex subject, not a simple subject made needlessly complex.

There is an art to painting and varnishing — a science, too — and the key to both comes from direct, personal experience and advice from others, most preferably experts. The former, the experience, you can get on your own; the latter, advice from experts, you can get right here in this book. Every one of our authors, all dedicated wooden boat enthusiasts, has been there and back.

Their topics are endless and their advice doesn't quit. Scraping and sanding. Filling and sealing. Dusting and cleaning. Choosing a brush. Rolling, tipping, brushing, touching up, recoating. One-part and two-part paints and varnishes. Working in cool climates, hot climates, humid weather, in the shade, under the sun. Cleaning and storing the tools. Topside paints, bottom paints, the boottop, planning a color scheme, solvents, applicators, maintenance schedules, aiming for the long haul, the short haul, confronting special situations.... You name it.

Perhaps the most interesting aspect of our authors' advice is the variety of it. Some favor one technique, others another. Some seem monomaniacal on certain subjects. Others have tried, and recommend, several methods and materials for the same application. In a way, that may seem like conflicting advice, but when you think about it, it is not. As in all aspects of boating, we are individuals looking for options, not scribed-in-stone rules.

Generally speaking, there are two approaches to painting and varnishing that are discussed in this book, and one that is not. The first is the utilitarian approach for a lasting, utilitarian finish and a fine-looking boat. The second is the all-stops-pulled-out approach for a gold-plated finish and an exceptional, award-winning craft. Think of them as different in the way a boat is different from a yacht. Each has its place; each has its enthusiasts; each will make you proud. Not discussed, however, is the slapdash approach — the one that produces an acceptable-looking finish that lasts for fifteen minutes after the boat is launched and peels, flakes, bubbles, and creeps forever after.

But there is one thing to keep in mind. The finish on a boat is one thing; the performance of the boat is another. When push comes to shove the boat itself will see you through a foul day at sea, not the depth of the varnish or the freshness of the paint. Boat finishing is not all floss and gloss; the integrity of the boat is the key.

Yes, a purpose of painting and varnishing is to delight the eye with the result, but that is only secondary. The primary purpose is to protect the boat. A cabinhouse coated with eight coats of varnish may be so deeply beautiful that it invites you to take a half-gainer right into it — it might even win the boat-of-the-year award at the WoodenBoat Show — but that is not the point. The point is that such a varnished surface is protected from the ravages of water, salt, sun, grit, and more, and the wood will therefore not weather, check, crack, or rot. In short, a properly painted and varnished boat will last.

And how is a boat properly painted and varnished? The answer lies in the following pages.

—Peter H. Spectre
Camden, Maine

About the Authors

ANNE BRAY, noted for her expert finish work, has lived with wooden boats for years. She is Director of Research at *WoodenBoat* magazine in Brooklin, Maine.

MAYNARD BRAY, former shipyard supervisor at Mystic Seaport Museum, is the author of numerous articles and books on wooden boat building and repair. A contributing editor of *WoodenBoat* magazine, he lives in Brooklin, Maine.

IAN BRUCE, known for his painting and varnishing skill, has spent years as a professional yachtsman in the Caribbean and the Mediterranean, and on the East Coast of the United States.

E. BARTON CHAPIN III, who has owned and maintained several wooden boats over the years, operates a boat-repair shop in Arrowsic, Maine.

DAN CONNER of Tequesta, Florida, has lived on, crewed on, and worked on boats for years. He has worked professionally in several boatyards repairing and maintaining wooden boats.

GEORGE FATULA, who has a background in chemistry and biology, is a long-time instructor in the Marine Finishing Program of the Washington County Technical College in Eastport, Maine.

AIMÉ ONTARIO FRASER, a marine writer, is the director of the boat-building program of The Maritime Center in Norwalk, Connecticut.

G.W. "GIFFY" FULL has spent a working lifetime as a professional skipper and one of the premier marine surveyors on the East Coast. A long-time resident of Marblehead, Massachusetts, he now lives in Brooklin, Maine.

DAVID L. JACKSON is the owner of Freya Boat Works in Anacortes, Washington, a licensed captain, and a marine surveyor.

RICHARD JAGELS, the long-time author of the "Wood Technology" column in *WoodenBoat* magazine, is a professor in the Department of Forestry at the University of Maine in Orono, Maine.

KARL MACKEEMAN of Montague, Prince Edward Island, Canada, is an artist, photographer, and sign painter.

DAN MACNAUGHTON is an owner/operator of Eastport Boat Yard & Supply of Eastport, Maine. He served as Associate Editor of *WoodenBoat* magazine for many years.

About the Authors continued

NICHOLAS K. MANGO is an experienced yachtsman and the owner of an immaculately maintained Riva runabout. He lives in Marblehead, Massachusetts.

SAMUEL F. MANNING of Camden, Maine, is an artist, writer, and illustrator specializing in traditional maritime subjects. He has illustrated many articles and books, including John Gardner's *Dory Book* and Bud McIntosh's *How to Build a Wooden Boat*.

EDWARD F. MCCLAVE of Noank, Connecticut, has been building and restoring wooden boats for more than two decades. A member of the Society of Naval Architects and Marine Engineers, he has contributed many articles to *WoodenBoat* magazine.

DEAN STEPHENS of Fort Bragg, California, has spent a lifetime building and repairing wooden boats; for many years he operated a boatbuilding school in northern California.

DOUG TEMPLIN, a resident of Newport Beach, California, and the president of DETCO Marine, is an enthusiastic owner of wooden boats.

Table of Contents

Chapter I.........Quick Steps to Spring Painting..1
    Pre-Launch Painting Kit 2
    The Disc Sander 3
    Selecting and Mixing Paint 4
    Brush Care 5
    Painting Technique 6
    Fillers 7
    Scraping 8
    Rescribing and Painting the Waterline 9
    Above the Rail 10
    The First Session's Work 10
    The Second Session's Work 11
    Things to Think About 11
    Scraping and Sanding 12
    About Varnish 14
    Oiled Finishes 15
    Canvas-Covered Decks 15
    Teak Deck Care 15

Chapter II.......Paint Adhesion..17

Chapter III.....The Wood/Paint Interface: Will It Stick?......................................19
    Fillers and Sealers 19
    Effects of Sunlight 19
    Pressure-Treated Lumber 20

Chapter IV......Mildew, and Lots of It!...21
    Is It Mildew? 21
    Mold Versus Stain 21
    A Persistent Beast 21
    Mildewcides 22
    Health Risks 22

Chapter V........Painting for Longevity..23
    Painting as a Construction Technique..........23
    Painting to Prevent Decay 23
    Painting to Prevent or Slow Down
        Dimensional Change 24
    When to Paint? 25
    Where to Paint? 26
    Construction Design Considerations 27
    Painting Faying Surfaces
        of Deck Joinerwork 27

continues

What Kind of Paint? 27
Paint as a Primer for Bedding Compounds ..28
Using Paint to Isolate Metal from Wood 28
Driving Screws with Paint 28
Setting Bungs in Paint 29
Other Coatings 29

Chapter VI......Painting for Decoration...31
Alden O-Boat 32
Biscayne Bay 14 33
Acorn 15 Sailing Dinghy 34
Egret 35
Asa Thomson Skiff 36
Acorn 10 Yacht Tender 36
Amphibi-Con 37
Cape Cod Catboat 38
Concordia 33 39
Some Very Opinionated Guidelines 40
Selecting and Mixing Colors 40

Chapter VII.....Rolling and Tipping..41
Tools and Materials 42
Preparations 42
Technique 42

Chapter VIII...Paintbrush Care...45
Preparing a New Brush 45
Cleaning a Used Brush 46

Chapter IX......For Her Name's Sake...47
Alternatives 47
Tools 47
Preliminary Work 48
Carving 48
Hand Painting 48
What's Your Style? 49

Chapter X.......Name in Gold, Hail in Black...51
Layout 51
Applying the Size 52
Checking the "Tack" 53
Applying the Gold 53
Burnishing 53
Painting the Outline 54
Painted Letters 55
Changes to Painted Letters 55
Finishing Up 55
Some Final Thoughts 56

Chapter XI....The Fine Art of Stripping Paint...57
Heat 58
Liquid Remover 58
Sanding 58
Preparing the New Surface 59

Chapter XII....Taking It Off with Chemical Strippers..................61
    Methylene Chloride 61
    Organic Solvent Mixtures 62
    Dibasic Esters 62
    N-Methyl-2-Pyrollidone (NMP) 62

Chapter XIII....Scrapers................................63
    Rough Scraping 65
    Deep Scraping 65
    Adapting and Sharpening
      Replaceable Blades 66
    Filing the Edge 67
    Serrated Scrapers 68
    Sculpting Wood with a Scraper 69
    Fine Scraping 70
    Sharpening Cabinet Scrapers 71

Chapter XIV....Looking Good Again......................73
    Power Sanding 74
    Scribing the Waterline 75
    Stripping the Brightwork 76
    Sanding the Brightwork 77
    Filling and Surfacing 78
    Buildup 79
    Final Sanding 79
    Final Cleaning 80
    Final Varnishing 80
    Final Coats of Paint 82
    Completion 83

Chapter XV....Linear Polyurethanes.....................87
    What's a Urethane? 88
    Marine Urethanes 88
    The Right Conditions 89
    Safety Considerations 90
    Why Sterling? 90
    For a Colored Application 90
    For a Clear Application 92
    Maintenance and Repair 92
    Now the Bad News, or Is It Good? 93

Chapter XVI..Water-Based Clear Coatings................95
    Testing Three Water-Based Varnishes 95
    Advantages and Disadvantages 96

Chapter XVII..Antifouling Paints.......................99
    The Basic Types of Copper Paint 100
    Choosing the Appropriate Protection 101

Chapter XVIII..Quick Steps to Spring Varnishing.......103
    Brushes 104
    Brush Care 104
    Varnish 104

continues

Sanding 104
Avoiding Dust 106
Applying Varnish 107
Additives 108
Repairing Damaged Varnish 109
Care 110
Frequency of Recoating 111
Stripping Varnish 111
Sealers 112
Fillers 112
Woods for Varnishing 113
Parting Thoughts 113

Chapter XIX...Hot-Weather Varnishing..115
Stripping 115
Priming 116
Sanding 116
Brushing Technique 116
Types of Varnish 117
Additives 118
Suggestions 118
Preventing Deterioration
    Due to Sunlight 119

Chapter XX...Two-Can Finishes, or One?..121
Characteristics 122
Life/Longevity 122
Application 123
Safety 126
Recommended Uses 126
Repair 127

Chapter XXI...A Lasting Finish..129
Which Paint? 129
The Varnish/Epoxy Combination 130
Proper Bedding 131
A Repair in Time 131
Protection from Salt and Sun 132
Protection from Chafe 132
Protection from Bumps 133

Chapter XXII...Mast Protection...135
Preparations 135
Cleaning, Tacking, and Varnishing 135

Chapter XXIII..Arabol..137
Advantages and Disadvantages 137
Application 138

Chapter XXIV...Maintenance with Meaning...139
Brightwork 139
Paintwork 143

I

Quick Steps to Spring Painting

—— by Anne and Maynard Bray ——

It's April. A Saturday. You're thinking about your boat. About getting her painted and overboard — early this year. No more end-of-June launchings.

What to do, then, with the day (the weekend, the spring)?

You need a plan — a realistic one where you never lose sight of the main objective: getting the boat overboard so you can use her.

Most owner-maintained boats are stored outside, so your plan, like it or not, will be largely controlled by the spring weather, and what you decide to do must be adjusted almost hourly, depending on whether it's warm or cold, rainy or sunny, early or late in the day, windy or calm. If your launching objective is to be met, you'd better figure on cooperating with the weather instead of ignoring it.

What has to be done before launching? Not as much as you think. How much time will it take? Nowhere near as long as you believe it will. This chapter is about scraping, sanding, and painting — the normal routine you have to go through each and every spring — and how to do it quickly and still have your boat look perfectly okay. Not ready for a show, perhaps, but nothing to be ashamed of, either.

These ideas for a quick fit-out are for the many, many owners who are frustrated because it takes so long to get their boats sailing — the people who love boating, but who can devote only a couple of weekends to spring outfitting each year. Painting seems to be their big problem.

For paint to look good and protect the wood underneath, certain conditions have to be met:

1. The wood must be dry and...
2. ...the surface must be reasonably clean and smooth before you start to paint.
3. The paint selected must be suitable for the job and used with the right additives.
4. There must be at least two coats over the bare wood.
5. Application must be even, without runs or "holidays."
6. Paint must have a chance to dry without the presence of fog, rain, or dew.

Far too many people concentrate on one or two of the above factors and ignore the rest. You have to keep them all at least somewhat in mind, along with a realistic idea of how much total time you're willing to spend. Hours and hours of preparing the surface, for example, can't be justified if you don't apply the paint with an equal commitment to quality.

Think topsides. They're what show most when the boat is overboard, even though you see more of the bottom in the boatyard. You want your topsides to be smooth and perhaps even to shine a little. The plank seams shouldn't be obvious, and you don't want digs, nicks, or gouges to show too much. The appearance of the boat's bottom, by comparison, is less critical, because most of it is hidden underwater after launching. The deck and trim above the rail can be worked on afloat. It's usually the topsides that hold up your launching schedule. Think topsides.

A typical pre-launch painting kit consists of:

2,000-2,500 rpm disc sander with 8-inch foam pad
Plenty of pre-cut sanding discs (80-, 100- and 120-grit) and disc adhesive
Extension cord
Cloth wiping rags
Dusting brush
Painters' tack rags
Cardboard paint buckets and/or tin cans
Gloves

Paint for topsides, boottop, and bottom
Additives for paint (retarder, lubricant, accelerator thinner, turpentine)
Solvent for cleaning brushes
Stirring sticks
Brushes for topsides, boottops, and bottom
Paintbrush spinner
Putty knives
Trowel cement
Seam compound or putty

Whiting
Lampblack
Dust mask for face
Batten for marking waterline
Brads or small nails for batten
Hammer
Power hacksaw blade or other scribing tool
Serrated scraper
Mill file for sharpening scraper
Opener for paint cans
Goggles

Check the weather radio. If the day promises fair, you should focus on painting topsides. Sure, there is always some scraping and sanding to be done, but keep this preparation to a minimum and plan on giving the boat two coats of paint in that one good day. This technique is a little uncommon, but it can be done.

Get an early start. Show up with a box full of tools and materials such as those in the photograph of the pre-launch painting kit. There'll be more work than you can handle alone, so bring one or two helpers. Your first task will be to wipe the topsides thoroughly dry of dew. You'll need a dry surface early in the day for the first coat of paint.

Then gather up sawhorses and planks, and set up a good staging all around the boat. While your helpers are finishing this task, start disc sanding on the driest side — that is, the side facing the sun. (See "The Disc Sander.") Remember, you're not trying to strip the hull to the bare wood, only to clean off and smooth up the old paint. Before smoothing, however, a rough sanding with 80- or 100-grit paper may be needed in some places. You rough-sand only to feather or fair.

Feathering is cutting away the loose paint and making a smooth transition between the bare areas and the rest of the hull where the paint is still good. Fairing is cutting down high places in the planking itself. (Minor ones, in this case; planing and grinding are the proper techniques for really unfair hulls, and these operations take more skill than most boat owners can be expected to have.)

After feathering and fairing, switch to a finer paper, say, 120 grit, and smooth up the rest of the topsides — or start with this grit if the hull doesn't need any rough sanding. Leave last year's name intact on the transom and the registration numbers on the bow; sand up close, not over them. Painted lettering is usually good for several seasons. Varnished transoms should be carefully hand-sanded so you don't break through to the lettering underneath.

Sanding by hand will be needed near corners, guardrails, and other places where the disc machine can't or shouldn't be used.

Disc sanding topsides on a 35-foot boat should take no more than an hour. Get one of your helpers to dust off (with a rag or a brush) the topsides after they're sanded, and to tack them so they're dust-free. (Tack rags are available from a hardware store or auto body shop; they're cheap, so forget about making your own.) Your job in the meantime will be mixing the paint. (See "Selecting and Mixing Paint.")

You'll be using regular oil-based marine paint — a semigloss, nothing exotic — and you're going to give

The Disc Sander

Compared with the other methods of sanding topsides, the disc sander is a real whiz. Don't use the rubber pad that comes with the machine, however, or you'll end up with telltale rings on the surface. Instead, replace the rubber pad with an 8-inch foam backing pad to which the discs of sandpaper are stuck with a special disc adhesive. Norton and 3-M make these pads and the adhesives, and hardware stores usually carry them.

You should use a sander that turns at about 2,000 or 2,500 rpm. The friction of higher-speed units softens the paint, which clogs the sandpaper. The Rockwell model 661 draws 10 amps and is powerful enough not to lose speed under load.

You can buy ready-made 8-inch discs; otherwise, it's a simple matter to cut your own out of standard 9- by 11-inch sheets. Use aluminum oxide production paper. When a disc wears out, peel it off (heating will soften the adhesive), and slap on a new disc, reusing the adhesive already there on the pad. You can go through three or four discs before more adhesive will be needed.

For topsides work, 120-grit paper is about right in average conditions. For feathering and fairing, 80- or 100-grit works well. (For extensive fairing, a phenolic pad should be used, rather than a soft foam or rubber one, and a higher-speed grinder, rather than a sander, is a better tool.)

Disc sanding produces a lot of dust, so wear a face mask and eye protection.

Hold the sander flat and keep it moving. You'll get those rings on the surface if you tip the disc, and you'll melt the paint if you stay in one place too long. Keep stopping, looking, and feeling. Without this kind of care, the disc sander becomes a weapon instead of a labor-saving tool. REPLACE THE DISCS WHEN THEY ARE DULL! Keep the sander an inch or so away from

adjoining woodwork, such as guardrails, and be sure to stay back from sharp corners, such as those at the stem and the transom, or you will round off their crispness. Hand-sand these fussy places afterwards.

You'll be amazed at how fast you can go with a powerful disc sander. Once more for the record:

1. Use a foam pad.
2. Don't tilt the machine.
3. Keep moving.
4. Don't sand with dull paper.

The disc sander has a bad reputation because of the crescent-shaped telltales it sometimes leaves, and those telltales come from not observing the above points.

The authors are indebted to Paul Bryant of the Riverside Boat Yard in Newcastle, Maine, for sharing his disc-sanding techniques. Having ourselves adopted Paul's methods for the past several seasons, we're convinced of their superior speed and results. With a fresh disc of 100-grit production paper, feathering flaking paint takes only seconds.

Selecting and Mixing Paint

Before deciding what paint to use, consider its purpose. A film of paint shields the wood from the weather, uniformly colors the surface, and creates a smooth and generally shiny appearance. If we could get these results in a single coat, we would all be in utopia, but that coat would have to be put on so thick that it would sag and run before it ever dried. That's why at least two coats have to be applied over bare wood. The more coats, in fact, the better — to a point — but here, we're trying to move the task of outfitting along rapidly and therefore want to put on as few coats of paint as we can get away with. This tells us that each coat should be as thick as we can make it and that the paint itself should have good hiding ability.

The modern high-gloss oil-based marine paints work really well, in that they tend to be self-leveling so the brushmarks flow together and disappear, and in that they dry fast. But for these very reasons, these enamel-like gloss paints go on thin and are slow to build up or become uniform in color. For a two-coats-in-a-day paint job, you'll find that semigloss paint gives better coverage than gloss, and that it works effectively right over the bare wood. A flat undercoater might also be used as a first coat, but because it's not a self-leveling paint, you will have to sand out the brush marks. For you to do that the paint has to be completely dry. And there goes your two-coats-in-a-day painting plan!

Semigloss, unfortunately, comes only in white. If you have dark topsides, you have to make your own semigloss first coat by mixing the gloss finish paint with flat undercoat — either white or black or some combination of the two — to get a close match with the final color. (Some companies make a neutral undercoat for this purpose.)

Using paint directly as it comes from the can, without thinning, is usually bad practice. It's just too thick to spread well; your brush drags, and applying the paint is slow work and just no fun. Paint companies make thinners that tend to accelerate drying, for use in poor drying conditions — nothing like the weather on this beautiful spring day. They also make brushing liquid thinners, such as Interlux 333 or Pettit 12172 or 9077, that slow the drying as well as lubricate the paint for easier brushing and better leveling. This is the stuff you want — but only a little bit of it, say a couple of capfuls in a quart to start with. Stir it in well, divide the resultant mix between two containers, and start painting. Get one of your helpers to add more to the idle container if your brush drags, then switch containers. Give your paint another dose every so often as you work along, whenever your brush starts to drag or the wet edge doesn't stay wet.

There may be times when paint needs lubricating or thinning for easy brushing, but when you shouldn't slow down the natural drying. Paint applied in the afternoon, for example, runs the risk of being flattened by falling dew if drying is retarded. Turpentine or Penetrol, rather than brushing liquid, are better choices here, even if you have to deal with a stickier wet edge.

Boottop paint is selected and mixed just like the topside paint, although you can sometimes get by with a single coat of it. (Try the heavily pigmented paint that sign painters use if you want to be sure of a one-coat job.) For the bottom, oil-based copper paint is far less tricky to deal with, so if you've mastered the topsides, you'll have no trouble here. More sophisticated antifouling paints use special thinners, so read and follow the label instructions.

Holes punched in the paint can's gutter keep it from overflowing if you decide to paint directly from the original container. When you're through painting, wipe the rim clean before putting the cover back on.

A dried paint film in a partly used can should be removed before the paint is stirred.

Straining paint into a separate container after stirring it is a good idea, particularly if you're using leftovers. A rag tied around the container keeps your hands free of rim dribbles.

the entire topsides a coat of it now and another later in the day. You've broken through to the bare wood in a number of places while sanding, and these spots will need two coats. You could touch them up, but you'd have to sand again to smooth out these spots before the final coat, so it makes sense to do the whole boat. She probably needs it, anyhow. This first coat should be put on fast and be finished in an hour or so. (See "Painting Technique.") Start with the shady side of the boat, so the paint there will have the longest to dry. Make certain before you start painting, however, that the hull surface is dry to the touch. A high moisture content in the wood beneath the surface is okay, but if you can feel or see any moisture on the surface itself, the paint will soon blister.

Judgment and experience help, and you're getting them here on this first coat. The second coat, to be put on this afternoon, should be much improved.

So far, the timing has been about like this:

Initial wipedown — 10 minutes
Disc sanding — 1 hour
Dusting hull and mixing paint — 15 minutes
Painting topsides — 1 hour
Time completed — 10 to 11 a.m.
(Bear in mind this is spring, when the days are long.)

While the topside paint is drying, you can work on the bottom — puttying, painting, and first-coating the boottop if that's needed. Just don't raise dust that will land in the wet topside paint. But first, clean your paintbrushes and cover the paint so it doesn't thicken in the can. (See "Brush Care.") Whatever other work you start, don't let it take your mind off those topsides. They are the primary task of this day.

As soon as the first coat of topside paint is dry to the touch (two to three hours), you should begin "facing up" the imperfections with a filler of your choice. (See "Fillers.") Here again, several people working at once will speed up the process.

By now, it's mid-afternoon and you must get on with the final coat, so there will be time for it to set up before the dew falls. Plan on finishing no later than 4 p.m. The first coat will probably be smooth enough to need only a light hand-sanding with fine paper over the wood fuzz or trowel cement or putty. (You don't have to roughen the whole surface or give it "tooth" to make the second coat stick to the first one; surface smoothness should be the only criterion.) Remember when hand-sanding here that the first coat hasn't dried fully hard and that there's only one coat over the bare wood in places. Go easy.

With the morning's practice, the second and final coat should be a great success. Chances are it's warmer now; to brush well, the paint will need a good dose

Brush Care

Good brushes are worth their extra cost, because they'll give you a better job, faster. Protect your investment by thoroughly cleaning them after each use, working solvent through the bristles by hand to dissolve and flush away all traces of paint, then spinning the brush dry. Do this twice after each use, and your brushes will last for years.

Clean your brushes right after using them! Here's how.

Flush out the leftover paint, alternately dipping the brush in solvent and working that solvent all through the bristles with your fingers. For a solvent, use kerosene and cheap thinner. Spin out the brush after each of two rinses, using clean solvent for each one. Wipe off the handle and metal ferrule after the final spin — the only part of this operation requiring rags.

Without a paintbrush spinner, however, you have to use the "shake-and-wipe" method, which requires a lot of rags and doesn't get the brushes as clean.

That's about all there is to it, unless you want to give your brushes a final rinse with warm water and detergent, as the books say. Store your brushes dry, unless you're using them daily. It's more convenient.

of lubricant — maybe more for use on the sunny side of the hull than on the shady one. (Turpentine is a better bet for this important last coat than brushing liquid; it will help the paint flow, but won't retard the drying.) Tack the hull free of dust before starting to paint, and once you do start, begin on the shady side and plan on spreading and brushing the paint out

Painting Technique

Use a full-bodied natural-bristle brush such as Hamiltons for the topsides and boottop, about 3-inch and 1 ½-inch respectively. You can't get a good job with a cheap brush, let alone a fast job, because the bristles are so coarse they leave big brush marks behind, they're always falling out, and there are so few of them that the brush doesn't hold much paint.

The technique for painting the topsides goes about like this: Start at one end of the hull and work toward the other. Dip your brush into the paint about halfway, wipe off only enough of the excess to stop the dripping, and start rapidly spreading the paint.

If you use firm, rapid strokes, mostly fore and aft, you can lay a band of paint that will be about 2- to 4-feet long and 6- to 12-inches wide. Each new brushful should hit the hull midway along this band, where it can be efficiently spread out to a uniform film thickness. One end of each band will be brushed back into the wet edge of the portion you've already painted; the other will head off in the opposite direction.

The coating should be as thick as you can make it without runs or sags developing. After spreading a brushful, go over it, stroking lightly this time, with a back-and-forth motion (always paralleling the wood grain) to get rid of the brushmarks. The final leveling stroke should be toward the wet edge to achieve a smooth, tapered transition. You won't eliminate all the brushmarks, even with the gentlest of stroking, but the paint will flow a bit afterwards to level itself — and any marks that still show will at least be running in a natural fore-and-aft direction. Your technique will improve as you go along; don't slow the job to learn it all in the first 6 feet of hull length.

Start the first band of paint, at the bow or stern, up near the sheer, then work downward with successive bands, each representing one brushful. The result will be a panel 2-to 4-feet long covering the entire height of the topsides. After completing one panel, move along to the next one. Stand up to paint; don't sit on the staging. Standing gives you more control and better speed.

Keeping a wet edge to avoid lap marks means working fast. You have to join up with and continue your last applied brushful before it sets up. Lap marks are the price you pay for not observing this. Two people, or sometimes even three, working one above another, spreading paint from bow to stern or stern to bow, help hold the wet edge. On a large boat this is sometimes the only way to get a good job. Keep looking back at what you've just done, checking for sags, runs, and bare places. If you catch these while the paint is still wet, you can brush them out. Left too long, your "repair work" will show.

Avoid painting topsides on days that are noticeably hot, cold, damp, or windy. A "shirt-sleeve" day, sunny with a gentle breeze, provides the best results.

Lapmarks in topside paint are avoided by always having a "wet edge" to work from. This means laying on the paint fast enough so what you've just painted doesn't get tacky before you "pick it up" and continue onward with your next brushful. Work from one end of the boat to the other, use large brushes, and spread and smooth the paint rapidly — with several people painting at once if the surface is a large one.

rapidly, as before. (Again, see ""Painting Technique."")

Masking tape along the waterline and rail will save time — you won't have to be as careful as you would if you were cutting in. Make sure to pull the tape off at the end of the day; there's nothing as permanent as masking tape that is old and sunbaked or that has been dampened by dew or rain.

So far, the afternoon has gone about like this:

Facing up the topsides — ½ hour
Smoothing up any rough places by hand-sanding — ½ hour
Dusting and tacking down topsides/mixing paint — 15 minutes
Painting topsides — 1 hour
Time at finish — 4 p.m.

Congratulations! You're done with the most critical painting of all. What remains — the bottom, the waterline, and the boottop — can be carried out in less-than-perfect conditions. And the painting and varnishing on deck can take place after the boat is waterborne.

What we've pushed for here is an early launching to ensure as little drying out of the planking and opening of the hull seams as possible. Just as soon as your topsides are complete, finish up the bottom work within a day or so, then plan on launching promptly. Do what work on deck you have time for, but don't let it interfere with the priority tasks below the rail.

Antifouling paints for the bottom are so diverse in their makeup and application techniques that it's simply not possible here to describe how to deal with all of them. Traditional oil-based copper bottom paint is what we'll be talking about — the kind that is easy to apply, doesn't build up because it wears away, and will inhibit marine growth for a normal season in northern waters. If you're using another type, be guided by the instructions on the can label.

Don't waste time sanding the bottom; it's an unnecessary and messy operation. If last year's bottom paint

Fillers

There are two approaches to choosing a filler. You can use a hard, quick-drying, trowel cement, or you can use a white lead or similar putty or seam compound, which won't dry while you wait, but which, if thickened with whiting, will be firm enough to stay in place for painting over. The trowel cement is probably best for shallow nicks, putty best for the deeper gouges and for the plank seams. In fact, if the seams have opened up, you should definitely use putty rather than cement. The putty will, of course, squeeze out after launching, but the planking, meanwhile, can swell naturally without overstressing the frames or fastenings.

There is an overwhelming variety of fillers on the market today. After deciding between cement (the hard stuff) or putty (the soft stuff), you have to select a specific substance. There's merit in using whatever is inexpensive to buy and is easily applied. Nothing lasts forever; most fillers will last at least a season — you'll get another chance next spring.

Use flexible putty knives that are 3 inches wide; narrow ones are okay, too, but they'll slow you down. Press the filler in, then scrape off the excess. Use your hand to smooth out what's left in order to avoid the need to sand later. Fillers stick better if applied over fresh, but dry, paint. (Both putties and seam compounds stay flexible longer if the wood is first prime-painted; bare wood is absorbent and will draw out the oil in the putty.)

Filler that is too gooey can be thickened with painters' whiting — a powdered, chalk-like substance that can be found in hardware or paint stores. By mixing white-lead paste with whiting, you can make up old-fashioned putty — as you need it.

Fillers are usually white, but can be tinted a dark shade with powdered lampblack, also obtainable in a paint or hardware store. Underwater seam compounds can be bought already darkened and with antifouling properties.

Use fillers not from the can they come in, but from a small board that you can hold close to your work as you go along. Your knife can be scraped off and reloaded more easily; you will have a place to mix in some whiting if needed; and with the can cover closed, the supply won't dry out or become contaminated.

Using fillers from a flat board, instead of from the can, is much faster, allows the use of a wide putty knife, and doesn't contaminate the can's contents. If thickening is needed, the filler can be mixed with painter's whiting on the flat board as well.

Scraping

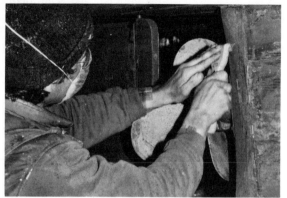

Scraping is sufficient preparation for traditional copper bottom paint, effectively removing the loose paint without all the toxic dust of sanding. Use a serrated scraper kept sharp by frequent filing, and don't forget a face mask and eye protection.

A serrated scraper, if kept reasonably sharp by filing, will efficiently claw off loose bottom paint. Using this tool on a boat's bottom isn't what you would call pleasant work, but compared to power sanding, hand scraping is quiet, quick, and relatively dustless. For a racing-type smoothness, you'll have to resort to sanding, but for normal use — cruising and day-tripping — this type of dry scraping yields a surface that is perfectly acceptable and can be directly painted over.

Stroke with the grain or diagonally, not crosswise, so the scraper doesn't chatter or dig in. The photograph shows a 2 ½-inch serrated scraper at work; this size is about right for most work. Wear a face mask and goggles for protection against paint chips.

Painting the bottom follows scraping and filling. (If you're using two coats on the bottom, do the filling after the first coat). Big brushes, say 3 to 4 inches, make for efficient painting, and rollers also work well for bottoms if you don't mind the pebbly surface they leave behind. You can paint the waterline very rapidly and well with a 3- or 4-inch brush, by holding it somewhat vertically and using its tip. A good scribe line also makes for efficient painting here. (See "Rescribing and Painting the Waterline.") Copper bottom paint pigment settles quickly to the bottom of the can, so keep stirring every so often while you paint. Try to get a couple of coats along the waterline where the worst fouling takes place, even if the rest of the bottom gets painted only once.

If your boat has a boottop, you'll be slowed down a bit. Painting it is an added operation, and there's another color to deal with. Boottop painting is best done after the topsides and before the bottom, although, with care, you can paint it last of all. Sometimes, if you don't thin the boottop paint too much, you can get by with a single coat — even over the bare wood. What you're looking for is a crisp line of uniform color; whether or not the paint surface shines can't easily be detected once the boat is overboard.

You were warned at the beginning that this was not for perfectionists. It is one way to get a good job in a couple of weekends. A close examination of such a boat readied for launching will show some imperfections. There's no harm done to the boat, however, and after the normal wear from a couple of weeks' use, it's our bet that you could hardly find the difference between the job described here and one that started out near-perfect.

is still firmly attached and if it was given a thorough scrubbing last fall, you can paint right over what's there. If there is loose paint, scrape it off — don't sand it — with a serrated scraper kept sharp by frequent filing. (See "Scraping.")

If the seams have opened up, use an underwater seam compound or other filler that stays soft and allows the planking to swell and the seams to close together naturally after the boat is launched. If your boat is severely dried out, try to do some pre-launch swelling before you fill or paint. Remember, the purpose of a seam filler is to protect the cotton caulking, give the hull a smooth surface, and reduce leakage when the boat is first launched; the caulking and the wood-to-wood contact between planks are what ultimately keep the water out. Some, if not most, of this year's filler will be squeezed out, so don't waste a lot of time or money fussing with it — the chances are good that whatever you use will do its job for the season.

Specific Products Referred to

	Gloucester	Interlux	Pettit	Woolsey	Z-Spar	Flood
Topside paint (oil-based semigloss white)	100	220	2146	761	101	NA
Lubricants (retarders)	NA	333	12172 or 9077	NA	M1050	Marine Penetrol
Thinners (accelerators)	NA	216	12120	NA	T10	NA
Fillers (hard, white)	715	93 or 4389	7164	890	NA	NA
Seam compounds (soft, white)	742	31	7110	896	NA	NA
Seam compounds (bottom)	743	30 or 35	7611 or 7510	895	NA	NA

Rescribing and Painting the Waterline

A straight, crisp, painted waterline makes the difference between a boat that looks sharp, and one that doesn't. Rescribing a faint waterline is no big deal; painting to that scribe line is even less so. Chances are good that your existing painted waterline is basically level and there's enough of it left to be used as a guide for a new scribe line.

For simple rescribing, you'll need a long wooden fairing batten, some brads to nail it on with, and a fine saw of some kind to do the actual scribing. The batten should be stiff enough to stay fair between the brads, yet flexible enough to bend around the hull without breaking. A ³⁄₁₆-inch or ¼-inch strip sawn off the straight edge of a ¾-inch or ⅞-inch by 12-, 14-, or 16-foot pine board makes a usable batten. Aft, where the waterline takes on a tighter curve, you'll probably need another, more flexible, short batten.

Rescribing your waterline should be done before you do any painting. It's a good job for one of those less-than-perfect days.

Starting at the bow on one side, nail on the batten so its top edge is in the right place for guiding the saw. Use only a few widely spaced brads until you have sighted along the batten in both directions and have adjusted it to get a fair line. Then drive in more brads to hold the batten firmly for the scribing tool.

Now for the scribing. You'll probably have the best results with an industrial hacksaw blade, although the end teeth of a regular handsaw will also do a good job. Other tools will work as well, including those with a scraping or slicing action. Use what you will to produce an evenly formed groove that's about ¹⁄₁₆-inch wide and equally deep — one whose edges are crisp so they'll show a crisp paint line.

Stop your scribing a few feet short of the end of the batten, pull the brads, and move the batten along the hull, allowing it to overlap your newly scribed line a little. Nail the batten, fair it, and scribe a line along its top edge as before, making a smooth transition with the line you've already scribed.

In painting to a scribe line, you run the lower color — usually the bottom paint — up to fill the groove. In other words, the top corner of the scribe line is where the color break takes place. With natural light from above, the shadow cast by this top corner helps hide any minor waviness in your paint line.

The best brush for painting a waterline is bigger — a lot bigger — than you'd think: 2 ½ inches to as large as 4 inches can be used. But whatever the brush, it has to take a good lay, without groups of bristles sticking out randomly all over the place. Painting to a scribe line is surprisingly rapid with a brush big enough to hold a supply of paint and with paint that's thin enough to spread well. As one might imagine, working from the top down (topsides first, then the bottom) is easiest, although with care you can go the other way.

If your boat has a boottop, it simply means that you have two scribings to do and another color to deal with. A smaller brush has to be used here — 1 inch or 1 ½ inches — and the prepping and painting will be as for the topsides. With or without a boottop, you should keep topside paint pretty much within its final boundaries. That means masking tape along the waterline while the topsides are being painted — not to establish the exact line, but to keep the paint from overspreading.

The temporary brads that held the scribing batten made tiny holes in the planking, of course, but these will disappear with the use of a little putty.

From the start, this freshly cut groove, or scribe line, begins filling up with paint. It can't be helped, and every four or five years you have to rescribe. Learn to do it with confidence, and never again will you have a ripply waterline.

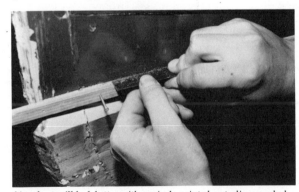

Your boat will look better with a crisply painted waterline, marked by a small scribe line. Cut the scribe line with a hacksaw blade (or other tool of your choice), guided by a batten temporarily nailed to the hull as shown.

Paint the lower color last, so it completely fills the scribe line and looks sharp (below). Otherwise, an uneven waterline (above) results.

A staging set up around the hull allows one to work from a comfortable standing position, yielding a better job in less time.

Above the Rail

It's still spring, and you've painted the hull; you may even have launched the boat, in which case you won't have to worry about the planking drying out. The painting has taken only a couple of days so far; if you keep pushing, you can complete the job in a couple more. But, as with the hull work, they have to be good weather days. It's time now to attend to the deck and everything else above the rails.

You should still keep in mind that we're talking about a practical approach here. We're sacrificing a little perfection to hasten your commissioning day, feeling that it's better to get the boat thoroughly painted and sailing than to fuss meticulously in one area while ignoring the others, or to stretch the spring outfitting into summer.

The main secret to working efficiently on deck is good programming — applying the paint early enough in the day for it to dry before the evening dew can settle on it and ruin the gloss. If you've decided to give this above-the-rail part of your spring outfitting two days of your time and no more, you'll generally be sanding, scraping, and priming on the first day, and priming (second coat) and applying the finish coats of paint and varnish on the second day.

The First Session's Work

Keep an eye on the clock and on the work remaining to finish all sanding and scraping, if possible, by 4:00 p.m. on the first day. If you start at the bow and work toward the stern, someone can begin vacuuming and priming at the bow even earlier than 4:00 while the areas farther aft are still being prepared. If you realize by early afternoon that you can't get everything sanded and scraped by 4:00, concentrate on the varnish (which needs at least two coats under the final one). In any event, the prime coats should all be in place by 5:00.

How do you begin? By sanding and scraping everything — everything — that you intend to paint or varnish. For appearance as well as for surface protection, you should plan on recoating just about everything in sight; it's a rare coating that will survive on the exterior of a wooden boat for more than one season. While the disc sander was indispensable for the topsides, you'll find little use for it here on deck, because there are so few flat surfaces and so many corners. There are some areas where a small vibrating sander might be useful, but generally you'll find that the work goes faster and that it's quieter and more pleasant with simple hand-sanding. This is a time when you can use all the helping hands you can get. The sanding technique isn't difficult, but there are some basic rules for doing a good job. (See "Scraping and Sanding.")

Places where the paint or varnish has flaked or lifted should be scraped and feathered rather than sanded (unless you're able to use a disc sander) — it's much faster. Scraping requires more skill, however, so take care who you put on the end of a scraper. You, for example, might choose to do all the scraping while others are at work with sandpaper.

Two people in a day should be able to completely sand and scrape everything above the rail on a typical 35-foot boat and prime-coat the bare places. Boats with teak decks or with oiled (instead of painted or varnished) surfaces should take even less time.

Areas left bare of paint or varnish from either the sanding or scraping process can be marked with chalk (on the adjacent surface, not on the bare wood itself) to indicate they need to be prime-coated.

You'll need at least one coat of paint and two of varnish as a primer over the bare spots before you apply a final finish. There won't be time to sand all the spots that have been primed, so the same self-leveling paint you'll be using for the finish coat, rather than high-build undercoater, works best here. Hasten the drying by adding about 10 percent accelerator/thinner, such as Interlux No. 216, to a small container of whatever paint or varnish you're using as a primer over bare wood.

In summary:

1. Decide what you intend to accomplish before leaving home; make certain you bring the necessary tools and materials with you. Time at the boatyard is precious; use it for scraping and painting, not for searching and shopping.
2. Pick a good-weather day and start early.
3. Scrape and sand everything on deck before starting to paint.

4. Clean up the dust by vacuuming, if possible; otherwise, give everything a very thorough sweeping and dusting.
5. Prime-coat all bare wood before you leave for the day — in time for the paint to dry before the dew falls.

So endeth day number one above the rail (or weekend number one, if your boat is a big one or one whose paint work is unusually rough). The second session will focus on painting and varnishing, on applying the finish coats; the objective here will be to have everything on deck finish-coated by, say, 4:00 p.m.

The Second Session's Work

Begin early in the day by wiping off the dew. If yesterday's primed areas need a bit of sanding to blend them in, do that next. Then clean up the dust (vacuum cleaner and tack rag — once again), and get your paint mixed and your brushes ready. This is a good time — just before painting, that is — to apply filler over dings, gouges, and open seams. This is also the time for giving the varnished areas a second, touch-up coat. If the boat hasn't yet been launched and there's no staging set up around her, take this opportunity to set up staging that is high enough to allow good access to what's on deck.

As with the topsides, or anywhere else for that matter, make certain the surface is dry before you start to apply paint or varnish. Where to start? A precise answer depends, of course, on the particular boat, but generally you should begin with the cabintop structures, such as skylights and hatches, then the cockpit, the cabintop itself, the cabin side's and coamings, the rails, and finally, the deck. The idea is to plan things so you don't have to stretch across your freshly painted work and jeopardize it with dribbles and hand prints.

Cutting in one color against another that hasn't yet dried — say, the deck paint against the freshly painted cabin sides — can be done if you're careful and use masking tape. Run tape along the deck to control the overspread when painting the cabin sides, then strip off the tape. When you're ready to paint the deck, carefully cut in the paint to the base of the cabin sides, using the end of the brush, as shown in the photograph. A little overlapping of the two colors is better than not having them meet, even if the color change isn't as crisp as you'd like it to be; these joints at seams where a color change takes place are vulnerable to the weather, and it's important that they be protected with a fresh coat of paint or varnish each season.

Almost any paint will need additives to make it spread well and/or dry quickly. Varnish occasionally needs this treatment as well. Remember that drying is faster (you'll lose the wet edge sooner) on horizontal surfaces such as decks and cabintops, and

"Tacking down" follows vacuuming as the final step to eliminate dust before beginning to paint.

Two or more painters always speed the work along, but it takes some planning to avoid working across freshly painted surfaces or painting oneself into a corner.

This is how you hold the brush for cutting one color in against another.

that the paint for them has to be thinned more than for vertical areas, such as cabin sides.

Things to Think About

As on the hull itself, we're talking about the use of traditional oil-based yacht paints — not the more sophisticated (and more expensive) types. The newer paints are great on a stable surface, retaining their gloss for several years, even in the southern sunlight. But, generally, there's too much movement around the seams and joints of a traditional plank-on-frame wooden boat for these paints to adhere long enough to be worth their extra cost.

To get your boat painted and sailing in a short time with minimum effort has been our goal. Our focus has been on protecting the worn-out finish and the exposed wood with a fresh coating of paint or varnish, being practical rather than fussy.

Not fussing, however, isn't the same as working without standards. When you paint or varnish, see that there aren't "holidays" or runs; when you sand, do it thoroughly; when you cut one color in against another, take care to get a crisp, fair line; when you apply filler, keep

Scraping and Sanding

If a film of paint or varnish has peeled and lifted, and lost its bond with the wood, it can no longer protect the surface. In fact, quite the reverse is true; moisture gets trapped underneath and tends to discolor and rot the wood. The only solution is to strip away the loosened areas of paint to expose the bare wood underneath, then build up a new film of two or three or more coats. You'll find that dry scraping is the most effective way to strip away this peeled and lifted paint.

Scrapers, even though used for rough work, are edge tools and must be kept sharp. Use a flat 8- or 10-inch mill file for sharpening, and use it frequently; your scraper will give much better results with less effort.

Scraping is a two-step operation. Clawing off the old finish with heavy strokes is first, then comes the feathering and smoothing, using lighter, more focused strokes. The objective of the second step is to blend the surface of the adjacent, intact paint work into the exposed area of bare wood in a smooth, tapered transition. The bare wood itself may need some careful scraping as well, either to make it smooth or to remove black water stains if it is to be varnished. Rough scraping is best done with a fairly narrow, 1 ½- or 2-inch Red Devil-type scraper so that you can build up some pressure, even though these scrapers sometimes chatter and leave telltale ridges behind. You can, with care and a delicate touch, use this same tool for fairing and tapering, but a flat-plate cabinet scraper with a rolled edge will give you more control. If you're not completely satisfied with the results of scraping, you can follow it up with a block-sanding, starting with about 80-grit paper and working through the numbers up to 120-or 150-grit.

The rest of the on-deck areas where the paint is still

The basic scraping tools are a hook-type scraper, 1 ½ inches or so wide, a flat-plate cabinet scraper, about 2 ½ inches in width, and an 8-inch mill file for keeping their edges sharp. A burnishing tool should be added if you want to roll the cabinet scraper's edge to make it cut better.

With the hook-type scraper resting on a firm surface, sharpen it by stroking diagonally downward with a file until the cutting edge is brought to a point that reflects no light. The edge bevel should be 30 to 45 degrees; after sharpening, the two corners should be rounded a bit to keep them from digging in.

Cabinet scrapers are sharpened like hook-type scrapers, but their edges can be rolled to form a tiny hook, which makes them easier to control and more effective for finish scraping. Use a burnisher with heavy strokes to roll the edges, starting at the angle shown and gradually bringing the strokes to a horizontal position.

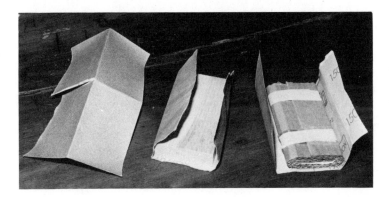

Fold a half-sheet of sand-paper as shown on the left if you plan on using no block or pad. For fairing and feathering an uneven surface, a wooden block (center) is helpful; for more effective sanding, a pad of cardboard or Ensolite (right) works well.

well stuck should be sanded; scraping is not needed. If you're careful, you can use a disc sander on flat areas, such as the deck; generally speaking, though, hand-sanding is quickest and most effective — better even than using a palm-sized orbital sander. Use a half-sheet of production paper, folded as shown in the photo, and perhaps a soft-but-firm backing pad — say, a piece of Ensolite cut to size or a piece of corrugated cardboard cut and folded as shown

For paint work, a 120-grit production paper is good to start with, but for rough surfaces, you may have to go to a coarser grit — 100 or even 80. Varnish work should be sanded with a finer grit so the scratches don't show — say, 150. If you do use coarser papers to knock down a surface, go over it with progressively finer grits until 120 is reached for paint and 150 for varnish.

Sand in the grooves; don't sand on the ridges — all as shown in the photos. Sand with the grain of the wood, not across it; that way, any scratches left behind aren't as obvious.

The main reason for sanding is to clean and smooth a painted or varnished surface so the new paint will go on evenly and adhere well. You don't need to sand through to the bare wood to achieve this. Remember, every place you break through has to be prime-coated, so don't be too heavy-handed. As soon as last year's sheen has been dulled by sanding in one area, you can move on to the next.

This is where you can use a whole army of helpers; just make sure you've made them aware of the above guidelines.

Finally, clean up all the sanding dust, or you'll end up with a nonskid finish, whether you want it or not, and with brushes so full of dust that they'll be useless for gloss work again. A sweep-down, followed by a vacuuming, followed by a tack-rag rub-down (just before the final coat), and you're ready for painting.

Sand in the grooves and inside corners, where varnish tends to build up and dirt tends to collect.

Exterior corners should not be sanded; they get worn down enough naturally and need all the buildup they can get.

About Varnish

Here's a practical approach to taking care of your varnishwork. Because varnish is a high-gloss finish, it needs more of a buildup over bare wood than do most paints — at least two coats underneath the final one for the standards we're talking about here. Touching up the bare spots with the first coat of "primer" (varnish cut with 10 percent accelerator/thinner) comes at the end of the first session, along with all the other touching up. That coat will have dried enough for sanding early the next day (you always have to gently sand the first coat to knock down the wood fuzz that comes through), after which a second prime coat can be applied.

Both these buildup layers can be laced with the accelerator or drier (accelerator for the first layer, which will also thin the varnish for good penetration, and Japan drier, which won't dilute the varnish — for the second coat), so they'll set up quickly; in touching up small areas, there's generally no "wet edge" to worry about — thus, a quick setup time is not a disadvantage. You should, however, try to taper the touch-up coats and blend them into the existing varnish work to some extent, so the final coat will be reasonably smooth if it has to be applied without sanding. Don't thin the varnish for the second touch-up or the final coat; you're after maximum buildup. For the same reason, don't sand excessively — hardly at all, in fact — just lightly after the first touch-up and generally not at all after the second, since that coat probably won't be dry enough.

The technique for brushing on the final coat of varnish is much like that for paint, described previously. You're after a uniform film thickness, as thick as you can get it without the wet varnish sagging from its own weight. You're also after a dust-free job, so vacuuming and tacking are important, as are clean brushes and clean varnish. Unlike paint, varnish used for the finish coat can generally be used without additives.

Getting an even layer without sags or runs is much easier if you use a fine-bristled brush. Badger-hair brushes are the standard for varnish work, although they're expensive. Unless your boat has vast, unbroken areas of brightwork, you can get by with smaller-sized brushes than for painting — say, a 2-inch-wide brush for general use, and a 1-inch brush for tight places. By its nature, varnish will level itself of brush marks before it starts to dry; your attention should be directed toward applying it quickly and brushing it out to an even and substantial film thickness — one that is thick enough, yet thin enough not to sag.

Varnish brushes are best stored with their bristles fully immersed in raw linseed oil, rather than put

Store your varnish brush submerged in a small can of raw linseed oil. Wipe out the excess oil on the edge of the can and flush out the rest of it in turpentine before each use. Reverse the procedure when going from use to storage.

away dry. They pick up less dust that way, and the cleaning process is ever so much easier. Flush the linseed oil out of the brush with turpentine (work the brush back and forth in a small can of it, then slat off the excess) before each use. Give it another turpentine rinse after you've finished varnishing, so that you don't contaminate the linseed oil with the varnish still contained in the brush. (Otherwise, you'll get a skin of dried varnish on the top of the nondrying oil and risk contaminating the brush with it.)

That's all there is to varnish brush care, except that you'll have to add linseed oil every few months to replace that which has evaporated so the bristles always stay fully submerged. It's also a good idea to suspend the brush, rather than let it rest on its bristles.

Although we've only allotted time for a single finish coat of varnish, a second finish coat applied right over the first one (after the first has dried, of course) is a great idea if there's time. Don't sand between coats unless you need to get rid of dust (shame, shame!), or smooth up areas that are too rough for a good shine. As mentioned earlier, there's no sense in sanding away one bit more than you have to of the varnish you've worked so hard to apply; we're after a good buildup for maximum protection.

Natural spar varnish, which is the only kind we're talking about here, is a flexible coating, which, if thick enough, is quite durable. Because it is flexible, it will generally expand and contract with the wood and stay in place after other, less resilient coatings have cracked. Varnish has enough body to act as its own filler to some extent. Varnish is a also an effective moisture barrier, and a good buildup will stabilize the wood underneath and eliminate much of the shrinking and swelling that would otherwise take place with changes in temperature and humidity. Failures come from two sources: from not keeping a fresh topcoat, and from moisture that gets underneath the film (oftentimes at joints in the wood), freezes, and fractures the varnish-to-wood bond.

it within the boundaries of the area being filled. You're trying to hold your boat's condition at the status quo with an annual painting; this is routine maintenance that should be repeated each season. Projects for the purpose of upgrading, such as the wholesale stripping of paint, refastening the hull planking, and recanvas-ing the deck, are best planned separately, with additional time set aside for accomplishing them.

Taking care of a wooden boat needn't be frustrating or time-consuming, if you develop an understanding of how to go about it effectively. Keep searching for a balance between speed and quality that suits you best.

Oiled Finishes

There are several coatings that fall into this category; the theory behind all of them is that they penetrate the wood surface, at least to some degree, and therefore don't depend on surface adhesion to keep them in place. For this reason, oil-type finishes don't lift and peel like paints and varnishes. Most oils darken the wood considerably more than varnish, and some, like linseed oil, become almost black in a few years. Their finish is matte or flat, rather than high gloss, so you don't have to fuss as much with the preparation or application.

Tung oil, linseed oil (often mixed with pine tar and turpentine), Deks Olje, and Watco are some of the more common oils in use today for wood trim work on boats. Oiled finishes keep out moisture by bulking the wood fibers near the surface with their water-repellent properties, while varnishes and paints give protection by sealing the surface with a moisture barrier-type coating. While both finishes have their strengths and weaknesses, there has to be a sufficient number of coats of either to give adequate protection and a good appearance.

You can apply oil-type finishes with almost any kind of brush, and for small areas, even a rag will work. A smooth surface under the final coat isn't vital, because high gloss isn't an objective. Some oils, like Deks Olje No. 1 and Watco, are very thin and require repeated coats for an adequate protective buildup.

Either boiled or raw linseed oil will work as the main ingredient of a homemade oil-type finish. Boiled oil is thicker than raw oil and dries — at least to some extent — in a reasonable length of time. Raw oil penetrates more deeply because it is thin, and it is very slow to dry; but by adding a little turpentine, boiled oil can be made to penetrate about as well as raw oil, and the mixture will be reasonably dry in a few days. Pine tar (a good coating, although probably too gummy by itself for pleasure-boat use) added to the linseed oil mixture increases its durability and darkens it to a more even tone. One part pine tar, one part turpentine, and four parts boiled linseed oil is a good mixture for a general-purpose homemade oil-type mix, but these proportions are not critical.

Canvas-Covered Decks

If your deck is canvas covered and painted, go easy on the heavy scraping to avoid tearing it. Give it a good sanding instead, using, say, 80-grit paper and a block or pad, or you can perhaps use a disc sander in open areas. If there's a heavy buildup of paint that has cracked, fill those cracks with seam compound after sanding and vacuuming. (Deck paint, by itself, will eventually fill cracks in canvas, but you won't be giving the deck enough coats of it this year for that to happen.)

Although the technique of stripping paint from deck canvas is beyond the scope of this chapter, be aware that it can be done, often eliminating — or at least delaying — the need to recanvas. Torn places in deck canvas can be repaired, usually by gluing the flaps back down to the deck (with epoxy or white glue) and filling over the area with a mixture of glue and sawdust until it's flush. Sometimes a patch under the tear to back it up is a good approach, and at least one boatyard uses thin aircraft-type fabric over tears as reinforcement, gluing such patches into place, then fairing in the result with trowel cement.

Just keep in mind that if you're going to fuss with tears and cracked paint, you'll need more time than the two sessions we've allotted for the work above the rail.

Teak Deck Care

Teak is a wonderfully stable wood because of the natural oil it contains; it doesn't shrink much in the hot sun or swell when it gets rained on. A protective coating is not necessary. If a teak deck is treated with anything, it is usually for the purpose of cleaning and bleaching — appearance considerations only. Scrubbed and bleached teak looks great, but the work can be overdone, abrading the surface away; the deck eventually becomes so thin that the fastenings begin to stick up and the caulking no longer stays in the seams of the thinned-down planks. Some bleaches are so strong that they chemically damage the seam fillers and perhaps even the surrounding paint work. An occasional scrubbing with warm, soapy water may be the best treatment in the long run. In any event, if you have teak decks that don't leak, their care can be minimal if you're willing to forego a bit of elegance.

Paint Adhesion

—— by Richard Jagels ——

An ancient Chinese formula for red paint uses the sap from the sumac tree as the basic vehicle. I recently examined a small oriental wooden bowl that had, presumably, lain for more than 800 years buried in wet soil. The wood was badly deteriorated, but the red paint, including the fine decorative detailing, was unblemished. I wonder if future archaeologists will see the same pristine preservation when they unearth our synthetic-finished treasures.

We all have our own favorite type or brand of paint, and for the method of application and the intended usage, it probably is the best, though it may not be perfect. I have yet to find the perfect paint, so I won't bore you by listing my own favorites. Instead, I'll discuss some wood characteristics that are often overlooked in the process of finishing or refinishing a boat — characteristics that should be considered before a boat is built or rebuilt.

Looking at the label on a can of paint has definite educational value. The better paint companies describe quite an array of characteristics for their coatings, either directly on the label or in free-for-the-asking descriptive literature. You may discover, for example, how resistant the paint is to ultraviolet light degradation, or to chemical and biological attack. Or you may discover how quickly it will dry, what kind of moisture resistance it has, or how tough the resultant paint film will be. You may even find that the paint is incompatible with certain materials, such as epoxy resins or aluminum. But I'm willing to bet my Adirondack guideboat that you won't discover much information about the paint's adhesion properties — or resistance to lifting characteristics — on different woods or woods treated in various ways. You may see a comment or two about getting rid of oil or moisture from the wood surface to be painted, but that's about it.

Yet probably the most often heard complaint about paint on wood surfaces has nothing to do with normal wear or to external factors such as ultraviolet light or chemicals or mildew, but is related to adhesion, the failure of which leads to blistering and peeling.

The wood characteristics primarily responsible for poor paint adhesion are: (1) presence of soluble wood extractives, (2) dimensional instability (the propensity for wood to shrink or swell with changing moisture conditions), and (3) the amount of exposed latewood. This last feature is primarily a problem with softwoods, especially woods that have very dense, wide bands of latewood.

Water in wood can act in concert with each of the above wood characteristics and indirectly affect paint adhesion. But water can also act directly on paint by migrating through wood and applying pressure to the back side of the paint film. Water movement is greatly enhanced by a temperature differential. If one side of a board is cold and the other side is hot, moisture in the wood will migrate toward the hot side. The explanation for this phenomenon is fairly simple: Water vaporizes when heated, leaves the wood cell walls, and enters the hollow cavities or lumens of the cells. In such a case there will be less water in the walls of the heated cells than in the walls of the cold cells. Given such conditions liquids migrate from the higher concentration (cold cell walls) to the lower concentration (warm cell walls), just like water moves up a cotton wick from an area of high concentration to an area of low.

The heated water vapor, in the cell cavities, expands and exerts a gaseous pressure behind the paint film. This causes blistering and eventual peeling. The process is accentuated if the hot side of the board faces upward and the cold side faces downward, as in boat decking and cabin roofs. This is because heated, energized water vapor tends to rise, as from a teakettle.

Armed with this information it is easy to see why

certain paint adhesion problems occur on boats. Why, for instance, cabintops and decks are extremely prone to paint failure, while planking below the waterline, if properly applied, rarely has paint failure resulting from film separation (the bilge side of planking is almost always warmer than the exterior, painted surface).

An exception occurs in trailered boats, when the exterior may be subjected to considerable heating. Pete Culler, in his book, *Boats, Oars and Rowing*, recommended painting the outside of a trailered boat white to reflect as much heat as possible — a sound suggestion.

The best remedy for floating craft, of course, is adequate ventilation of cabins and other closed areas. What is adequate ventilation? Use your paint film as a test meter —if it blisters or peels in one season, ventilation is inadequate.

So we've seen what water alone can do. Let's return to the role of wood characteristics — extractives, dimensional stability, and presence of latewood. When south Louisiana boatbuilders had to relinquish their time-honored lead-based paints a few years ago, they found that unleaded paints refused to dry properly and subsequent paint separation was common. Cypress and Spanish cedar are the prime boatbuilding woods used in that region. Both contain water-soluble extractives, which interfere with the drying and adhesion characteristics of paint, especially under damp conditions. In the past white lead overcame the problem by enhancing the drying and hardening properties of paint. Since the Louisiana boatbuilders discovered problems with non-lead-based paints, zinc sulfide has been found to be a reasonable substitute for white lead. For woods like cypress, cedar, and redwood, therefore, a primer containing zinc sulfide is essential.

Wood in the presence of fluctuating moisture conditions is dimensionally unstable; or, more simply, as all boatbuilders know, it shrinks and swells. Paints that are designed to be used on wooden boats are formulated to have a built-in flexibility, which compensates for dimensional changes on the wood surface. But as paint ages it loses some flexibility and eventually cracks. This kind of failure is hastened by the use of woods with poor dimensional stability.

Wood shrinks and swells in all directions but is most dimensionally stable in the longitudinal axis. Quartered or edge-grain (radial) surfaces are more stable than flat-sawn (tangential) surfaces. Ideally, flat-sawn planking should be avoided.

Most marine-grade plywood manufactured in this country is made either from Douglas-fir or Southern yellow pine veneer cut on a rotary lathe. Therefore, all exposed surfaces are tangential. Because of the deservedly poor reputation this type of plywood has for holding paint, manufacturers have produced plywoods with coatings or paper overlays that improve paint-holding capabilities. Many of these are now available in exterior grades, which have been used successfully by some boatbuilders for above-water applications, such as cabins and bulkheads.

Another critical problem often occurs with many softwoods that contain a dense latewood. Southern yellow pine is perhaps the most notorious for containing this condition, but it is certainly not unique. Part of the problem results from the different abilities of porous earlywood and dense latewood to absorb paint. This results in a paint film that is thinner and less firmly adhered over the latewood areas, and is, therefore, more easily eroded.

A less well-known quirk of dense latewood species arises when kiln-dried, flat-sawn lumber is planed under a dull knife or when rotary-cut plywood veneer is peeled with a dull blade. Under these conditions, the less dense earlywood is compressed by the more dense latewood. If a paint film is applied before the wood reaches equilibrium with the moisture conditions found in a boat, the crushed earlywood will later absorb moisture, swell, lift the latewood, and cause paint separation at the juncture between the earlywood and the latewood. For this reason kiln-dried lumber is best treated by permitting it to reach ambient moisture content before final sanding and painting; or if that is not possible the surface should be wetted prior to finishing.

End Grain of Flat-Sawn Boards

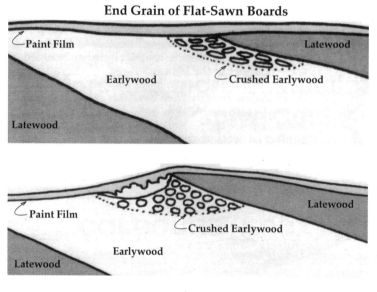

The Wood/Paint Interface: Will It Stick?

by Richard Jagels

Much has been made of the compatibility of different wood species with paints and varnishes. Surprisingly, housebuilders seem more concerned with this issue than boatbuilders, perhaps because boatbuilders have simply become habituated to the annual spring chore of scraping and painting. Of course, other wood properties — strength or decay-resistance, for instance — can have higher priority than paintability when a boatbuilder chooses wood for boat construction.

For example, oaks are notoriously poor at holding paint, yet the decay resistance, strength, and bending properties of white oak outweigh this defect. Abrupt-transition softwoods with dense latewood — woods such as Southern yellow pine, Douglas-fir, and tamarack — also show early paint failure. (Abrupt-transition woods are those species in which the boundary between low-density wood, produced early in the season, and high-density wood, produced later in the season, is very distinct.) These woods, like the porous hardwoods, have large coefficients of shrinking and swelling. Flat-sawn boards shrink and swell more than quartersawn boards, and thus the stability of the paint film is better on quartersawn surfaces. Paint films lose flexibility with age and are more likely to fracture as the wood beneath shrinks and swells.

Fillers and Sealers

The paintability of very porous woods, such as oaks, ash, and elms, can be improved by using a wood filler before painting or between the prime coat and top coats. If the pores are not filled, the paint film is suspended over large openings, enhancing the likelihood of film fracture. In Douglas-fir, Southern pine, and tamarack, there is more chance for paint failure, particularly on the flat-sawn (tangential) surface. The softer earlywood cells are crushed by overlaying denser latewood when boards are planed. Dull knives or heavy roller pressure accentuate this cell crushing. After paint or varnish is applied, the crushed earlywood cells may swell if the wood becomes wet and may push the latewood upward as raised grain, causing paint to flake off or peel.

Extractives in woods like cedar and redwood can bleed through some paints, but any paint primer that contains zinc sulfide will eliminate this problem. Resins in pines can also bleed through films. Seasoning the wood longer at higher temperatures can partially alleviate this problem.

Setting aside the problems of extractive or resin bleeding, gradual-transition softwoods with low density (cedars, redwood, cypress, and soft pines) have good paint-holding properties. These woods absorb paint evenly and do not shrink and swell as much as denser woods.

Effects of Sunlight

The choice of a particular species of wood does not guarantee good paint adhesion, though. Recent research with Southern pine, Douglas-fir, spruce, and Western red cedar has shown significantly reduced paint adhesion for oil-based (alkyd) paints if the wood was exposed to sunlight for eight weeks before painting. For latex paints, adhesion was reduced after only four weeks of sun exposure. The ultraviolet (UV) rays in sunlight photodegrade lignin — the "glue" that binds the cellulosic wood fibers together. And when paint is applied, it bonds to these "loose," broken-down surface fibers.

If UV-transparent varnish is applied to untreated wood, UV degradation of lignin can continue after the varnish is applied. This is the major reason why varnishes do not last as long as paints when exposed to sunlight. Refinishing varnished surfaces requires careful sanding, because all the wood has been exposed to UV light through the varnish. The same care needs to be taken with areas of bare, weathered wood on an otherwise painted surface.

The new evidence demonstrating problems with wood/paint adhesion on wood exposed to sunlight for only a few weeks may be an incentive for boatbuilders to build under cover. (But keep in mind that clear plastic may be UV-transparent.) If UV protection during construction is not possible, complete and thorough sanding of all surfaces should be done just before painting. Experiments have shown that treating bare wood surfaces with chromic acid (chromium trioxide) before painting or varnishing reduces photodegradation. Care must be taken to protect skin and eyes from chromic acid.

Pressure-Treated Lumber

Pressure-treated wood that is preserved with CCA salts (chrome, copper, and arsenic) should be a good substrate for paint, since CCA (type C) contains about 47 percent chromium trioxide. Early results from long-term tests seem to confirm that paint adhesion is at least as good on CCA pressure-treated wood as on untreated wood. One precaution should be noted, however. If the treated wood contains surface-deposited salts, these must be removed before finishing. Since they are water-soluble, wiping the surface, then giving it a light sanding will do the job. When sanding CCA-treated wood, use an approved respirator.

UV light degradation of wood is not the only environmental factor with which boatbuilders must contend. Recent research has shown that acidic deposition may speed up the weathering of wood. On the coast of Maine, we face not only acid rain, but also extremely acidic fogs. To what degree these accelerate UV degradation can only be guessed. But a prudent boatbuilder will build under cover if possible, and thoroughly sand surfaces shortly before painting.

Mildew, and Lots of It!

by Richard Jagels

As the wood-technology columnist for *WoodenBoat* magazine, I received a letter awhile ago from a reader concerned about mildew problems:

"A year ago I purchased an FD-35, a fiberglass boat. Yes, I know that may come as a disappointment to you, but the boat has beautiful teak woodwork. The interior is all teak, no fiberglass in sight anywhere! Here is my problem: Mildew [on the wood]. Lots of it!

"It was there when we bought the boat. We thought that the previous owner might not have been careful keeping the interior dry. We cleaned it all up during the winter, using Lysol and tung oil. It came back. We are careful to keep the interior dry! She has four Dorade vents. The cabin door is ventilated. The bilge is dry. The deck does not leak. We keep her at our yacht club. Can you give advice? I would greatly appreciate your opinion and suggestions. We love the boat! Don't tell me that we should buy one made of wood."

Is It Mildew?

First off, fiberglass has nothing to do with this boat's problem.

Mildew is caused by a fungus, and its presence can often be confirmed by its distinctive smell, although absolute identification requires microscopic examination. Mildew, more commonly referred to as mold when it occurs on wood, may appear as a fluffy, whitish or grayish bloom or may range in color from red or yellow to blue-green or even black. In boats, the black discoloration is quite common. The color is a result of spore production by the fungus, with different species producing different-colored spores.

Although the spores, and hence the discoloration, are produced only on the surface of the wood, the fungus usually penetrates the wood to some depth with colorless hyphae (microscopic threadlike structures). Scraping or wiping the surface may remove the discoloration, but when conditions are right again, the colorless fungus remaining in the wood will produce more spores on the surface and more surface discoloration.

Mold Versus Stain

The group of fungi that cause mold or mildew are called Ascomycetes. Certain members of this group are known as "staining" fungi, because they produce colored spores within the wood rather than on the wood surface. Both mold fungi and staining fungi use starches and sugars stored in specialized wood cells as their food source. However, under the right conditions of moisture and temperature, if Ascomycete fungi (particularly the stain fungi) persist in the wood long enough to deplete these easily digestible carbohydrates, they will attack the walls of the wood cell and slowly weaken the surface of the wood — a process known as soft rot.

Mold fungi generally do not penetrate deeply into wood, because they require abundant oxygen (more than the Basidiomycetes, which cause interior decay of wood). As long as the stored starches are available near the wood surface, the mold fungus will persist. When this food supply dwindles, the fungus may enter a resting stage or simply die. If new food sources (such as linseed oil or tung oil) are added to the wood, the mold will persist as long as air humidity or wood moisture content remain high enough.

A Persistent Beast

Although Lysol and other disinfectants can kill some bacteria and perhaps some surface mildews, they have little penetrating effect on wood. Once the mold fungus has become as well established as it seems to be in your teak, a surface application of Lysol would have little effect, particularly if you did not first remove the old finish. I can recommend a couple of possible remedies, but cannot guarantee their efficacy since persistent and well-established mold fungi are very difficult to eradicate.

Being fastidious about keeping the boat well ventilated all year around and using the tried-and-true method of going over the boat once a year with a solution of one part household chlorine bleach to five to ten parts water can solve the problem for many a wooden boat. Bleach, however, will give oiled or unfinished teak a whitish-gray look. You can avoid this by using an oxalic acid solution instead. Oxalic acid is much less volatile than chlorine bleach and, therefore, less of a health hazard in enclosed spaces. Never mix chlorine bleach with other cleaning solutions — toxic fumes could be generated.

Another way to attack the problem is to strip the woodwork, apply a mildewcide, and refinish it. The time to do this is when the wood is at its driest, perhaps after winter storage, depending on how and where the boat is stored. Scrape and sand all wood surfaces to remove any trace of finish. If your woodwork is extremely damp and if your boat, like the letter writer's, is a fiberglass boat, you could then heat up the interior of the boat to as high a temperature as is practical (90 degrees F or higher, if possible) and maintain that temperature for a minimum of a week in an attempt to bring the moisture content of the wood below 15 percent.

Caution: This kind of severe and prolonged heating may be difficult to achieve, and, of course, it is not recommended for wooden boats.

When you are confident that the wood is as dry as possible, apply a surface treatment of a mildewcide (more on this later). If the mildewcide is water based, again dry the wood, this time with localized heating. A hair dryer or a heat gun used for removing paint may be appropriate here.

For final finishing of the wood, apply varnish or an oil that does not have a natural seed-oil base; if it does, a mold inhibitor should be incorporated into the finish. A hard, glossy finish like varnish can be cleaned periodically and is less likely to attract more surface mold. Another advantage of varnish is that it is better at excluding oxygen from the wood beneath it, and thus better at preventing microorganisms from growing. Natural-oil finishes always remain a little tacky and, therefore, are magnets for dirt and mold spores. Oil finishes also tend to be slightly more hydroscopic (water attracting). If you must have an oil finish, then incorporate a mildewcide into it.

Mildewcides

The effectiveness of a mildewcide is directly proportional to its toxicity to mold fungi. Unfortunately, many of the most effective mildewcides are also hazardous to human health — pentachlorophenol (PCP) being the most blatant example. I do not recommend the use of PCP under any circumstances.

Several other less toxic chemicals are also reasonably effective in controlling mold growth: copper naphthenate; zinc naphthenate; copper-8-quinolinolate; bis-(tri-n-butyltin) oxide (TBTO); 2-(4-thiazolyl) benzi-midazol; 3-iodo-2-propynyl-butyl-carbamate (Polyphase); and chromium trioxide (chromic acid).

With the exception of chromium trioxide (which is dissolved in water), the above chemicals are usually dissolved in mineral spirits and hence can be incorporated into the final finish as well as used as a pretreatment on the stripped wood. The copper-containing preservatives will turn the wood slightly green, and the chromium trioxide will either darken the natural wood color or turn it slightly green or yellow, depending on the wood species. If you cannot adequately reduce the moisture content of the wood, then I would recommend using chromium trioxide. Otherwise, one of the other preservatives would be preferable.

Probably the most effective chemicals that are readily available and do not appreciably change the natural color of woods are Polyphase and TBTO (or combinations of the two). The following companies produce clear or tinted versions of these wood preservatives, alone or in combinations: Cabot, Cuprinol, Lucas, Magicolor, Minwax, Olympic, and Sherwin Williams. I am sure this is not an exhaustive list.

Health Risks

The chemical mildewcides that I have listed are thought to have minimal health risks. (TBTO can cause skin irritation for some individuals.) However, many of these chemicals, particularly Polyphase, are relatively new on the market, and we do not know the long-term health risks associated with using them. Avoid using any of these preservatives in areas where food is prepared or stored. I would certainly advise wearing appropriate respiratory and skin protection (face masks, gloves, etc.) when applying these chemicals. Forced ventilation with fans is highly recommended when working with wood preservatives or household chlorine bleach in the interior of a boat. Maintain forced ventilation for several days after application to ensure removal of residual volatiles.

■ V ■

Painting for Longevity

by Ed McClave   Drawings by Greg Summers

Wooden boats are expensive — expensive to build, to repair, and to maintain — but they needn't be nearly so expensive as they are. The bad reputation that wooden boats have today, which has contributed to the decline of the business, comes in part from the high cost of caring for and repairing boats that were expected to last only about 15 years, yet have survived half a century or more. For existing wooden boats to survive and for the building of new ones to be a viable option, construction design, material selection, and maintenance and repair techniques must be geared toward a long, easily maintainable, repairable life. New construction and restoration work should be done with the goal of a 50-year intended life span.

Painting a boat's structural members during construction can increase its life span and decrease maintenance costs.

arate trades. A woodworker wasn't likely ever to pick up a paintbrush; painting was considered less-skilled work and beneath the dignity of a real boatbuilder.

The result of this caste system was that most of the structure of a boat, and virtually all of the cut fits, went together "dry" (that is, without application of any protective coating to the bare wood). This situation prevails today in some shops and in a lot of repair yards, and the quality of a lot of boatbuilding and repair work suffers because of it. There's no doubt that painting as you fit is messy and seems inefficient, but I'm quite convinced that the effect on the quality of the finished product makes it all worthwhile. There's no room today in the wooden boat business for the sort of arrogance that makes boatbuilders want to avoid the mundane task of getting dirty.

Painting as a Construction Technique

In the process of taking apart many old boats for repair or restoration, I've often thought about how much better many of those boats would have fared over the years had more attention been paid to painting during the construction process and during the execution of various repairs. It's not surprising, however, that painting isn't generally considered to be an integral part of wooden boat construction; boatbuilding for better or worse, is a tradition-bound business, and boat painting and boatbuilding were traditionally sep-

Painting to Prevent Decay

One of the primary aging processes in wood is biological decay. Biological decay, of which rot is the best-known form, requires fairly high freshwater moisture contents (but below saturation level), reasonably high temperatures, and oxygen. Paint is quite effective in preventing water and oxygen from entering wood surfaces.

A second, and much slower, type of deterioration is chemical hydrolysis — the dissolution of the cellu-

— 23 —

lose component of wood into the water. It's most apparent on frame heels, near the end-grain of floor timbers, inside centerboard trunks and slots, and in other places where bare wood is immersed in water all the time the boat is in the water. A simple coat of paint provides very effective protection against this for many years — indefinitely, if the paint film can be maintained.

Painting joints before assembly makes rot's "domino effect" a lot less likely. When fresh water gets into a wood component in sufficient quantity to initiate rot, the rot often spreads to adjacent pieces of wood. Accordingly, every joint where wood touches wood should be painted on both surfaces.

Painting to Prevent or
Slow Down Dimensional Change

Another effect of aging in wooden boats, and, indeed, in any wood structure, is failure related to the swelling and shrinking due to changes in moisture content. This problem is more critical for the underbodies of boats that are hauled out for the winter than for those that stay in the water all the time, but all wooden boats, in any circumstance, are subject to long- and short-term changes in the moisture content of their components.

A certain amount of swelling and shrinking is unavoidable in wooden boat components. Any change in moisture content below the fiber-saturation point will cause dimensional change across the grain direction of boards that are free to deform, or it will cause transverse stresses in boards that are restrained from deformation. (Virtually all the individual wooden pieces that make up a boat are at least partially restrained from swelling or warping.) These stresses can damage the wood directly through transverse

checking, or they can cause failure by crushing the wood under the heads of restraining fastenings, which in turn allows some deformation, which can weaken the structure, allow seams to open, etc. In many cases, the damage can be minimized or even completely eliminated if changes in the wood's moisture content can be made to happen more slowly. Using paint is a very effective way to slow things down.

A wide board will warp or cup for two reasons when its moisture content changes. First, if it is slash-sawn and there's significant curvature in the rings, the difference between the shrinkage/swelling rate along the annual rings (the tangential direction) and across the annual rings (the radial direction) will cause the board to warp (Figure 1). (The tangential shrinkage/swelling rate is about twice the radial rate for most woods.) Any damage done by deformation or stress due to this process will happen no matter how quickly the moisture content of the wood changes. The problem can be minimized by: the selection of species that have low rates of dimensional change or that have nearly equal radial and tangential shrinkage rates; the use of rift-grain (vertical-grain) lumber; and the selection of boards with only slight ring curvature (in other words, boards from big trees). Unfortunately, paint isn't a lot of help here in preventing this kind of deformation (or stress, if the board is prevented from deforming by the structure around it).

There's another way for a board to warp, however. If one side gets wet and swells while the other stays dry, a board will warp, or, if restrained, it will develop internal stresses. The deformation and stresses resulting from this condition have the same result as in the previous case, except that in this case, when the moisture content of the board equalizes at a new level throughout, the board will flatten out again, which

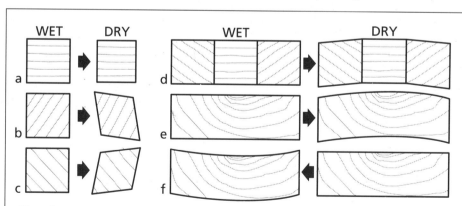

Figure 1
These end-grain views illustrate the consequences of the difference between wood's radial (across the rings) and tangential (along the rings) shrinkage and swelling rate. Painting will slow the rate at which this happens, but it won't prevent it.
(a) A square section with flat or vertical ring alignment shrinks to a rectangular section. (b & c) A square section with diagonal rings shrinks to a diamond section. (d) End-grain sections are combined to show why a flat board with curving rings shrinks (e) or swells (f) to a cupped, or warped, section.

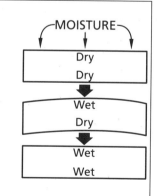

Figure 2
Uneven wetting and drying can cause a board to cup regardless of the ring alignment. Painting can prevent this.

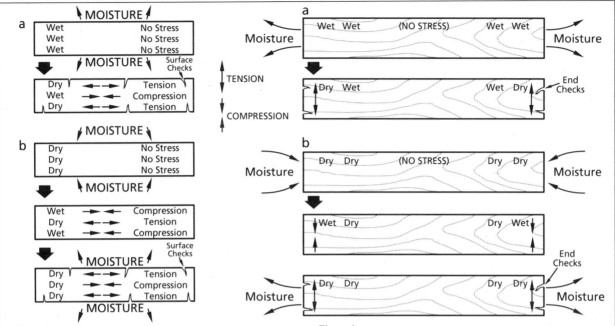

Figure 3
These end-grain views illustrate the effect of rapid changes in the moisture content of a board's surface, while the interior wood responds much more slowly. Painting would slow the rate of change of the surface moisture content, allowing the interior more of a chance to "keep up."
(a) When the surface of a board is dried rapidly, cross-grain tension develops on the surfaces and causes surface checks.
(b) If a board (or part of a board) is restrained from swelling because of an increase in moisture content the resulting cross-grain compression stress may cause permanent deformation of the cell structure (compressive set), and the board, when brought back to its original moisture content, will be narrower than it was originally at the same moisture level. If it is restrained from shrinking to this narrower dimension, it develops cross-grain tension, which will cause checking. In the illustrated case, the interior wood restrains the surface wood from swelling and then from shrinking, resulting in surface checks.

Figure 4
These side views illustrate the effect of rapid moisture changes at the ends of boards. Because of the directional cell structure, water moves much more freely along the grain of wood than across the grain. Rapid drying or rapid wetting of the ends causes end-checking. Painting the end-grain prevents the problem in either case.
(a) Rapid drying of the ends of a board will cause cross-grain tension, since the shrinkage across the end will be restrained by the wet adjacent wood. This tension will cause end-checking.
(b) This is another illustration of compressive set. The ends gain moisture rapidly but are restrained from swelling by the drier adjacent wood. This restraint causes cross-grain compressive failure at the ends, and upon subsequent drying the ends want to shrink to be narrower than they were originally. This shrinkage is restrained by the adjacent wood (which didn't get wet, and wasn't crushed by compression), and the ends develop cross-grain tension that causes end-checking.

may cause more problems. Again, restraint from deformation doesn't eliminate the problem; it only changes it (Figure 2).

A related problem occurs when the surface of a board swells rapidly due to a humidity change in the air while the inside of the board stays dry, or when the surface of a wet board dries rapidly while the inside remains swelled up. In the first case, the surface fibers may become permanently crushed, since they are restrained from swelling by the unswelled wood inside. When the board reaches a uniform moisture content throughout, the surface will check (fail in transverse tension). In the second case, the surface fibers are restrained from shrinking freely by the still-swelled wood inside the board, and again, checks develop on the surface (Figure 3).

Still another problem occurs near the ends of boards. Here, moisture can move in and out of the board longitudinally through the open pores (cell cavities) of the end-grain much faster than it can where it must diffuse transversely across cell boundaries. The wood near uncoated end-grain responds much more rapidly (by swelling and shrinking) to moisture changes than does the rest of the board, causing end checking, which is often structurally damaging (Figure 4).

In any of the cases mentioned above where a difference in moisture content through the thickness or along the length of a board causes problems, these problems can be almost completely prevented by applying a uniform coat of paint all over the board. If the paint film is sufficient, the moisture will diffuse more slowly through the paint than through the wood itself. The moisture content of the board will change slowly and uniformly across its width and thickness, and along its length, and deformation or stress due to non-uniform dimensional change will be eliminated.

When to Paint?
The best time to paint is when a piece of wood is freshly milled, or when a joint is newly cut and fitted.

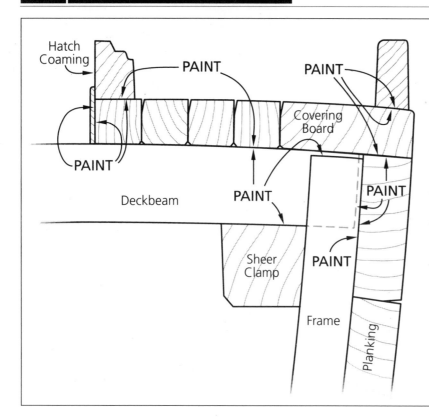

Figure 5
Places to paint before assembly:
Underside of decking and covering boards*
Tops and ends of deckbeams
Edges of exposed decking inside deck openings*
Back face of trim in hatch opening*
Underside of hatch coamings and toerails (varnish is often preferable here)*
Deck surface under hatch coamings and toerails*
Tops and outboard surfaces of frames
Top of sheer clamp
Inside planking

* Necessary to prevent drying of bedding compounds in these locations

Like most adhesives, paint sticks best to fresh surfaces. This makes a good case for painting as you go along during construction. Paint applied later, to surfaces that may be weathered, salty, or oil-soaked, hasn't the same long-lasting, protective effect.

Where to Paint?

Wood is designed to transfer moisture longitudinally, along the grain, parallel to the cells. Therefore, end-grain surfaces are the big chink in the armor, because moisture moves into and out of wood most rapidly through the end-grain. End-grain is the place where paint can do the most good, and where the lack of it can do the most harm.

The tops and the bottoms of frames, the ends of deckbeams, and the end-grain surfaces of wood floor timbers and butt blocks are all particularly susceptible to the entry of deck leakage or fresh water that might find its way into the bilge. These are very important places to paint. Unfortunately, they're often not very likely to get any paint during the construction process. They're also impossible to paint once the boat is completed. It is very important as well to paint the end-grain of those components whose grain penetrates the deck and provides an end-grain path for moisture to get under the deck; knightheads, hawse timbers, samson posts, and stanchions should be sealed on all surfaces before they are fastened in place and their end-grain covered by railcaps, etc.

Along with wooden components that penetrate the deck, the insides of the holes through which those components pass should also be thoroughly painted; mast holes, ventilator holes, chainplate slots, and the like are also weak spots in which end-grain is exposed to likely deck leakage.

Horizontal or nearly horizontal surfaces are also critical locations for paint: the tops of sheer clamps before the deckbeams go down, frame tops, floor-timber tops, breasthooks, and quarter knees. These are all places where water can lie and penetrate if there isn't a barrier. The rotting of many a deckbeam could have been avoided if the top surface of the beam had been painted before the deck was laid. A leak that's only a nuisance over a painted beam means certain trouble when it's over a beam of unpainted oak. Those little chamfers on the underside edges of laid decking aren't just there for looks; they're drains. If water leaks through the seam, it is supposed to escape along the groove formed by the chamfers before it soaks into, and rots, the deckbeam. If the top of the beam is painted, then the leakage has a chance to dry out before it saturates the beam (Figure 5).

If possible, all wood-to-wood faying surfaces in a boat, whether end-grain is involved or not, should be painted. This includes the outside surfaces of the frames where they contact the planking (yes, frames can be steam-bent with paint on them — the steam box provides the heat for bending, and the moisture should be in the wood already). Floor-timber-to-frame surfaces are also important.

Every piece of the deadwood and backbone of any boat should be completely painted before assembly, including the faying surfaces of joints or scarfs in the backbone. The only surfaces that should be left bare are the edges of plank and deck seams, and rabbets against which cotton or oakum caulking will bear — a painted surface is too slippery for a caulked seam. End-grain of planking should, however, be painted.

Construction Design Considerations

As I've already pointed out, paint in the right places can eliminate the rapid swelling and shrinking of wood in response to changing environmental conditions and slow the aging process. Construction that is designed to allow painting in those places, both initially and periodically later on, also helps. Although paint is particularly important on end-grain surfaces like frame heads and heels, it unfortunately peels, chips, or wears away in time. If the boat is constructed to allow the occasional paintbrush access to such places, the protective paint film can be maintained indefinitely. Frame heads get wet from deck leaks and are more apt to rot. Paint here will just about eliminate the problem, and if the frames are cut off ⅛ inch to ³⁄₁₆ inch below the underside of the deck, the paint protection can be maintained. (Frame tops should be cut off a bit below the top edge of the sheerstrake, anyway, in case the sheerstrake shrinks. Then an unexpected dry season out of the water won't result in the frame heads jacking the covering boards off the boat.)

Exposed (i.e., unpocketed) frame heels are also a place where paint makes a big difference. If frames are cut off ½ inch or so above the keel surface, or centerboard trunk log, or whatever, the paint on the heels, and the protection it affords, can be maintained indefinitely (Figure 6).

Painting Faying Surfaces of Deck Joinerwork

Deck joinerwork (such as cabin sides, cockpit coamings, hatch coamings, and toerails) will hold its finish a lot longer if the bottom surfaces are given a good coat of paint or varnish after being fitted and before permanent attachment to the deck. Careful priming of deck joinerwork, especially if it's to be finished bright (varnished), can have a tremendous effect on annual maintenance costs over a boat's entire lifetime. In the same spirit, the edges of transoms should be well painted or varnished during construction before those edges are covered up by the plank ends (Figure 5).

What Kind of Paint?

For any applications below the waterline, red lead primer is my favorite sealant. Red lead is heavy-bodied, with a high percentage of pigment, so a single coat provides a good moisture barrier. (We generally try for two coats, however, especially on end-grain.) Red lead seems to stick better and last longer than other, more glossy paints. It dries fast, too, an important factor when joints must be cut, painted, and assembled without delay. And because red lead contains only a moderate amount of hardening oil, it doesn't tend to crack and peel as easily as, say, porch and deck enamel.

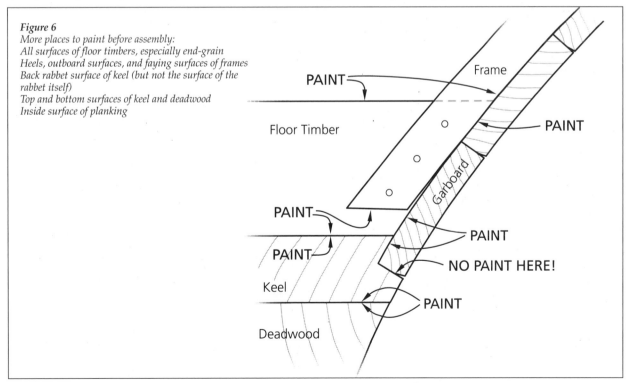

Figure 6
More places to paint before assembly:
All surfaces of floor timbers, especially end-grain
Heels, outboard surfaces, and faying surfaces of frames
Back rabbet surface of keel (but not the surface of the rabbet itself)
Top and bottom surfaces of keel and deadwood
Inside surface of planking

PAINT — Frame

Floor Timber

PAINT —

Garboard

PAINT —

PAINT —

PAINT —

Keel

PAINT

NO PAINT HERE!

PAINT

Deadwood

Above decks, varnish should be used on the bottom surfaces of any deck joinerwork to be finished bright. If time permits, two or three good coats, lapped up well onto the side surfaces, will keep out the moisture and prevent the wood from staining or the exposed film from peeling. Although the exposed surfaces will need annual revarnishing, those that are completely out of reach of the sun will not. Varnish under a piece of joinerwork lasts a very long time.

There are many cases, particularly when fitting interior components, when some kind of sealer coating can greatly enhance the longevity of the subsequent finish and sometimes extend the life of the piece itself, but the drying time of red lead or varnish presents an unacceptable delay in the construction process. In such cases, shellac (3- or 4-pound-cut orange shellac) or the quick-drying acrylic sealer sold by many of the paint companies will save the day. Either one will dry in a few minutes and will allow the fitting and assembly work to continue uninterrupted. The acrylic sealer gives off noxious fumes, but it is pretty much invisible under varnish. Shellac is a lot more pleasant to use, but it gives wood a dark color under a clear finish.

Paint as a Primer for Bedding Compounds

Although polysulfide and polyurethane bedding compounds have made inroads into the wooden boat business (and they're certainly useful in many instances), a number of us traditionalists still prefer oil-based bedding compounds for their ease of handling, their lower viscosity, and their lack of adhesive properties (which makes structures more readily maintainable and repairable). Oil-based bedding compounds can provide long and effective service, but only when all the wood in contact with them is sealed with a barrier coat such as paint, varnish, or shellac. If the bare wood is directly in contact with an oil-based bedding compound, the bedding turns to powder a few years down the road after the wood sucks the oil right out of it. Only the hard, inflexible filler material is left behind.

What goes for bedding compound goes for seam putty as well. If you use an oil-based seam compound or glazing putty, great care should be taken to prevent it from contacting bare wood. In caulked seams, both the cotton caulking and the edges of the seams should be well primed with paint before the putty is put in.

Using Paint to Isolate Metal from Wood

Another very important place for paint during the construction process, also often neglected, is between metal and wood. Diagonal hull or deck straps, metal floors, or any other metal components or fittings such as seacocks, struts, and stuffing boxes should be isolated from direct contact with wood. A couple of thick coats of red lead seem to work best for this purpose. I always try to paint both the wood and the metal. It's even worthwhile to paint underneath washers.

Damp, salty wood in contact with metal provides the electrolyte (the ion-conducting solution) needed for corrosion of the metal. In turn, the chemical products of the corrosion can break down the wood. Hydroxyl ions produced at cathodic sites on corroding metal are delignifiers; they break down the resin (lignin) that holds the cellulose fibers of wood together, destroying the wood. When metal fittings are protected from corrosion by being connected either directly or through a boat's bonding system to a sacrificial zinc anode, the wood around them is often destroyed. The chemical reaction responsible for the damage takes place where the metal and wet wood make contact, and painting both the metal and the wood at and near their contact surface deprives the metal of ready access to the water in the damp wood (the electrolyte) and stifles the oxygen supply, thus preventing the reaction from occurring. This simple act of painting can go a long way toward protecting the wood from corrosion damage.

Driving Screws with Paint

Another place where paint is useful during construction is as a lubricant and protective coating for wood screws used as plank fastenings below or near the waterline. (Although this isn't a new idea, it's not at all popular with boatbuilders who prefer to stay clean.) Driving screws with paint serves several functions: First, thick red lead is a good lubricant, and, unlike soap, grease, etc., is totally nontoxic to the wood. Second, the paint fills any voids between the plank and the frame, and fills any threads that are not fully engaged in the wood due to an oversized or misshapen pilot hole. Third, the paint seals around the screw shank, eliminating the possibility of leakage along it, which is not as uncommon a problem as you might think since many screw pilot bits drill oversized shank holes. Fourth, the paint squeezes back out at you around the screw head and protects the slot from corrosion, making removal of the screw many years later much easier.

Of all the uses of paint during construction, driving screws with it is certainly the messiest; the stuff gets all over you, your drills, power drivers, bit braces, and clothes. But I think it's worth the mess. We use old thick red lead paint for this purpose, thickened up even more with 8-pound-cut shellac until it will cling to the screws without dripping off. (It is hard to believe, but red lead and shellac mix together just fine.) The screw is dipped up to the top of the threads and then driven. Some of the paint may squeeze out between the plank and the frame; some of it fills voids between the threads; and the rest squeezes out and ends up on your clothes. (Note: I'm talking here about silicon-bronze screws. Zinc chromate paint should be used with galvanized screws.)

Setting Bungs in Paint

Larger boats generally have the heads of their plank fastenings countersunk and covered by wooden bungs. A wooden bung, especially if it is cut from scraps of the same plank it's in, swells and shrinks the same as the plank does, and thus remains invisible under the paint. My partners and I have found that the best way to set bungs in a hull, assuming that the bungs are a good fit in their holes, is in a mixture of paint and heavy shellac. This mixture holds up well, and, best of all, it allows clean removal of the bung should repair ever be necessary. We use red lead paint mixed about 50-50 with the same 8-pound-cut shellac that we use as a double-planking cement. Where the red color is a problem, white lead paste is substituted for the red lead.

Other Coatings

Until now, I've been talking a lot about paint and not much about alternative coatings. Advocates, like me, of using paint everywhere in the construction of a wooden hull are under fire from two diverse groups: traditionalists, who believe that everything should be coated with linseed oil, pine tar, and other sticky, smelly substances that turn black, and the modern-materials crowd, who like to cover everything, including themselves, with epoxy.

Yes, linseed oil and epoxy are coatings and will do most of the things that paint and shellac will do. However, oils and tars don't contain the pigments that contribute substantially to any coating's moisture-barrier properties, they don't dry very quickly, and they tend not to form the kind of thick, durable film that paint does.

Epoxy has no advantages over a paint film of the same thickness. Both paint molecules and epoxy molecules are big, with spaces between them, whereas water molecules are small, have interesting electrostatic properties, and can diffuse at about the same rate through either paint or epoxy. Epoxy dries more slowly than red lead, and it often tends to peel off wood that undergoes dimensional change. I use epoxy a lot as an adhesive, but since I believe in coating everything, there is a lot of surface area to deal with. I don't care to expand my usage of epoxy to that extent.

In conclusion, for wooden boat building to survive as a trade in these times of high labor costs, the boats being built today must be built in such a way that they last a long time, continue to have only moderate main-tenance costs well into their old age, and remain easily repairable throughout a long, useful lifetime. This longevity, maintainability, and repairability must be designed and built into new boats from the ground up. With this in mind, it's difficult to justify the cutting of any corners in the name of construction efficiency. Painting during construction has been, historically, the most commonly cut corner of all, but it's one of the easiest to avoid cutting.

Painting for Decoration

By Maynard Bray   Illustrations by Kathy Bray

*I*t's wonderful how well a wooden boat lends itself to decoration and adornment. Its structure abounds with sharp corners, and projecting and receding planes, and its material is soft and thick enough for carving names, scrolls, and cove stripes, and for scribing crisp lines where one color meets another. Wooden boats present opportunities in painting that simply don't exist in thin-skinned, rounded-off fiberglass craft.

In our preoccupation with painting for preservation and high gloss, we tend to forget what joy can be had when working with color and decoration. Most wooden boats require seasonal repainting, so every year you have a chance to try out something new in the way of color, or else fine-tune what remains from your last effort. As a boat-owner friend once said, "Through my spring painting, I get a new boat every year." And, as an old-time boat painter told me, "The good thing about paint is that if you don't like the color, you can always change it."

Try thinking of painting as an opportunity instead of a chore. Be a little less concerned with how much your wooden boat shines (leave high-gloss paints to the fiberglass crowd and to the few wooden boat owners who can really afford that luxury), and devote more attention to attractive and unique color schemes. You might find the rewards of wooden boat ownership significantly enhanced.

When it comes choosing colors, a look at marine paintings depicting seventeenth- and eighteenth-cen-

tury small craft may help. Bright colors and decorative paint schemes were common back then, whereas recent times have seen boats become more conservative and sober in their appearance — in this country, anyway. European working craft are still brightly painted, using mostly the primary colors of red, yellow, and blue, along with white, black, orange, and bright green.

As with any object that's painted with all bright colors, there can be too much of a good thing. That intensity gets tiresome pretty quickly. In my view a garish appearance is not what we're after in our boats at least. And since white is one of the best colors for preserving a wooden boat's topsides, I wouldn't want to stray very often from light tones for topsides, or for decks, either, for that matter.

Color and decoration can be used to emphasize the attractive features of your boat or to help play down what doesn't look so good. I think the brightest colors should be used sparingly for accent, while most areas should be painted subdued shades that can live with each other in peaceful neighborliness. Your own personal taste has to be satisfied, of course — that's the whole point of painting for decoration. But right now, since I'm the one who is writing on this subject, it's my personal taste that you must endure. Some color schemes that I think attractive show up in the following examples. I hope these will prove helpful in showing some of the possibilities — and pitfalls to avoid — in painting for decoration.

Hull: White
Bottom: Copper-brown antifouling
Sheerstrake: Deep, rich buff
Deck: Warm, light gray or tan
Coaming: Dark oil
Tiller and booms: Varnished
Mast: Light buff, varnished, or oiled
Hull interior: Off-white or warm,
  light gray
Floorboards: Buff like the mast
  or gray that is darker than
  the inside of the hull

Alden O-Boat

Here is a hull with a rather flat sheer, so I've given her a mildly contrasting sheerstrake to perk up her sheer line and provide an accent. Because of her low freeboard, which appears to be even lower because of the contrasting sheerstrake, there is no need for a boottop. There is good contrast between the white topsides and the copper-brown antifouling bottom paint. Brown competes less with the sheerstrake than copper-red would have, and was used for that reason. I wanted the vivid buff sheerstrake — a beautifully tapering line — to be the dominant accent for this boat. Brown bottom paint, if not available as such, can be made by mixing red and green antifouling paints together.

If there is to be any brightwork, I'd suggest varnishing the tiller and the two booms. These are high-visibility pieces that can be taken home and varnished. The steam-bent coaming's handsome shape should be emphasized by being contrasted against the deck. Because the coaming is of oak, which stains from moisture, a dark oil (boiled linseed oil, colored with pine tar and thinned with turpentine) may be a more practical finish than varnish. The deck should be a warm, light shade — perhaps a gray or a tan — so it will be easy on the eyes and will not show the dirt, yet will reflect most of the sun's heat.

The mast would look fine varnished, or, for lower maintenance, painted a lighter buff than the sheerstrake. Woolsey Mast Buff is always reliable here. Alternatively, the mast could be oiled. The masthead and tops of the booms would look great painted white. Decorative stars, carved into the after ends of both booms, in red, blue, or gold leaf would be a nice touch. I'd do the hull interior in an off-white or light gray, and the floorboards in a darker gray or a buff like the mast.

Biscayne Bay 14

For this boat we did several color studies on paper — each one using a different family of colors — before selecting the scheme shown here. The hull is knuckle-sided, providing natural breaks for the stripes, and it has handsome, tapering planks, so it made sense to use a colored sheerstrake, even though it is exceptionally wide. Because of the strake's width, however, too much contrast between it and the rest of the hull would have been a mistake, so we picked a rich, almost golden buff, then used a cream for the rest of the hull below it, down to the antifouling bottom paint. Copper-red was a logical choice for the latter, although brown would also have worked.

The deck is planked with cedar boards and only the foredeck is canvas-covered, so to stabilize the shrinking and swelling as much as possible, a good coating of white paint was used. And, since the decking ran out over the guardrails without a well-defined break (toerails terminate at the shrouds), the guardrails were also painted white. Neither the low coamings nor the short toerails are much of a presence, so we used a teak-like wood and left them to weather for low maintenance.

Since the interior is fairly busy, with chine stringers, bent frames, floorboards, and a centerboard trunk, we painted it all the same inconspicuous color: a type of duck-boat drab. Only the spars and tiller were varnished.

Sheerstrake: Deep, rich gold
Topsides from sheerstrake to painted waterline: Rich cream
Bottom: Copper-red antifouling
Deck and guardrails: White
Interior: Duck-boat drab
Mast and spars: Varnished
Tiller: Varnished
Coaming, toerails, and miscellaneous trim: Weathered

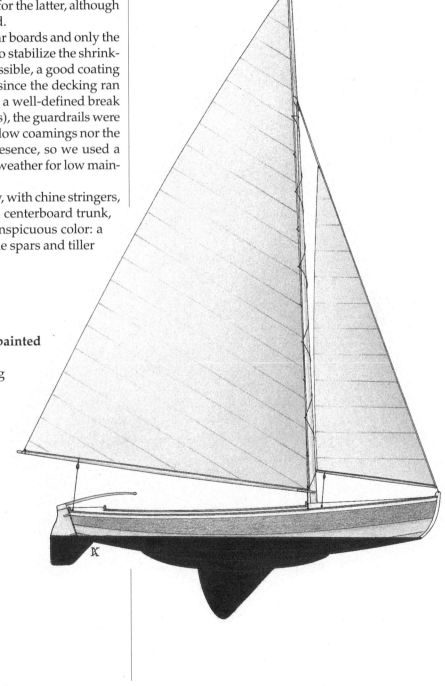

Hull: Cream

Bottom: Copper-green (not blue-green) antifouling

Second or "binder" strake: White, with red bead along lower corner

Sheerstrake bead: Red

"Mustache": Red

Rudder, tiller, transom, daggerboard, rails, and seats: Varnished

Mast and sprit: Oiled, with white tips, or varnished

Seats: Varnished, or painted rich tan

Hull interior: White, warmed up with a dash of cream

Floorboards: Weathered, varnished, or deep tan

Acorn 15 Sailing Dinghy

If the planks are uniformly tapered toward the bow and the stern, lapstrake boats are best painted a light color to show them off. Bad plank lines, however, can be downplayed with a dark-colored hull. Varnish work could be lavishly used on a small boat like this, because she is small enough to be taken into the shop for her annual finishing. Spars, masts, rudder, tiller, transom, guardrails, inwales, seat risers, and even the floorboards would look good varnished. But, for lowest maintenance, all this could be painted instead.

Level, painted waterlines on lapstrake boats are tough to make look right, and difficult to paint, besides. I'd avoid them, if possible, but sometimes there's no choice for boats that stay overboard. On the other hand, lapped planking offers some wonderful possibilities for full-length color bands and stripes, an example of which has been used here. The band is, of course, created by painting the second strake white. That strake's lower edge is beaded to facilitate striping. A similar bead has been planed into the lower corner of the sheerstrake, and both beads have been done in red. Since it's very easy to do, I've called for a red-painted "mustache" within the triangular space bounded by the stem rabbet, the scribed waterline, and a plank lap. I've left the stem above the waterline white — an easy matter with this boat, since her planking fairs to the rabbet line, leaving a natural paint break there.

For this boat, which we've assumed needs antifouling bottom paint, copper-green was selected. It should be a yellow-green, rather than bluish-green, however, so it will harmonize with the cream topsides. Since neither the rudder nor the daggerboard will be in place except when sailing, they can be varnished all over; this avoids the task of cutting in one color against another. Guardrails and inwales should probably be varnished — maybe the seats as well — and the spars could be oiled, with white-painted tips. A warm white would be good for the hull interior, along with tan or weathered floorboards. Stars, diamonds or other decorations could be applied to the seats. The boat's name would look great carved into either the forward (if there's no interfering stern knee) or after face of a varnished transom, then gilded.

Egret

Here is a boat that, in spite of her flat bottom and topsides, is inherently pretty from nearly any vantage point. Although she'd look just fine in the traditional all-white commonly used for old-time working sharpies, I couldn't resist trying out one of my favorite combinations: gray, white, buff, and copper-red.

To complement the strong sheer, I thought a sheered boottop would look good, and decided that its white color could be carried up the stem and sternpost to advantage. At the deck edge, there are toerails, along with guardrails with a beaded trim strip beneath them, giving all kinds of opportunity for striping. I've shown a buff trim strip with a black bead, and have simply oiled the guardrails and toerails, but there are hundreds of other good combinations. Browns, greens, reds, and yellows, for example, could work well here.

Both the uninterrupted cabintop and the oval shapes of the cabin sides and coamings cry out to be accented. Rather than have too much going on, I've emphasized only the cabintop by painting it buff to match the sheer trim, and pretty much left all else on deck white. The cabintop edge molding, however, I've shown darkly oiled as a means of further pointing up the lovely, curved shape of the cabin.

Topsides: Warm, light-to-medium gray
Bottom: Copper-red antifouling
Boottop, stem, counter, and sternpost: White
Sheer trim: Rich yellow-buff
Bead: Black, red, yellow, or harmonizing accent color of choice
Guardrail and toerail: Dark oil, or gray like the topsides
Deck: White, or a gray that is lighter than the topsides
Cabin sides and coaming: White
Cabintop: Buff, like the sheer, with dark oil on edge molding
Masts and sprits: Oiled, with white tips

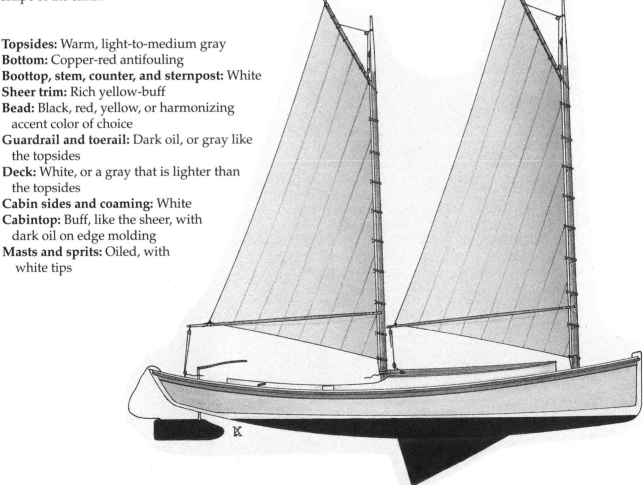

Asa Thomson Skiff

There are a couple of good ways to paint dory-type boats if the lowest lap clears the water so it isn't subject to fouling. The easiest way, shown here, is to paint the garboards as well as the flat bottom with the same antifouling paint. Alternatively, a level waterline can be scribed into the garboard planks, and the antifouling paint can be stopped there. With this second approach, the sheerstrake can be highlighted without making the color scheme too busy.

Although small craft can be brightly painted and still look good, subtle use of color works on them as well. Here, very bright lime green has been used as an accent stripe along a plank lap, while the rest of the boat is fairly plain. For a little additional interest, I've painted the outer stem and the sternpost white.

Generally, in a small, open boat, there is enough interior busy work for the eye to take in without fooling around with too many color variations. In this boat, the seats could be different — perhaps white — and maybe the inside of the flat bottom, but I'd not recommend doing the interior sides in anything but a single, easy-to-take color — probably the same gray as used outside.

Bottom and garboard: Copper-red antifouling
Topsides: Warm, medium gray
Stripe: Bright lime green or bead yellow
Stem and sternpost: White, or gray like the
  topsides
Interior: Gray like the topsides
Rail: White, or gray like the topsides

Acorn 10 Yacht Tender

Because this boat will be spending most of her time hoisted clear of the water, antifouling bottom paint is unnecessary, and the difficult task of striking and painting a level waterline on her lapstrake hull can be avoided. And because, for my friend Debbie, teal blue had to make an appearance, that is the dominant exterior color. So as not to obscure the handsome, tapering plank lines, a lighter shade was selected, however.

To show off her already jaunty sheer, there's a contrasting sheerstrake in white, along with a tapered accent stripe along its lower edge. And, since there was a natural break in structure along the rabbet, it seemed logical that she be given a white-painted backbone — all the way from the stem head to the transom.

Her service as a tender will require a canvas-covered rubber fender rail, so there was a limit on what could be done at the sheer itself, except inside, where the inwales are varnished.

The mahogany plywood, which forms the lapstrake planking of this craft, is not especially attractive when finished bright, so the interior as well as the exterior of the hull has been painted. White, softened by adding a bit of ochre, is the interior hull color, and that is set off by varnished seats and floorboards of "real" mahogany. A gilded name will add a touch of elegance to her varnished transom, and there will be small elliptical badges with carved and gilded acorns, as called for on the plans, gracing her bows.

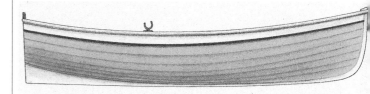

Hull exterior: Medium teal blue
Sheerstrake: White, with harmonizing accent
  stripe along its lower edge
Backbone exterior: White
Hull interior: Warm white
Seats, transom, floorboards, inwales, and oars:
  Varnished

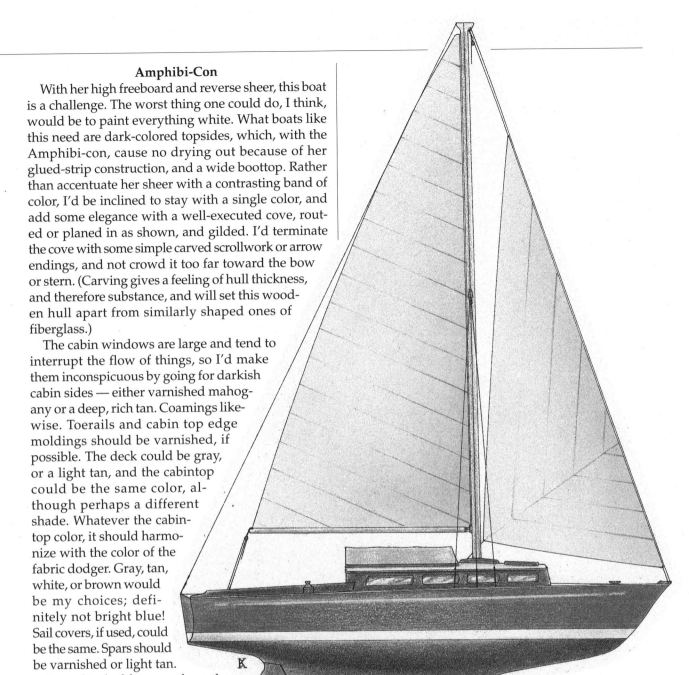

Amphibi-Con

With her high freeboard and reverse sheer, this boat is a challenge. The worst thing one could do, I think, would be to paint everything white. What boats like this need are dark-colored topsides, which, with the Amphibi-con, cause no drying out because of her glued-strip construction, and a wide boottop. Rather than accentuate her sheer with a contrasting band of color, I'd be inclined to stay with a single color, and add some elegance with a well-executed cove, routed or planed in as shown, and gilded. I'd terminate the cove with some simple carved scrollwork or arrow endings, and not crowd it too far toward the bow or stern. (Carving gives a feeling of hull thickness, and therefore substance, and will set this wooden hull apart from similarly shaped ones of fiberglass.)

The cabin windows are large and tend to interrupt the flow of things, so I'd make them inconspicuous by going for darkish cabin sides — either varnished mahogany or a deep, rich tan. Coamings likewise. Toerails and cabin top edge moldings should be varnished, if possible. The deck could be gray, or a light tan, and the cabintop could be the same color, although perhaps a different shade. Whatever the cabintop color, it should harmonize with the color of the fabric dodger. Gray, tan, white, or brown would be my choices; definitely not bright blue! Sail covers, if used, could be the same. Spars should be varnished or light tan.

Some kind of fancywork on the transom could be used to advantage. A simple carved and gilded nameboard, along with a carved or painted border design, might be worth considering.

Hull: Dark blue
Bottom: Black or blue antifouling
Boottop: White
Deck: Light gray or tan
Cabin sides and coaming: Varnished or deep, rich tan
Cabintop: Rich tan, gray, or a blue lighter than the hull

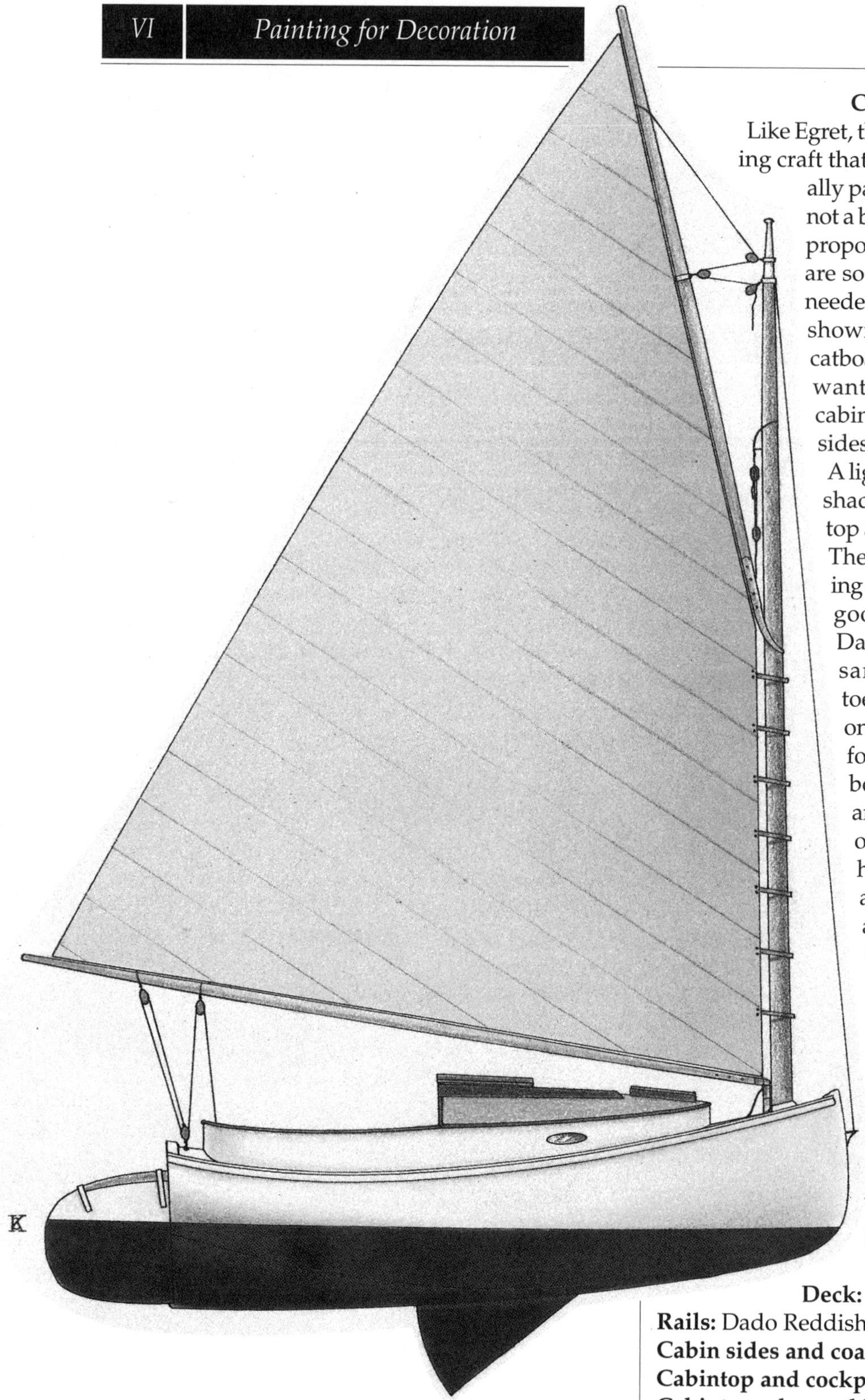

Cape Cod Catboat

Like Egret, this catboat developed from working craft that were, for practical reasons, usually painted mostly in white. That's still not a bad idea, because this boat's shape, proportions, and detailing, like Egret's, are so perfect that colors are not really needed. It's hard to beat plain white for showing off the shadows cast by the catboat's hollow bow. And who would want to hide the elliptical cat's-eye cabin window by painting the cabin sides a dark color?

A light tan for the deck, with a darker shade of the same color for the cabintop and cockpit sole, would be good. The cabintop edge molding, coaming caps, and hatch slides would look good either varnished or painted Dado Reddish Brown, as shown; same with the guardrails and toerails. If there's a practical limit on what is to be varnished, I'd go for the sliding hatch and the tiller, both of which can be easily seen and appreciated, yet can be taken off the boat and worked on at home during the winter. The mast and spars would look just about as good painted buff or tan as they would varnished.

This boat needs no boottop, and, with the neutral color scheme described above, her bottom could be painted either red, green, or brown copper antifouling.

Topsides: White

Bottom: Brown, red, or green copper antifouling

Deck: Light tan or white

Rails: Dado Reddish Brown or white

Cabin sides and coamings: White

Cabintop and cockpit sole: Warm, rich tan

Cabintop edge molding and coaming caps: Dado Reddish Brown or varnished

Hatch slides and hatch coamings: Dado Reddish Brown or varnished

Sliding hatch and tiller: Varnished

Gaff and boom: Varnished, or painted a tan that is lighter than the cabintop

Mast and hoops: Varnished or oiled, with white masthead

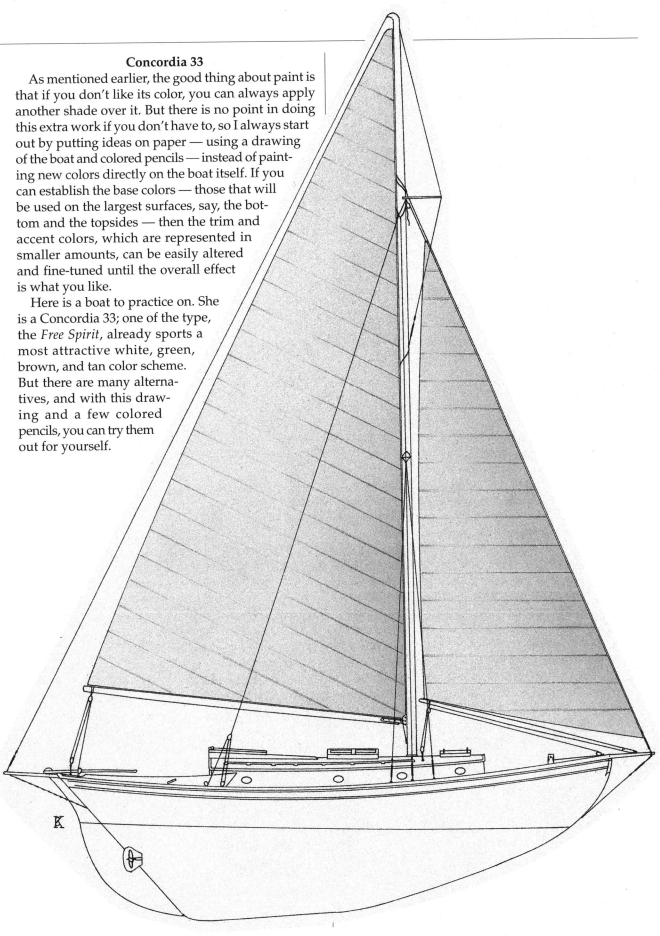

Concordia 33

As mentioned earlier, the good thing about paint is that if you don't like its color, you can always apply another shade over it. But there is no point in doing this extra work if you don't have to, so I always start out by putting ideas on paper — using a drawing of the boat and colored pencils — instead of painting new colors directly on the boat itself. If you can establish the base colors — those that will be used on the largest surfaces, say, the bottom and the topsides — then the trim and accent colors, which are represented in smaller amounts, can be easily altered and fine-tuned until the overall effect is what you like.

Here is a boat to practice on. She is a Concordia 33; one of the type, the *Free Spirit*, already sports a most attractive white, green, brown, and tan color scheme. But there are many alternatives, and with this drawing and a few colored pencils, you can try them out for yourself.

Some Very Opinionated Guidelines

• Lots of contrast between topside color and bottom or boottop color always looks good, but without a fair and level waterline with a crisply painted edge, no boat looks her best. For information on marking and scribing the waterline, see Chapter XIV, Looking Good Again.

• Light-colored topsides and decks are desirable to reflect the sun's radiant heat. Hot sun is especially hard on carvel construction with single-thickness topsides, and caulked, painted decks. They are far more apt to open their seams and leak if painted dark colors.

• Fore-and-aft bands and stripes, of varying widths, are good on boats with high topsides or sheers that are too flat. Tapering stripes are more interesting than parallel bands.

• Tone down cluttery deck structures by painting them a neutral tone.

• Avoid, where possible, painting level waterlines on lapstrake hulls. Painting them properly is tedious work.

• Warm, muted colors (not pastels) or whites are a good choice for large expanses, with brighter colors used for accent. A boat painted with all accents, say bright reds, yellows, and blues, is usually garish.

• A touch of genuine gold leaf used in a cove stripe, scrollwork, or name gives a touch of elegance. Gold leaf is durable as well, and can last for several years without renewal. Stay away from gold paint (and other forms of fake gold, such as stick-on tape or letters), however. It's a masquerade. If you can't use gold leaf, you're better off with a color.

• Flat or semi-gloss paint will cover and hide surface imperfections better than high gloss, saving you time in preparation that can be used elsewhere to better advantage. Most paint companies offer flattening agents that, when mixed with the paint, will knock gloss down to at least semi-gloss.

• White paint, because shadows show up well on it, looks good on the bottoms of boats. Consider using it on craft that are dry-sailed or where marine fouling is not a problem. A boottop used as an accent sets it off very well.

• Where possible, change from one color to another at a break in the boat's structure, such as at the topside seams, plank laps, guardrails, etc. The "cutting in" will be easier, and the result will look more natural. Scribe a line for easier cutting-in where there's no structural break.

• If, as in the case of a chafed cove stripe, cutting-in has to be against a ragged edge, go for minimum contrast between colors; that way, the ragged paint line won't be as noticeable as it would be if there were a marked contrast between colors.

• Masts and spars are best varnished, oiled, or painted buff or tan. Whites and grays (including aluminum) don't look natural.

• Painted tips on booms, and sometimes on the tops of masts, look good.

• Warm, creamy whites give a more natural and friendly feeling than cold, bluish ones.

• Bright blue sail covers are an invention of the devil. Canvas work is best in white or natural tan.

• To look their best, registration numbers (usually required by law on each side of the boat) should have space around them instead of being crowded up against the sheer. Stick-on numbers never look very good. Painted numbers look the best, especially if raked a little to harmonize with the rake of the stem.

• Just a touch of well-kept varnish work, polished brass, and genuine gold leaf can transform a plain boat into one that's special, whereas acres of run-down bright work show old age and neglect.

• Well-kept paint work looks far better than neglected varnish.

• Accent yellows should be bold, like Caterpillar yellow instead of lemon yellow.

• Most laminated members are better painted than varnished. Since the layers generally don't flow with the shape of the piece, it's best if they don't show.

Selecting and Mixing Colors

When I picked up the color charts of the major paint companies the other day, I was saddened to learn how few good color choices there are — at least in the oil-based paints that most wooden boat owners still use. Some of my old favorites — Interlux Sunset Buff, and Dado Reddish Brown — have been dropped, and the emphasis has clearly shifted to sophisticated antifouling bottom paints and to higher-priced epoxy and urethane topside finishes, where durability and gloss are paramount. That's tough on us old-timers who enjoy doing an annual paint job and don't want to fuss too much preparing the surface. Nowadays, to get the color we want, we might have to buy the nearest thing available, then doctor it up by stirring in something else.

It's really not all that bad, however. I've been keeping on hand small bottles of strongly pigmented sign-painter's paint in the three primary colors — red, yellow, and blue — plus black. A touch of one or more of them stirred into paint that is already close to what I'm looking for will produce the desired color. It's fun, really. Universal tinting colors can also be used in the same manner. A color wheel, or a color map, available from any art supply store, can help a lot here. When starting off, you may want to mix just a small batch to make sure you're on the right track, rather than risk an entire quart or gallon.

Rolling and Tipping

by Dan MacNaughton

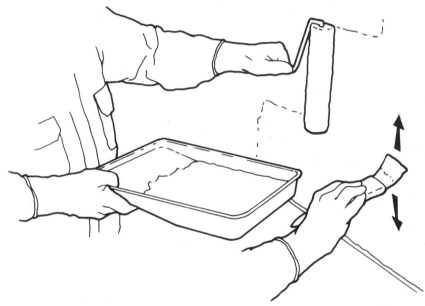

The roller stays just ahead of the brusher. Vertical brush strokes seem to sag or run less, but some painters prefer to smooth the paint horizontally.

"Rolling and tipping," as it's sometimes known in the trade, is a technique that rolls a finish onto a wide surface so quickly that there's time for a second worker to come along right behind and easily smooth it all out to perfection. It's an especially popular and valuable technique for applying quick-drying coatings like two-part polyurethanes, which is where the method seems to have gotten its start, but it will also work well for you with more traditional paints and varnishes.

If you're lucky, the surface you're painting will be narrow, the conditions perfect, and the paint or varnish easy to handle — a brush painter's paradise —and in that case a good brush will give good results without the need for a roller. But when the surface is too broad, the drying conditions too

quick, and the brushing time of the paint too short to easily retain that all-important "wet edge," your only options are to add more painters working in the same area, or spray the paint on, or roll and tip.

While few people would notice (or care about) the difference, the best sprayed job is likely to come out a little better than the best rolled-and-tipped job. However, when a sprayed paint job goes wrong it often seems to go wrong in a big way. This is partly because when spraying, the paint has to be at just the right consistency, and once it's in the gun and you've started painting, you're committed. Also when you're spraying you're not in direct contact with the surface, so if you find yourself with a run, a holiday, or a June bug, there's little you can do. Spraying greatly increases the possibility that the painter will absorb paint through the skin and lungs, making the most toxic paints potentially deadly, and raising conventional finishes from somewhat dangerous to very dangerous.

At our yard, we get such consistently good results with rolled and tipped finishes, with so little trouble and in so little time, that we don't consider spraying finishes except on very complex surfaces. We roll and tip instead of conventionally brushing all paint and varnish, wherever the surface is large enough to make it convenient.

One of the advantages of the roll-and-tip method is that it allows the application of most finishes at closer to package consistency than other methods. In other words, you are less likely to thin or otherwise modify the paint to make it handle properly or to extend the drying time. The less you have to thin the paint, the better it covers and the better the gloss, if you're using gloss paints. Rolling and tipping is so fast that it is actually helpful to have the paint dry rapidly, as it reduces any chance of a run or damage to the paint from bugs, the boss's fingerprints, etc.

Tools and Materials

If you'll be working with polyurethanes, be sure to purchase the accessory products intended to aid brushing, as opposed to spraying, such as a special catalyst, thinner, or accelerator. One of the advantages of a versatile and well-developed paint system is in your ability to adapt the product to your individual conditions and methods. So far we have had poor luck with products that claim to be good for both spray and brush applications without modification. We have come to the conclusion that expensive, highly toxic paints are only logical when the boat owner is willing to tolerate previous seasons' dings and scrapes until the paint begins to lose its gloss. Otherwise it is best to paint with regular paint every year or so, especially since rolled-and-tipped finishes can produce polyurethane-quality appearance with conventional paints.

Purchase low-nap foam rollers sold as suitable for the type of finish you are using. Use a clean, top-quality brush. Any decent brush will work, but we feel that badger hair brushes are best for all finishes. "Badger Style" is not badger hair. Some painters like to use disposable foam brushes for tipping, under the correct assumption that if there are no bristles, there can be no bristle marks, and those who are used to them can get good results. However, foam brushes do have a tendency to act like squeegees and make thin spots in the paint, and they don't offer the controlled release and absorption of paint that a good bristle brush provides. One of the secrets of good bristle brush painting lies in varying the brushing pressure according to the need to apply more or less paint, or even absorb paint off the surface, and it is this type of technique that badger hair is best at. However, this is less important if the surface is all flat and accessible to the roller, when little paint will be put on the surface by the brush in any case. The trick of tipping with the foam brush is to use extremely light pressure almost all the time.

Preparations

Plan to keep the paint and its additives off your skin and out of your eyes, and provide good ventilation at all times, taking particular care when using linear polyurethanes and their solvents.

If you are using scaffolding, make sure it is at a good working height and will not require much adjustment as you work. If you're applying polyurethanes, you may be working fast! Take pains to vacuum and tack-rag thoroughly just before you start to paint. Don't bear down on the tack rag, or you will transfer the sticky substance from the cloth to the surface, causing fish-eyes in the finish. If at all possible, work in the shade, out of the wind, early in the day. Dew or rain will dull the gloss unless the finish has had a few hours to cure. A combination of thorough, indirect lighting and direct lighting placed to shine along the length of the surface you're painting will best reveal holidays or sags.

Mix enough paint for the whole job, or at least enough to take you to your first "stopping place." Instructions for the two-part polyurethanes we have used say to let the mixture stand for a few minutes after mixing, and it is my impression that conventional finishes apply slightly better if they, too, sit for a few minutes after having been thinned and stirred. Don't put all the paint in the roller pan, as it is all too easy to spill the contents of the pan. Work with moderate amounts in the pan, adding fresh paint as you go along and keeping the remainder back under cover in the paint pot to avoid thickening due to solvent evaporation.

Technique

Usually one painter applies the paint with a roller and is followed by another brushing it out, but a third person can also be helpful to add reducer or mix more paint if it is needed, and to help spot holidays and sags in the still-brushable zone. If there are different skill levels among your painting gang, put your best painter on the brush, your second-best sighting for flaws and tending the brushes and paint, and your third-best on the roller. On very broad surfaces, it might be desirable to have a second person brushing. We also frequently roll-and-tip singlehanded when it is practical — it is still the fastest, easiest, and best method.

Wet the roller thoroughly, but don't be sloppy. Be careful when swinging the roller up to the surface, or drips may fly off onto areas you've already painted.

It is a mystery to me why brand-new paint brushes always arrive chock-full of dust, but they do. So even if your brush is new, firmly flip the bristles until no dust comes out, before dipping it in the paint. Wet the brush with the paint, wiping out the excess. Fully wetting the brush with paint before you start makes it handle more smoothly, and it will produce a more consistent paint film from the start. If there is the slightest residue of oil-based paint or varnish in your brush, don't consider using it with two-part polyurethanes. The more powerful solvents will pull granules of it off the bristles, and you'll have "idjums" in the paint.

As the person rolling moves ahead (rolling vertically on upright surfaces), the person with the brush lightly brushes the surface to even out the paint film, pop the bubbles left by the roller, and coat any areas the roller couldn't reach. Hold the brush like a pen, not a sword, and keep it as perpendicular to the surface as possible. When the area you are painting is wide enough to make it easy to do so, finish the area by brushing vertically. The brush marks will then heal up more quickly, with less chance of beginning sags or runs. Use the lightest pressure possible for your final strokes in each area — this is why they call this part "tipping."

The person brushing should be constantly sighting along the wet edge, moving up and down to view the reflections of the light in all areas of brushable paint, looking for dull spots (holidays) or ridges (developing sags). The person rolling works at the pace of the person brushing, staying just ahead of him—not so close that he has to stop and wait, but not so far ahead that the paint sets up before the brusher can get to it. As with any paint job, the brusher must constantly judge how large an area is still wet enough to brush, and must resist the temptation to go back and fiddle with areas that are too dry. With a little practise, the person on the roller will find they can precisely vary the thickness of the paint film according to the brushing person's instructions. On large jobs, the paint in the brush may start to set up before you're done. Or you could drop it in the dirt! A second brush should be held in reserve, ready to wet with paint as before and hand to the brusher on demand. As the work progresses, the first brush can be cleaned out for reuse if needed.

If this all sounds like a bit of a panic party, it can be, especially when the paint is drying fast, but after you've done one coat you'll have the hang of it, and you will appreciate what the technique can accomplish.

VIII

Paintbrush Care

———— by E. Barton Chapin III ————

*E*very year, it seems, the boating magazines publish a new collection of articles about painting and, to some extent, paintbrush care. Everyone has an opinion about and a method for taking care of brushes, and everyone seems to disagree strongly with everyone else. Here is my method, which I have not heretofore seen in print. It is not my method alone, however; it was taught to me by a third-generation painter from Colorado by the name of Alan Long.

In the mid-1970s, Alan showed me 10 or so brushes that his father had given to him. The brushes, with bristles that came from pre-Mao China, had seen heavy use for 25 years and, although worn, were without a trace of paint. They could have been used interchangeably for either paint or varnish without ill effect (although Alan, I am sure, would never recommend that).

Preparing a New Brush

Alan had a drill he would go through before he used a new brush. He would hold the brush out horizontally, with the flat part of the brush also horizontal. He would then tap the ferrule with his finger, and the bristles that were in wrong-end-to would hang down. Bristles are tapered with a flag on the narrow end, and even the best brushes have some bristles in backwards. If left in the brush, the reversed bristles would make a line in the paint. Because the fat end of a bristle is heavier, it hangs down when held horizontally; so, whenever Alan found a bristle hanging down, he would single it out and carefully bend it back against the ferrule and cut it off with a knife. He would repeat his search until he could find no more reversed bristles. This brush would then be suitable only for rough work until Alan deemed it smoothed out enough for more delicate jobs.

Cleaning a Used Brush

When it came to cleaning brushes, Alan also had a very definite method, a method I became all too familiar with when I worked for him. If we were using oil paint and would be working with that same paint first thing the next morning, we would wrap the brushes, while still full of paint, in a plastic bag and store them in a cool place. If we were not going to use them the next day, then we would clean them. At the time, we used mineral spirits, and our hands would dry out and crack. Now I use kerosene, which is cheaper. But, because I've learned more about the dangers of petroleum-based solvents, I avoid skin contact with any solvent and ensure plenty of ventilation during its use. Otherwise, I still take care of my brushes using Alan's method.

I keep four or five jugs in a row where I am cleaning brushes, and I rotate through them, leaving the unused ones to settle for a few days. I start the first wash with used kerosene, although I do not mix kerosene used for varnish and kerosene used for paint. Here's how it goes:

Pour out half a quart or so of used kerosene into a wide, shallow pan; a pan of this shape will catch more of the spillage than a can or paint pot will. Immerse the brush in the kerosene and pick it up by the handle, holding it over the pan with the bristles pointing up. Grab the bristles, and force the kerosene back into the ferrule. Re-dip the brush, and repeat this squeezing of the brush upside down about 15 times.

This technique is like milking a cow in reverse. You start at the end of the bristles, which are between your thumb and index finger, then bend the bristles over and squeeze with your remaining fingers, working the kerosene toward the ferrule. This forces the solvent into the ferrule, where paint can lurk.

Next, using a wire brush (I use a stainless-steel one), brush the bristles quite hard on all four sides of the brush. This is most easily done by resting the ferrule of the brush on the edge of a block and brushing away from yourself. This may sound rather brutal, but it is essential to get the paint out of the top part of the brush.

Rinse with kerosene once or twice after using the wire brush. Pour the kerosene into another jug, and shake the brush onto a piece of paper or plywood. Pour out some clean, used kerosene, and repeat the process three times more, including the wirebrushing. This sounds tedious, but if you are set up for the job, it will go quite quickly.

When the paint does not flow out over the ferrule as you squeeze it, wash the brush once more in clean, unused kerosene and skip the wire-brush treatment. During the washing process, it is important to keep the wire brush as clean as possible, for it can impart paint and dirt to the brush you are trying to clean.

It is quite difficult to determine when a varnish brush is clean, so it is best to overdo it. Five or six washes should make it clean if you are thorough enough with each wash. Numerous washes with small amounts of kerosene are better than a few washes with copious amounts of kerosene.

Because I use kerosene for brush cleaning, I do not find any need to oil the brushes after cleaning, nor do I find it necessary to wash the brushes in soap and water. Simply hanging them bristles-down for a day, wrapping them in clean paper, and storing them in a clean, dry place will keep them from harm.

This method may seem like more effort than you are willing to put into your brushes, but anyone who tries to do a good job of painting realizes the advantage of having a good brush, and a good brush is worth taking care of.

There is almost never a need to throw out any used kerosene. Used kerosene will settle out in a matter of a few days and can be used out of the jug it's in or decanted into a clean jug. Plastic milk jugs do not work well for the storage of kerosene, for they deteriorate and crack. I use jugs that once held antifreeze or windshield-washer fluid; they will last for years if not left in direct sunlight. Eventually, however, the jugs will fill up with paint residue. When this happens, the kerosene on top can be poured off into another jug, and if the top is left off the full jug for a while, the residue will solidify, making disposal safer and less messy.

If you think your brushes are getting clean enough, try this test. After you have been painting with a light-colored paint, wash your brush using the method you normally use. Then try a wash using Alan's method. If you see paint flowing out of the bristles over the ferrule, then your brush still has paint in it. If you let the brush dry with paint in it, it will eventually fill up with hardened paint and be ruined.

Sometimes dried paint can be washed out of a brush with lacquer thinner or a commercial brush cleaner, but these do not work all that well and they rob the bristles of their oil. Some people get around the problem of dried paint in their brushes by suspending them in oil or thinner, but when you use a brush again with paint in it, the paint is quite likely to bleed out. Of course, you could have a separate brush for each color paint you use, but good brushes are expensive. Furthermore, storing brushes in liquid on board a boat is a bit risky at best.

Remember, though, as with any rigid dogma, brush-care methods are subject to personal modification. But Alan's methods have worked for me for years, and they could for you.

For Her Name's Sake

—————— by Karl MacKeeman ——————

The "nit-picky" job of applying the name and number to a boat is one that many people put off. But the high cost for the services of a professional sign painter inspire many a boat owner to be a do-it-yourselfer. This makes sense.

Boat people generally are the sort who can learn new tricks. Most surprise themselves when they find they can do their own lettering and numbering with the proper equipment and a little know-how. I know that I was quite proud of my own first efforts on what was then the first boat I had ever owned. She was called *Mermaid B*, and her name was painted in three colors. She was also decorated with pictures of sharks, fish, mermaids, and other baroque trimmings. At the time she didn't seem a bit overdone, even though she was only a 7-foot rowboat!

Alternatives

When considering lettering your boat for the first time, the first area to explore might be the various alternatives to paint and a skillful hand. There are many forms of metal and plastic letters and numbers available in most marine and general hardware stores, usually applied with screws or nails. The disadvantage of going this route is that the letters are easily damaged, and sometimes deteriorate. They are, however, easy to replace and repair. Choose a very readable letter style; avoid the flowing italics that are often used for house numbers. Boat letters and numbers must be fairly straightforward and easy to read, for identification.

Stick-on lettering is also readily available in many styles and sizes. The metallic kind, with black lettering on a gold-colored background, is often used, though it doesn't last long and doesn't look very good. Stick-on lettering with a clear plastic backing seems best: Letrasign, Alpha-stick, and Formatt adhesive lettering systems are used by designers and commercial artists. Letrasign seems to be the best suited for boats and the outdoors; a coat of polyurethane varnish will prolong its life span. Letrasign is available in both black and white and in five sizes, from 1 inch in height to 6 inches. Each letter can be purchased in packages of five at most art and stationery stores.

Tools

While the above methods are relatively easy to work with, nothing will look as good as well-done hand application of letters and numbers. Given the proper tools and a little practice, most people can master the art well enough to fool the neighbors.

Let's have a look at tools. Sign painters do not use anything that you would call a brush for this kind of work, because the end bristles of a standard brush can spread and run dry in a single stroke. Such a brush can be made to work in a limited fashion, but the results are shaky at best. Even the best brush has its faults: it cannot hold and control a sufficient quantity of paint; it generally has a blunt or pointed tip, preventing it from making straight-edged strokes, and because only the tip is put to use, the pressure upon the working surface is difficult to control.

The right tool for hand lettering is the quill, a special little object that closely resembles a brush, but is used differently. It can be bought in any shop that carries sign painters' supplies; the cost is generally reasonable, especially in the smaller sizes. Imported from France, they are called quills because the ferrules are made of goose quills, although many are now made of plastic. Squirrel hair is mounted in the quill and held fast by a twist of brass wire; the hair, nearly 2 inches long, is very soft. Because most quills are imported without handles — except for the Grumbacher type — any old stick will do as a handle, whittled to fit.

The size of the quill is governed by the size of the letters chosen. Your craft's name is only meant to be read at polite distances, and you should not overdo it. A No. 6 quill and a few larger sizes should serve your needs.

To estimate the width of the stroke of a quill, wet it and bring it to a chisel edge. This is the working shape of the quill (some people try to hold that set in the hairs with a little Vaseline, when the quill is not in use); the width of the stroke will be the width of the chisel edge. The squirrel hairs are springy, and if you bend them, they will spring back to their original shape; this is known as "snap."

While you are out shopping for a good quill you might also pick up a small tin of "One Shot" sign painter's enamel. It may cost a little more than conventional paint, but it is certainly worth it. "One Shot" comes in different colors, covers in one coat, has the proper consistency for lettering, and weathers well. The only other items of basic equipment you will need are a pencil, carbon paper, turpentine, and some rags.

Preliminary Work

Measure the area where your boat's name will be, and do all your preliminary drawings on paper so that you can trace them onto the working surface with carbon paper. This allows you to use the same drawing repeatedly in different locations. In this way all the figuring, erasing, and messing about is done on a piece of paper instead of on the side or transom of your boat.

There are books available to help you choose different letter styles and formations. If you doubt your ability to get the proportions right, use stencils, which are available in most stationery shops, but be sure to join the bridges after you have traced out your words. They are there to hold the open areas of the letters together; joining these gaps makes a much more professional-looking job.

In all cases, consider spacing, which will help you to cover up some of your other sins. There are a few rules to follow: remember that it is not the distance between letters that is equal, but the blank space (the air) between each letter; the verticals, such as two I's, would have the most distance from each other; two O's would be closest in terms of distance; and the space between words is usually equal to a capital O. Squint at your word to see if the letters are equally spaced. Remember that the

gaps in your spacing will be more evident from a distance, or when studied upside down.

After completing your master drawing, transfer it to the surface for painting. If possible, hand letter on a wooden nameboard that can be screwed in place. Not only is it much easier to work on the flat surface of a workbench than on the vertical side of a boat, but when the letter is being repainted, the nameboard can be easily unscrewed and replaced when the work is finished.

Carving

If you happen to like carving wood, you could carve the letters into the nameboard with a "V" tool, though you must be careful not to carve the letters too deep. Paint the letters so that they show up better. Any surplus paint or splatters outside the letters themselves can be removed by sanding the board to a smooth finish, then the board can be given three or four coats of varnish.

I have seen signs and nameboards done in this manner with a rotary tool. In either case I would not recommend carving a nameboard when the lettering is less than 2 inches in height, as it will lose legibility.

If you must work directly on the boat, make sure it is done while she is hauled out. To letter a vessel that is moored even in very calm water is a task that often baffles the experts.

Place your carbon black-side-down on the working surface and tape the master drawing into position. Check the placement by measuring with your tape, making sure you have it exactly where you want it. If you are working on a black surface, chalk the underside of the master drawing instead of using the carbon paper. Now, trace over the master drawing; the outline will come through on the working surface. To make things easy for yourself in the future, you should then outline the lettering on the surface by using a scribe or tapping it in with the blade of a chisel. Following a scribed outline will simplify repainting the letters in the future.

Hand Painting

For the purist who wants to test his skill lettering a relatively flat surface, here are step-by-step instructions:

• First obtain a painted board or whatever is handy and test your quill on that.

• Make sure you are holding the quill in the proper position; it is not a pencil or a pen. The best position is one in which the quill can be held firmly upright, with the handle at right angles to your arm. Don't let your fingers take control. The direction of your line should be controlled by your wrist and arm.

This may seem awkward at first but try it out and you will see that it does work.

• Stir the paint well and dip a bit out on your pallet, which can be anything from a piece of cardboard to an old tin lid. Dip the quill in the color but don't soak it. Work the hairs to a chisel edge.

• When applying the paint use the hairs so they bend near the ferrule. Don't use the tip. Stroke downward to form verticals. The top edges of the brush strokes can be sharpened by using the chisel tip in a slight horizontal cut to the left and then down. This finishing off method will take a little practice, but it may not be necessary if the quill holds a good edge.

• Again, making the curved strokes should put your wrist and arm in action, not your fingers. Letters are formed in parts. For example, the letter O is made of two opposite curved strokes, both made with downward strokes of your quill. It is seldom necessary to stroke upward; generally, this is to be avoided. The letter S is formed by first making the center spine and adding the top and bottom curve, brushed left to right.

• The pressure of the hand is important for neat work. Most people steady their hand by using the knuckles of their little finger as a caster, and control the direction of the strokes with their wrist. Some sign painters use a maulstick to steady their hand. It can be made from an old mop handle with a rag balled around one end to protect the working surface on which it pivots. The stick must be held by one hand to provide a rest for the lettering hand. Its use is a matter of personal preference, but it does prevent one's hand from smudging the wet paint.

• While you're working, don't tense up — this produces a shaky line. Work smoothly and rhythmically with no hesitation in mid-stroke. You can letter carefully without being too slow and shaky. Don't be afraid to make mistakes; just keep a rag slightly moistened with turpentine handy. It is equivalent to your eraser and works fine while the paint is still wet.

• There are lots of ways to decorate your lettering with another color, such as outlining or shading. I'd advise the novice to stick to plain and simple lettering on the first try and save the fancy stuff for later.

• Enamel dries within a few hours, but it would be advisable to keep moisture off the lettering for a day or so.

There is tremendous satisfaction in doing the job yourself. Once the paint is dry, the hand lettered name should last the life of the boat with some occasional retouching. And because it's a job worth doing, it's worth doing well.

What's your style?

ascender limit
x-height top
baseline
descender limit

The preparation you do before the actual lettering goes on your boat can make all the difference in the outcome. A major consideration is the choice of a lettering style. Probably the best place to start is with a book of typefaces, such as the *Photo-Typositor Alphabet Library*. A fairly extensive book, it provides a number of faces from which to choose.

There are two basic kinds of typography — serif and sans-serif — with many families in each, such as the Avant Gardes, the Caslons, the Harrys, the Helveticas, the Vero Antiques, and on and on, *ad infinatum*. Sans-serif letters are usually of the same thickness throughout, while serif forms are comprised of thick and thin parts. The twist at the end of the letter is the actual serif. Any part of the letter normally written with an upward stroke is thin, whereas a downward stroke is thicker. Generally, sans-serif letters will be easier to apply to the boat.

In choosing the typeface, a number of items should be considered. First, and foremost, think about your boat's name. **Sans-Serif**

What images does the name bring to mind? The essence of the name should be reflected in the visual appearance of the letters. Some general guidelines can be followed — serif faces are more romantic (and traditional) than sans-serif faces. The relationship of the x-height to the ascenders and descenders is critical — a smaller x-height has a more traditional appearance than type with a larger x-height. The weight and slant of the type can enhance or detract from the name. Don't feel you must use only capital letters — upper and lower case can sometimes provide **Weight** better visual impact while maintaining good legibility.

Once you've decided which face to use, and with the typebook in front of you, start to rough out the name in

gull

A first rough, in pencil on tissue.

pencil — preferably on tracing paper. It's best to do the lettering four or five times on paper, beginning quite rough, and refining during each revision. If you're using tracing paper you can place the last rough underneath the one you're working on to serve as a pattern.

Draw a series of parallel lines to define the baseline, top of the x-height, and limits of the ascenders and descenders. Pay close attention to the shape of each letter's curves and where parts join. Curved surfaces sit below the baseline, giving the appearance of equal depth as a letter with a flat baseline.

Zeus

thistle

QUEST

Gypsy

Have your lettering reflect the boat's name.

The spacing between the letters is critical. As noted in the article, spaces have to be visually—not mechanically—equal. Two curved lines will be closer together than two parallel lines; both will appear to be spaced equally. Looking at the lettering upside down allows you to evaluate a visual form, instead of a name.

By doing the lettering first on paper, you can work out all the problems to be considered: size, spacing, color (the consistency of weight flowing from letter to letter). And after seeing your boat's name in the actual typeface, you may decide it's not the one to use after all. It's a lot less painful to grab another sheet of paper than it is to paint over the lettering that took you ten hours to do.

—Steve Ward

Wood Gull

Remember, spacing must be visually, not mechanically, equal. The space between two parallel lines will be more than that between two curved lines.

Name in Gold, Hail in Black

A MASTER SIGN PAINTER AT WORK

———— Story and how-to photographs by Maynard Bray ————

BENJAMIN MENDLOWITZ

*D*ave Gross of Penobscot, Maine, is well known Down East as the "Yankee Painter," which is the name painted in genuine gold leaf on the doors of his truck. Boatyards and boat owners from midcoast Maine to Jonesport call on him to paint their boats' names, registration numbers, hailing ports, and occasional graphics.

I encountered Dave while I was supervising the face-lift of the R.O. Davis motorsailer *Burma* at Billings Diesel and Marine in Stonington, Maine. When I asked Dave to paint *Burma*'s name and port of hail, we talked before he began about the techniques he uses (I've always imagined myself as a sign painter). One thing led to another, and the next thing I knew he had agreed to share his skills for publication.

For the most part, Dave could talk and work at the same time (his commentary slowed to a crawl, how-ever, while outlining the gilded letters, so great was his concentration), so in a matter of a couple of hours his work was complete, and I came away with two rolls of film, three sides of microcassette audio tape, and an education in the fine art of laying out letter-ing, applying gold leaf, and painting letters.

1. Layout

Overall placement of the name and the character of the letters were, in this case, to duplicate as nearly as possible the original lettering, shown in the 1950s-vintage photograph taped to the stern of the boat for reference. But even with such an aid, the idea is always to lay out tape guidelines above and below the loca-tion of the boat's name to the desired height of let-tering, leaving room underneath for similar treatment of the boat's hailing port. Then, the letters (and any

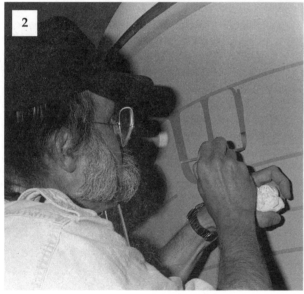

up the letters to the necessary size. The pen used for marking out the letters is a Stabilo. The outline being drawn here is to the outside of the area that will be filled with gold leaf, but you should remember that letters fatten up when the painted outline is added later. These 5 1/4-inch-high letters will measure 3/8 inch at the narrowest strokes and 1 inch at the widest.

Materials:

The pencil, called a Stabilo, makes marks that are water soluble and won't contaminate or weaken the bond of any paint that happens to go over them. Erasing is done with a damp rag.

The guideline tape is 1/4-inch 3M "Fineline," which can be peeled off afterwards without taking the paint, yet, if pressed on firmly, will keep the lettering paint from running under it. Do not use regular masking tape for this. Fineline tape is available at marine and auto supply stores.

Books on lettering styles can be found at art supply stores.

2. Applying the Size

The natural width of a single brushstroke should equal the narrowest part of the letter, or about 3/8 inch in this example. Before applying the gold size (a varnish mixture that the thin, delicate pieces of gold leaf adhere to), make sure that the base coat over which you'll be painting and gilding is completely dry; if there's a chance that the gold leaf might stick to the base, give the base a light dusting of talc. The Fineline tape described in step one will form the top and bottom lines of each letter (tape is a big help in making the sharp endings of the serifs), except for the curved parts of letters like "U." The letter "U" should extend about 1/8 inch beyond the line so it will look as tall as the neighboring letters. The smoother the surface, the more the gold leaf will shine, so apply the size with as much care as you would gloss paint or varnish — evenly, without brush marks. The guideline tapes can be pulled off as soon as you've completed the sizing.

Materials:

The brush is a No. 6 gray-squirrel lettering quill, obtainable at any artists' or sign painters' supply house for three to four dollars. These quills are laid up by hand from Russian squirrel hair, and each one is a little different. While this No. 6 gave the desired 3/8-inch width with half its hair length at work on the surface, another No. 6 might draw a somewhat different width of line. The loss of a few hairs through normal use will, in time, gradually narrow the line width as well.

Brushes last for years, if cared for. After flushing out the paint or size with mineral spirits, lubricate the bristles with motor oil, transmission fluid, or, best of all, lard oil. An occasional bath in warmed oil is a good idea, after which the softened hairs can be gently stretched out and flattened

graphics) within the guidelines should be laid out to appear balanced side-to-side and evenly spaced. For this, a good eye is better than precise measurements — and a lot faster. As Dave says, "It's more art than science; what looks right, is right."

Don't be afraid to start over again if your first attempt at layout doesn't look right. Dave made two tries with his tape spacing and lettering layouts before he was satisfied. For beginners, a name template, made beforehand, sometimes helps, as do individual letters cut out of cardboard and positioned by trial and error on the template or on the transom itself until they look okay, then traced.

The lettering style can be whatever you find attractive — *Burma*'s name will be modified Roman — and an enlarging photocopy machine can be used to blow to the desired chisel-tipped shape. (Cutting the hairs to improve the shape of the brush, however, doesn't work. Hairs are laid up so their natural tips are aligned with each other when the brush is made, and that's the way they have to stay for the brush to perform properly.)

The gold size is made by mixing spar varnish with a bit of dark chrome-yellow enamel so the size can be seen during application. Like varnish, the size should be thin enough to flow out of the brush and thick enough to level itself to a uniform film thickness without sagging. Thin the mixture, if required, with mineral spirits, a retarder such as Interlux 333, or the special stuff Dave uses (the very best there is, he claims), called Edge. It's manufactured by Chromatic and available at art supply and sign painters' stores.

3. Checking the "Tack"

After about an hour, the gold size will probably be dry enough to "snap" when touched, although the time varies with atmospheric conditions. Check it with your knuckle as shown so as not to contaminate the surface and diminish adhesion with finger oil or dirt. If you're outdoors, direct sunshine and/or wind should be avoided; you'll soon find out why, if you ignore this caveat. If the size gets away from you and becomes too hard to "snap," the gold leaf still may stick well enough, but the subsequent burnishing, or "coining," may be impossible. Hot water wiped over hardened size with a lintless cloth can be used, however, to recover the "snap." The tendency is to start gilding too soon; in most cases, the size stays "open" for several hours.

4. Applying the Gold

Lay on the gold leaf a sheet at a time by simply laying it gold-side-down on each letter and gently rubbing, as shown. Overlaps are not a problem, because only the first layer will "see" the size and stick to it. The excess may hang around for awhile, but can be blown off or gently wiped away. Go for full coverage of each letter and, because of the high cost of gold, try to make good use of the entire sheet.

Materials:
Patent gold leaf consists of thin leaves of pure gold loosely adhered to a waxed-paper backing. Packets of patent gold leaf can be ordered directly from the manufacturer or purchased from art supply or sign painters' stores.

5. Burnishing

Now, after the gold leaf is in place and before the letters are outlined, is the time for the optional burnishing process. If you want the "coined" effect being created here, use a piece of velvet, made into a round pad as shown. The motion is about a quarter turn at

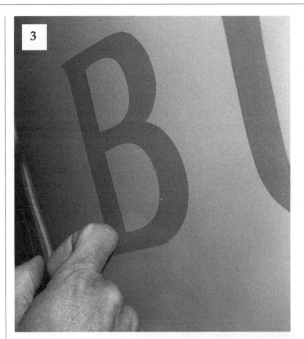

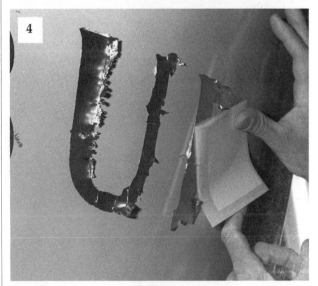

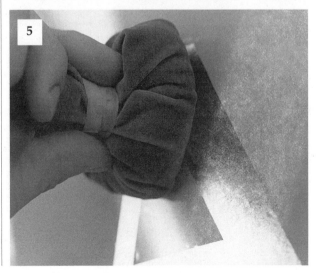

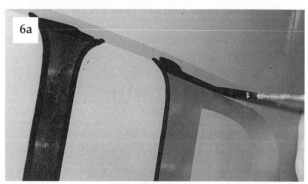

Tape makes painting the horizontal lines easier.

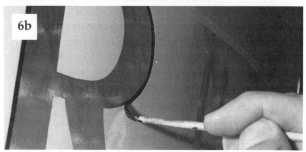

Roll the brush as it goes around a curve.

Use only moderate pressure, and concentrate on making fair lines of even width.

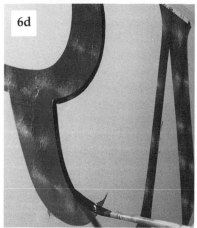

Vertical lines are easiest, horizontal lines most difficult.

each of the spots, using moderate pressure (after you've tested it first, softly). Like the overlapping grapes you used to draw on paper with a penny, these golden "coins" should lap over one another a little, and should be evenly spaced by eye (no fair measuring!).

Materials:
 The burnisher is a soft velvet cloth formed around a ball of cotton batting and held in shape with masking tape.

6. Painting the Outline

The outlining (or piping, as it is sometimes called) can be the color of your choice. Black paint covers best and is what is being used here. This outline will be about ⅛-inch wide. The first of these photos shows how new strips of Fineline tape have been pressed on ⅛ inch away from both the top and bottom of the gilded letters. Outlining is, by far, the trickiest part of the entire gold-leafing process, and horizontal lines are especially difficult; but with tape, all you have to watch is the outline's edge against the gold. That's the edge you should usually be looking at, anyway, even where there's no tape, because the other edge of the outline — the outside one — can always be wiped away and a new edge made if you mess it up.

What you're after is a fair curve of uniform width laid on in the proper place — and it's not easy to get. Practice your strokes on the pages of a magazine. Rolling your brush so it's always working "on the flat" holds the line width. Once you have a line going well, keep on with the stroke just as long as you can — until it feels awkward, or you can no longer see what you're doing, or the brush runs out of paint. If you load up your brush by working it back and forth on, say, a piece of paper, the reservoir of paint stored at the upper ends of the hairs will keep feeding the tips where replenishment is continuously needed, and you'll be able to run long lines between refills.

Paint consistency has to be "just right" here, not too thick and not too thin, and this is where Dave's Edge thinner comes into its own. (He keeps a small, open-topped can of it beside him while he does the outlining, so he can fine-tune the paint consistency.) Thick paint won't flow, and thin paint won't cover. With the possible exception of black, specially pigmented sign painters' paint, such as One-Shot, can stand more thinning than most other paints without losing its opacity.

Materials:
 The brush used here was similar to the one used for the gold size, a gray-squirrel quill, but smaller — a No. 4 that Dave has come to favor. Its natural width gives a ⅛-inch line, slightly wider if the brush is pushed on harder, or a

little narrower if rotated and held at an angle.

The outlining paint is One-Shot black, available in half-pint cans at almost any art supply store. Standard gloss topside paint will also work in black, and possibly in colors as well. Thin it so it flows, and check it for coverage before you go out and buy the special stuff.

The thinner Dave uses is Edge.

7. Painted Letters

Plain painted letters, as should be obvious by now, are much easier to do than gilded ones and are a good place to start building your skill and confidence. They'll be used here for the hailing port, done in what Dave calls Eurostyle, one of his favorite lettering styles. The painting is straightforward and the result is perfectly legible yet doesn't compete with the boat's name for attention. Eurostyle letters, with the exception of "I," are as wide as they are high (2 ¼ inches here) and are so simple in shape that only a roughly sketched layout is needed to establish the approximate spacing. Dave fine-tunes as he goes along, widening letters as appropriate to fill the available space rather than increasing the distance between them. "The real test of one's lettering skill is the letter 'S,' regardless of the chosen style," says Dave. "But unless you're doing a word where the 'S's are close together, as in 'Mississippi,' your 'S's don't have to be exactly alike."

Materials:

The brush is the same well-worn No. 6 gray-squirrel quill used for the gold size; Dave knows from experience that it will make the right ⅜-inch line.

Paint and thinner are the same as were used earlier for outlining.

8. Changes to Painted Letters

"Don't be intimidated," says Dave. "If you don't like the letter you've just made, wipe it off and start again." Use a dry rag for wiping away letters or parts of letters. This "F" looked too fat, so one edge is being wiped away as the first step in making it narrower. As long as the basic strokes look okay, keep forging ahead and get the entire name painted without fussing too much, then go back and tweak it here and there where refinement is called for.

Materials:

The "eraser" is a piece of clean, dry terrycloth or other absorbent rag, used, of course, while the paint is still wet.

9. Finishing Up

As before, pull off the tape as soon as you've finished painting the letters. Then stand back and look at what you've just accomplished. If the edges are a

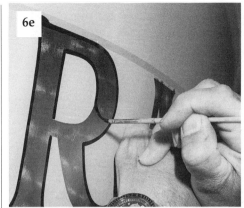
Hold the brush perpendicular to the surface being painted.

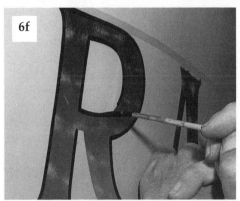
Outline curves in two operations if it feels more natural.

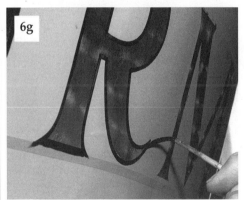
Get on with the basic stroke, but come back to touch up later.

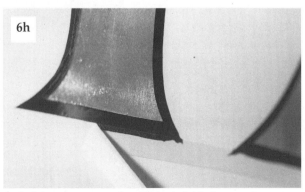
Peel off the tape as soon as the outlining is finished.

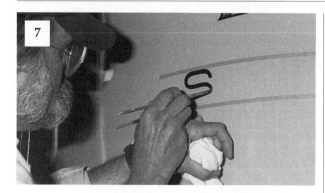

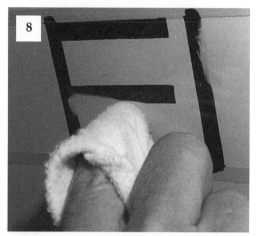

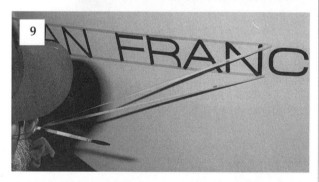

little wiggly, be assured that those wiggles won't show at normal distances; at least the parts painted against the tape are straight. And be confident that you'll do better next time.

Pure gold stays bright for years, but to protect it from scratching or other accidental abrasion, it's a good idea to lay a coat of varnish over it. Carefully brushed on over the gilded portion only of each letter, this coating can be applied before the outlining is fully dry, if you're careful.

Some Final Thoughts

- For raking transoms, letters have to be lengthened a little to look right when viewed from a normal vantage point. Letters at the bow of a boat look proper if somewhat slanted to follow the line of the stem — but don't overdo it.
- Use the largest brush that will work, so it can do at least some of its job in a single stroke. Long-haired brushes are more difficult to control, but they hold more paint.
- Dave is right-handed, so he paints the letters from left to right. Being a left-hander, I have to paint the letters from right to left in order to keep my hands out of the wet paint.
- A sign painter's "maulstick" can be used as a guide and as a hand rest if you find it more comfortable. You can make one yourself using a stiff wooden dowel with a ball on the end of it to keep it — and your hand — off the work.
- With this or any job, the gilding comes first, before the painted letters, so that extraneous gold leaf doesn't accidentally end up stuck to the wrong wet paint.
- Gilded lettering itself will last as long as the surface it's on, but that may be only a year for annually painted transoms. Varnished transoms with gold-leaf lettering on them, however, are different. You can keep adding coat after coat of varnish over the transom, lettering and all, and find that your boat's name stays looking just fine for years. Do your lettering and gilding on the sanded surface of the transom after the varnish has been built up to the next-to-last coat, then brush on the final coat over lettering and all. The sanding for next year's varnish will have to be done very lightly over the gold to avoid scratching it, but as the years go by and the varnish builds up, the risk of scratching through to the gold becomes less and less.

The materials listed above can be found at art supply or sign painters' stores, or they can be ordered directly from The Dick Blick Company, P.O. Box 1267, Galesburg, IL 61401, 800-447-8192.

The Fine Art of Stripping Paint

by Dan MacNaughton

While it takes years for professional refinishers to learn the intricacies of their trade, the novice must start somewhere. This chapter is for the beginner who needs to know what must be done to achieve adequate, respectable results, when stripping paint.

To begin with, you seldom have to strip all the paint off any given surface on a boat. Stripping is a drastic action to correct a widespread lack of adhesion of the paint to the wood, or to completely change coating systems — i.e., to change from paint to varnish, regular paints to two-part polyurethanes, etc. If there is a sensible way to avoid stripping a surface, aside from ignoring the problem, it will be best for you and the boat to do so.

It is widely believed that stripping a boat is somehow good for it, when in fact the reverse is usually true — it is common for boats to dry out considerably if they are allowed to stand for long without paint. This usually makes it impossible to get a good finish on the topsides until the second season afterwards, because the swelling action will squeeze putty out of the seams, and everything will move a little. I have seen many boats stripped that could have had fine finishes with just a heavy sanding, some filling with compound, and a few coats of paint.

Boats (or parts of boats) need to be stripped when for some reason the entire finish is no longer sticking to the wood, or when it is beginning to develop cracks that are unrelated to underlying seams and joints. The most frequent reason for this is that the paint has built up to such a thickness that it no longer comes and goes with the substrate. All this paint seems to have "a life of its own"; not only the surface coats have lifted from the wood, but

also the prime coats as well. Sometimes one of the older coats of paint will have been applied over a poorly sanded or damp surface, and while the peeling may only affect paint from that layer up, stripping the whole finish may be the best solution to the problem. Other reasons for poor finish adhesion might include a poorly ventilated compartment behind the affected area, or a joint that is admitting water to the structure, in which case it will be best if the problem is corrected before you start thinking about cosmetics.

I feel that none of the new non-lead-based paints adhere as well as the older lead-based paints, and this is another reason why I tend to leave the old paint on when I can. I believe that products that are added to paint to improve the brushing consistency without thinning the paint contribute to poor adhesion, particularly on non-epoxy sealed boats with a heated interior, in which case there is moisture being pushed out through the wood with a remarkably powerful force. Under these circumstances the less porous the paint, the more its tendency to lift, and in my opinion these additives make the paint less porous.

If the problem is in a small area, or if you only have time to do a small area at a time, it is acceptable to strip just part of a surface — the new paint surface can be faired into the surrounding area pretty well during the painting stage. If an entire surface must be stripped, it is still best to strip small areas at a time, getting prime coats on before stripping the next area. The idea is to keep the wood painted, to prevent its weathering and drying, which would certainly ruin the seams for at least one season. So do everything you can to keep her tight while you take her down, and you will minimize the tendency of the seams to show when she swells.

How thorough should you be in stripping away the old paint? It's a judgment call, but if the new paint is compatible with the old paint, in our yard we seldom worry about getting the last little bits of paint out of the pores of the wood. Any paint film that has penetrated that deeply seems to be holding as well as the new paint will. It is important to clean paint out of larger defects, however.

There are three ways to get the paint off the boat, all of which are physically unpleasant, though they may be mentally gratifying. They are heat, liquid paint remover, and sanding.

Heat

In almost all cases heat is the easiest, quickest, and safest way to go, and the most popular and best tool for applying it is a hot-air gun. These guns are very controllable and therefore less likely to scorch the wood than other heating devices, such as torches and electric coils. Furthermore, they seem to dry the surface of the wood quite nicely, an advantage if you are going to be immediately sanding and refinishing. In my opinion there is little point in using any other type of heating device for removing paint.

It is possible to scorch the wood with a heat gun, but the problem is easy to avoid. It is not necessary to wait for the paint to completely bubble up and smoke — it can be easily scraped off just prior to that extreme stage. You can quickly develop a pace, whereby with the gun in one hand and the scraper in the other, you move more or less steadily along, heating and scraping at the same time.

The heat gun is so safe and effective that we use it in our boatyard for almost all varnish stripping now, too. However, it is easy to become careless with the gun, especially when setting it down while it is running (or while standing and talking with it in your hand). A heat gun is very capable of starting a fire. I understand that it is common in house refinishing for a heat gun to blow a burning paint chip into a crack, where it starts a fire inside the structure!

Take care. Never allow a heat gun to remain running unattended.

Liquid Remover

If you are working on very thin paint, or metal (which draws heat away from the paint), or a delicate surface such as a canvased deck, or if you do not want to damage nearby areas that would be affected by heat, use liquid paint remover. Buy more than you think you'll need, and apply it thickly with an old brush. You won't save anything by using thin coats, because the remover needs to be thick to penetrate the paint layers. Work in small areas, so that you can scrape the paint off just after it stops bubbling, and before the remover dries.

Unlike heat, most paint removers will require several applications. Put the scrapings directly into a non-plastic bucket or jar, to keep them from sticking to the surface, your shoes, or another part of the boat.

Remember, paint remover works on people, too! Wear rubber gloves, work in a well ventilated area, and keep a rag handy to wipe up any remover that strays onto the wrong surface (like your skin). Before you use any product on a boat, read the entire label, and follow the directions. I have not yet had a chance to use any of the new, more environmentally sound paint removal products, but I do recommend that these be considered.

Scrapers play a major role in paint stripping, and can make the difference between a tolerable job and one that is frustrating and unpleasant. It is possible to use a putty knife with either heat or a liquid stripper, but its function then is really just to lift the paint off the surface, not to provide much scraping action. If you use a putty knife, it is best if the blade has no bevel, but has its edges sharpened square with a file. This will improve the lifting action and help prevent digging into the wood. It also helps to knock off the corners of the blade just a bit, with the file.

A regular paint scraper is the best choice for stripping paint. If it is to be used with a heat gun it must have a wooden or metal handle, or be a heat-resistant plastic, or it will melt. Keep the scraper sharp, and give it a slight convex curve along the cutting edge. Again, knock the corners off a little. A sharp scraper cuts well without much pressure, greatly reducing the chance of gouging the wood.

If you seem to be having any trouble keeping your scraper sharp, the problem is usually with the file. It is probably worth getting a nice new file for any big stripping job.

Sanding

It is possible to sand paint off by hand or with a power sander, but that is hard work and is not usually an economical proposition in terms of labor or material. Sanding is also the only method that carries with it a risk of making the substrate less fair.

When using a power sander use only an orbital or back-and-forth model. These are slower, but belt sanders and non-orbital disk sanders have no place in finish maintenance or removal. They are for rough work or woodworking, and when used on finely finished surfaces can cause bumps and hollows very easily. Many a boat has been permanently damaged with a belt sander or a non-orbital disk sander; while I have read about people who can get a good finish with these tools, most cannot, and certainly no amateur should attempt it. One thing to remember is that gloss paint reveals unfairness in a surface very clearly, and it is common to discover the defects too late in the refinishing process to do anything about them.

Always wear a respirator when doing any sanding, and add rubber gloves and rubber-soled shoes when using power tools outdoors. Electric shock is a real danger, as I discovered once when I grounded myself to an aluminum ladder through my arms, rubber boots and all!

Preparing the New Surface

Whatever stripping method you choose to use, sand the stripped surface thoroughly before priming. Check the directions on your seam and surfacing compounds to see if they should be applied before or after the prime coat. Never use a hard compound in any seam on the boat. Use only those that say something like "permanently flexible" on the label, lest you risk damaging the seams. For nicks and gouges use a good surfacing compound that doesn't dry in the can or on the putty knife too quickly, causing wasted compound. My favorite compound for small defects is 3M's fast-drying acrylic putty, mostly because it comes in a handy toothpaste-style tube and therefore won't harden in the container after it is opened. For larger defects we use Gougeon Brothers' epoxy with their Microlight filler.

I have gradually come to the conclusion that when using conventional single-part paints, the primers I've used were no improvement over the finish paint in terms of adhesion or paint film strength. While the primers usually sand up very nicely, it seems to me that the best technique is to work entirely with the finish paint, thinning the first coat a little more, for penetration.

Applying the paint is the fun part. Remember to follow these essential rules:

1. Clean the surface thoroughly with a vacuum cleaner and after the primer coat, a tack rag; if chemical paint remover was used, do whatever is recommended on the can. I seldom use any kind of solvent for cleaning, as it is difficult to be certain it has all evaporated, especially from bare wood. If it has not, it will inhibit adhesion.

2. Using a good brush, apply the paint in fairly thin coats.

3. When performing annual maintenance on the boat, try to sand off as much paint as you will apply, to reduce paint buildup. This should prevent having to strip her again for a very long time.

Taking It Off with Chemical Strippers

—————— by George Fatula ——————

Refinishing is at least 70 percent surface preparation, and we are always looking for ways to make this job easier, quicker, and safer. Chemical strippers seem to offer an "easy" way of removing old paint. We can avoid the dirty, back-breaking jobs of scraping, grinding, and sanding — just let the chemicals do the work! Apply some stripper, the paint comes off, and we are ready to paint again. Right?

Unfortunately, it's not that simple yet. Aggressive chemicals can damage adjacent surfaces, remove a gelcoat, attack metals, and dissolve many plastics. Spills can cause more work than the original project entailed. Some chemical strippers contain very hazardous compounds. Cleanup and disposal of the old finish may require compliance with hazardous-waste disposal regulations. There are human health considerations as well, and anyone using these products should read the Material Safety Data Sheet for the product before using it and comply with all safety precautions specified. Data sheets can be obtained from the product supplier.

There are hazards involved in any refinishing operation, and using chemicals to remove finishes requires some careful planning. Here is a comparison of four types of solvent-based paint strippers. We applied each of the strippers to five different, well-cured (three years) test panels:

Panel 1: Plywood with four coats of semi-gloss alkyd enamel.
Panel 2: Mahogany with five coats of spar varnish.
Panel 3: Etched aluminum with four coats of gloss alkyd enamel.
Panel 4: An aluminum spar with U.S. Paint's aluminum schedule, including two-part epoxy primer and two coats of Awlgrip topcoat.

Panel 5: A fiberglass panel with 20 mils of polyester gelcoat.

Methylene Chloride

Until fairly recently, chemical paint strippers have been dominated by solvent mixtures containing a high percentage of methylene chloride (dichloromethane). These products are very effective. They work quickly, removing most finishes in a matter of minutes, including two-part epoxies and urethanes, but they require special precautions if they are to be used safely. Besides their hazards to humans, they will soften and remove gelcoat and attack many plastics.

Methylene chloride is a hazardous chemical. The National Institute for Occupational Safety & Health (NIOSH) lists it as a suspected carcinogen, and its use has been banned in California. Organic-vapor cartridge-equipped negative-pressure respirators do not provide adequate protection from methylene chloride vapors. Air-supplied respiratory protection is specified on Material Safety Data Sheets for the use of these products without "adequate ventilation." Exposure can burn the skin and cause blindness; it can also affect the upper respiratory tract, central nervous system, cardiovascular system, and liver. The metabolic by-products of the vapors include carbon monoxide, which reaches the maximum concentrations in the body three to four hours after exposure and can produce symptoms ranging from headache to heart attack.

Paint strippers with methylene chloride are often formulated with methanol, another hazardous compound that increases the stripper's effectiveness and its toxicity.

The effectiveness of methylene chloride strippers must be weighed against the complexities of handling them safely. Consider carefully whether the job at hand requires or safely permits the use of these aggressive chemicals.

We used Sterling's 5f5 and Dumond Chemical's PeelAway 2 in our tests. Both products quickly removed all the finish on all of the test panels after one heavy application, with the exception of the AwlGripped spar, which required a second application. The surfaces required some scrubbing and light sanding to remove residue

PeelAway 2 is a thick paste. It is covered with a vinyl backing sheet after it has been spread over the surface to a thickness of about ⅛ inch. This backing prevents the stripper from drying out and makes cleaning up the residue much simpler.

Sterling's 5f5 is a thick liquid that requires agitation prior to use, since the component solvents tend to separate on standing. (The gelcoat panel was destroyed by these methylene chloride strippers, but the strippers that follow had little effect on it.)

Organic Solvent Mixtures

Another category of solvent-based strippers does away with methylene chloride but retains a mixture of organic solvents, including acetone, methyl ethyl ketone, toluene, and methanol. These are industrial solvents and should not be handled casually by any applicator. Not quite as effective as the methylene-chloride-based strippers, this group comes very close and can be handled safely with proper ventilation and/or organic-vapor cartridge-equipped respirators. Proper gloves, eye protection, and fire safety precautions must be followed. The risk to metal or fiberglass surfaces is reduced, but organic solvent strippers can still damage plastic.

Our test used Nu-Tec Paint Buster. Sprayed from an aerosol can, Paint Buster worked almost as fast as the methylene chloride products, but it had a faster drying rate and needed to be reapplied during the stripping process. The coatings were all softened and lifted in a matter of minutes.

Dibasic Esters

This third category of strippers relies on a group of solvents known as dibasic esters, or DBE. This is a much safer group of solvents, but it is not without hazards. DBE has been reported by its manufacturer, DuPont, to cause blurring of vision. Dibasic esters are flammable compounds and must be handled with care. Eye and skin protection are necessary, but no respiratory protection is required with proper ventilation. Dibasic esters are slow acting and may require up to 24 hours to penetrate a thoroughly cured paint film.

We tested Dumond Chemicals' Peel-Away Marine Safety Strip. At first, I was discouraged by the slow performance of this product. Like the other Peel-Away products, Marine Safety Strip has a backing sheet that covers the spread-out chemical paste. I occasionally peeked under the backing sheet during the first four hours, looking for results, but only saw some lifting at the edges of the test panels. However, 36 hours later, all of the coatings had been softened and lifted easily with the backing, exposing a very clean substrate. If you can plan your project around such slow working speed, Marine Safety Strip is a very effective and relatively safe product.

N-Methyl-2-Pyrollidone (NMP)

The safest category of solvent strippers that we looked at relies primarily on N-methyl-2-pyrollidone. This type of chemical stripper is safer than some household cleansers, but it is slow acting and, as with the DBE-based strippers, may not remove some two-part finishes.

We tested Chute Chemical Company's Magi-Sol, which is a very slow-acting stripper but effective given enough time. Forty-eight hours after application, this stripper lifted all of the coatings on our test panels, with the exception of the AwlGrip. The AwlGrip had lifted at the edges and was soft. Magi-Sol is a very safe product as strippers go, and it works if you can be patient with it. I tried it on another alkyd panel, this time lightly sanding the panel first. This speeded up the stripping process considerably.

I am not a big fan of chemical strippers and in the past have avoided using them whenever possible. I may, however, begin to rely on some of the safer products tested here to remove finishes that can't be easily taken off mechanically. (Sometimes, though, it is a good idea to leave the old finish right where it is.)

Sources

Chute Chemical Co.
233 Bomarc Rd.
Bangor, ME 04401
207-942-5228

Dumond Chemicals, Inc.
1501 Broadway
New York, NY 10036
212-869-5350

Nu-TecChemicals
P.O. Box 99815
Seattle, WA 98199
206-298-0128

Sterling Clark
Lurton Corp.
Malden, MA 02148
617-322-0163

Scrapers

Text and Illustrations by Sam Manning

A scraper is a hand-held blade — either flat or hooked — meant to be dragged. Its purpose is to strip a surface of paint or dirt, or to sculpt or flatten it. A scraper penetrates only as deeply as your body weight chooses to force it. It is the easiest and quickest cutting tool to sharpen. It is also the most abused and least understood cutting tool in most kits.

Most people have unpleasant memories of working with a scraper, particularly of scraping paint. The first few strokes with the new tool were almost fun; it cut broadly and well, planing the wood beneath the paint's surface. But lead paints are terribly abrasive to a tool's cutting edge, and soon the scraper would begin to dull, skipping over the hard areas and gouging into soft spots. If the user didn't stop to sharpen the scraper, the rest of the experience became too unpleasant to be recited. People trying to use dull scrapers quickly migrate to paint removers and sanding machines — and endure chemical fumes and clouds of dust.

Step back from that scraper and give it a fresh look. It's meant to be a cutting tool, not a scratcher. The cutting edge of a scraper is easily created with a few authoritative strokes of a sharp, flat file. The most effective scraper edge is quite fragile and somewhat ragged, yet the tool is meant to be thrust through dirt and grit that would instantly dull your saw or plane. One trick is to keep the scraper continually sharp. The other is to keep the scraper's edge working under the painted or gritty surface where the wood is clean and the scraper can survive. Kept sharp and employed with the skill that grows with doing, the scraper will become one of the most dependable and versatile tools in your kit. You'll look forward to deftly stripping paint from any

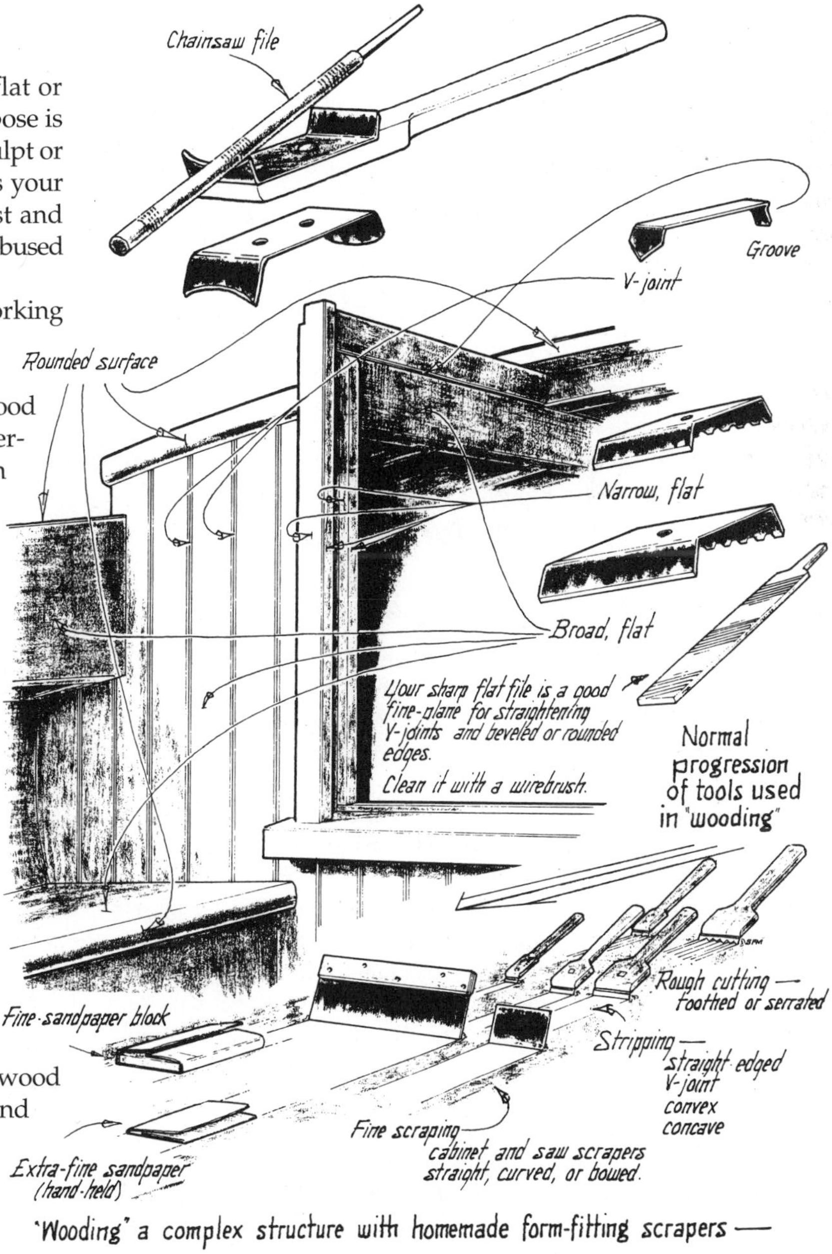

Chainsaw file

Groove

V-joint

Rounded surface

Narrow, flat

Broad, flat

Your sharp flat file is a good fine-plane for straightening V-joints and beveled or rounded edges.
Clean it with a wirebrush.

Normal progression of tools used in "wooding"

Fine-sandpaper block

Rough cutting — toothed or serrated

Stripping
straight-edged
V-joint
convex
concave

Fine scraping
cabinet and saw scrapers
straight, curved, or bowed.

Extra-fine sandpaper
(hand-held)

'Wooding' a complex structure with homemade form-fitting scrapers —

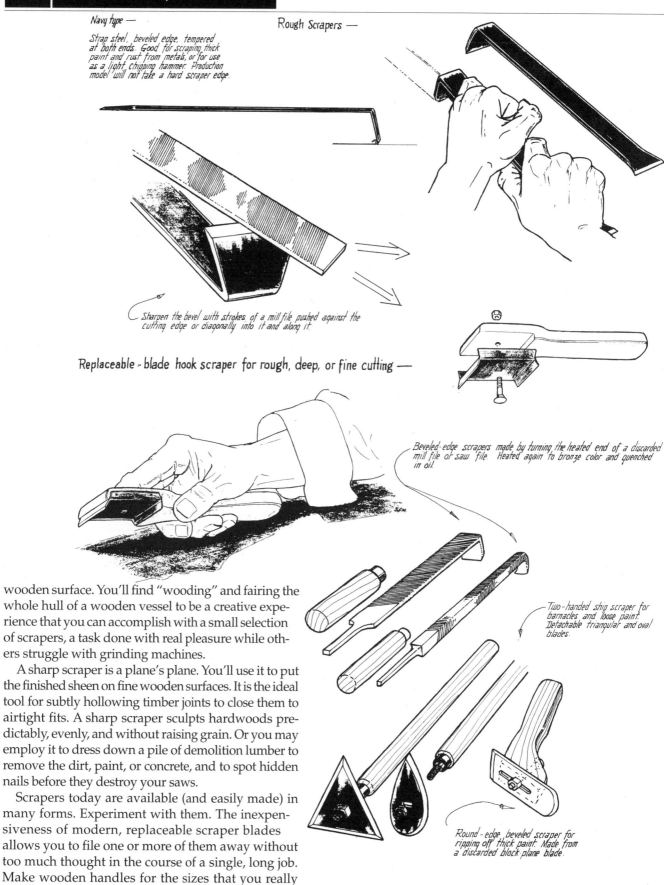

Navy type —

Strap steel, beveled edge, tempered at both ends. Good for scraping thick paint and rust from metals, or for use as a light chipping hammer. Production model will not take a hard scraper edge.

Rough Scrapers —

Sharpen the bevel with strokes of a mill file pushed against the cutting edge or diagonally into it and along it.

Replaceable-blade hook scraper for rough, deep, or fine cutting —

Beveled-edge scrapers made by turning the heated end of a discarded mill file or saw file. Heated again to bronze color and quenched in oil.

Two-handed ship scraper for barnacles and loose paint. Detachable triangular and oval blades.

Round-edge beveled scraper for ripping off thick paint. Made from a discarded block-plane blade.

wooden surface. You'll find "wooding" and fairing the whole hull of a wooden vessel to be a creative experience that you can accomplish with a small selection of scrapers, a task done with real pleasure while others struggle with grinding machines.

A sharp scraper is a plane's plane. You'll use it to put the finished sheen on fine wooden surfaces. It is the ideal tool for subtly hollowing timber joints to close them to airtight fits. A sharp scraper sculpts hardwoods predictably, evenly, and without raising grain. Or you may employ it to dress down a pile of demolition lumber to remove the dirt, paint, or concrete, and to spot hidden nails before they destroy your saws.

Scrapers today are available (and easily made) in many forms. Experiment with them. The inexpensiveness of modern, replaceable scraper blades allows you to file one or more of them away without too much thought in the course of a single, long job. Make wooden handles for the sizes that you really like. And keep those blades sharp!

Rough Scraping

What might be described as "rough" scraping is, frankly, hoe work done with a scraper. Barnacles off the bottom, paint blisters off the side of the house, tar off the garage floor. Hateful work because it leaves no finished, pleasurable results. With this kind of scraping, an existing finish is to be retained as a base for new coats. A dull scraper is best for this, as it slides over the established surface and breaks off the humps. Heavy-bladed scrapers with relatively soft steel in the scraping edge are the best type of tool for rough scraping: long-handled ship scrapers, Navy bars, and annealed file scrapers. Sanding usually follows.

Deep Scraping

"Deep" scraping is more creative than rough scraping. Here, the tool is doing cutting work, so it needs to have good steel and be kept sharp. The best steel I've found for scraping purposes is, oddly, easily available in the replaceable blades sold everywhere for scrapers. The most versatile of these is the replacement blade with four cutting edges: two of them bent upward, two downward, formed from a single, thin, steel plate. These are usually offered bolted to a wood or plastic handle. The handle is a simple one and can be easily duplicated for an array of other scrapers ground or narrowed for special purposes.

The main principle of deep scraping (through paint) is to push the cutting edge down to where it is working just beneath the paint or grit, and to keep it cutting wood, not grit, until the area is entirely stripped.

One way to keep the scraper working at the base of thick paint is to chip the surface with light hammer blows of a dull scraper to break up the surface and to present vertical paint edges for the scraper's edge to grab.

Another way is to cut parallel scratches, troughs, or "flutes" along the grain of the thick-painted wooden surface, using the sharp corner of your replaceable-blade hook scraper; then the full blade is able to shear off strings of remaining paint rather than cope with unbroken armor plate. Wider fluting can be done with a round- or oval-edged scraper before stripping the remainder with the straight blade. Or, if the paint or grit is relatively thin, do the fluting with a serrated-edge scraper that leaves corduroy to be scraped flat with the straight blade.

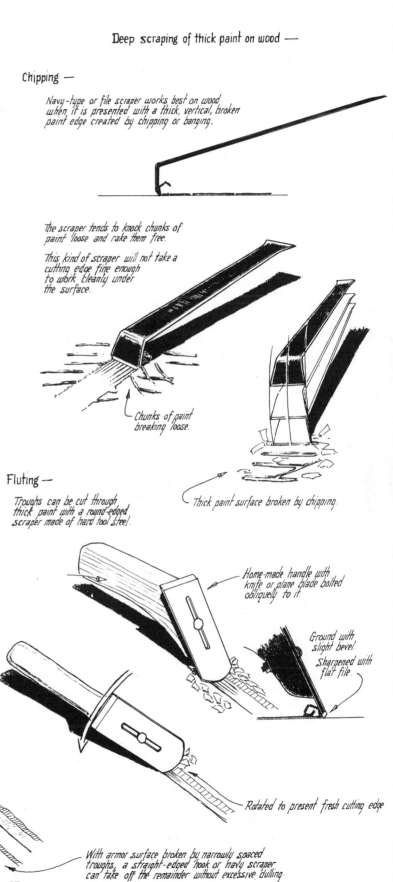

Deep scraping of thick paint on wood —

Chipping —

Navy-type or file scraper works best on wood when it is presented with a thick, vertical, broken paint edge created by chipping or banging.

The scraper tends to knock chunks of paint loose and rake them free.

This kind of scraper will not take a cutting edge fine enough to work cleanly under the surface.

Chunks of paint breaking loose.

Thick paint surface broken by chipping.

Fluting —

Troughs can be cut through thick paint with a round-edged scraper made of hard tool steel.

Home-made handle with knife or plane blade bolted obliquely to it.

Ground with slight bevel. Sharpened with flat file.

Rotated to present fresh cutting edge

With armor surface broken by narrowly spaced troughs, a straight-edged hook or navy scraper can take off the remainder without excessive dulling.

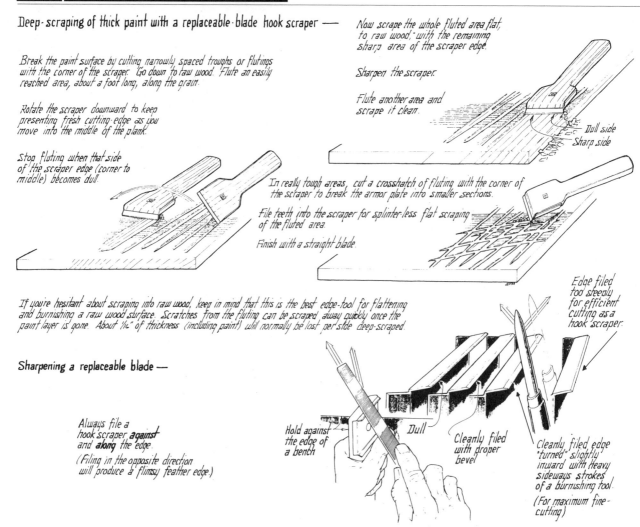

Deep-scraping of thick paint with a replaceable-blade hook scraper —

Break the paint surface by cutting narrowly spaced troughs or flutings with the corner of the scraper. Go down to raw wood. Flute an easily reached area, about a foot long, along the grain.

Rotate the scraper downward to keep presenting fresh cutting-edge as you move into the middle of the plank.

Stop fluting when that side of the scraper edge (corner to middle) becomes dull.

Now scrape the whole fluted area flat, to raw wood, with the remaining sharp area of the scraper edge.

Sharpen the scraper.

Flute another area and scrape it clean.

Dull side
Sharp side

In really tough areas, cut a crosshatch of fluting with the corner of the scraper to break the armor plate into smaller sections.

File teeth into the scraper for splinter-less flat scraping of the fluted area.

Finish with a straight blade.

If you're hesitant about scraping into raw wood, keep in mind that this is the best edge-tool for flattening and burnishing a raw wood surface. Scratches from the fluting can be scraped away quickly once the paint layer is gone. About 1/16" of thickness (including paint) will normally be lost per side deep-scraped.

Sharpening a replaceable blade —

Always file a hook scraper **against** and **along** the edge.
(Filing in the opposite direction will produce a flimsy feather edge.)

Hold against the edge of a bench

Dull

Cleanly filed with proper bevel

Edge filed too steeply for efficient cutting as a hook scraper.

Cleanly filed edge "turned" slightly inward with heavy sideways strokes of a burnishing tool.
(For maximum fine-cutting)

This four-eared replaceable-blade model seems to have the best steel and the most reserve of the various hook scrapers offered in stores today. As you become skillful with this tool, you'll gladly file an ear or two away in the course of a project while enjoying the finished work of a really sharp scraper.

Adapting and Sharpening Replaceable Blades

For those who enjoy blacksmithing, *The Making of Tools*, by Alexander G. Weygers, is an excellent paperback book that authoritatively discusses the making and tempering of edge tools such as scrapers. Making scrapers is a good way to use up your spent files and blades. Shipyard blacksmiths used to turn out a great many of these, shaped and tempered for specific jobs.

You can buy a pile of replacement scraper blades for the price of a single complete tool. The blades can be cut down with a hacksaw and cold chisel to any width wanted, and filed to any tip shape desired. Handles are easily made, and holes can be bored for improved bolting or riveting of a special blade to a special handle. In narrow widths, the replacement blade can be taped to the handle if it is suitably let into the wood to prevent movement. (I usually add half again to the usual length of a handle for comfortable two-handed gripping.)

If you have only one scraping tool, it should be your replaceable-blade hook scraper with the cutting edge modified by you for fine, coarse, or deep scraping. For fine scraping of flat surfaces, straighten the cutting edge by filing atop the point (thereby dulling it) until the cutting edge sights "straight." Then sharpen it by filing into and along the cutting edge, giving this fine scraper a little less bevel than was originally ground into it. Round the sharp corners to keep them from digging in.

For coarse scraping, a lightly convex cutting edge is desirable. Work the extremities of the blade down a bit and give the cutting edge a bevel of about 45 degrees. For deep scraping, continue sharpening to a 45-degree bevel in a toothed or serrated scraper.

Always file into and along the cutting edge of a hook scraper. This drags the cut steel cleanly inward from the point. Filing in the opposite direction (down the bevel, off the point, and into the air) will tend to gouge out the steel just behind the cutting edge and leave a sharp-feeling, but weak, "feather edge" that

Close-up view of what the file is doing —

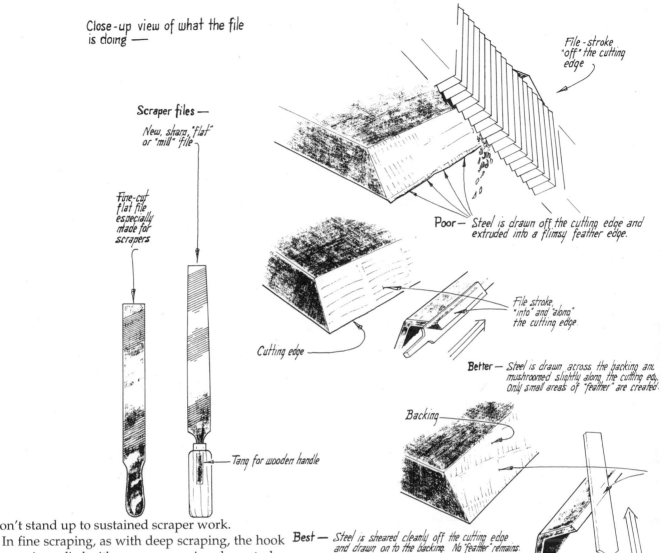

File-stroke "off" the cutting edge

Scraper files —

New, sharp, "flat" or "mill" file

Fine-cut flat file especially made for scrapers

Poor — Steel is drawn off the cutting edge and extruded into a flimsy feather edge.

File stroke, "into" and "along" the cutting edge.

Cutting edge —

Better — Steel is drawn across the backing and mushroomed slightly along the cutting edge. Only small areas of "feather" are created.

Backing —

Tang for wooden handle

won't stand up to sustained scraper work.

In fine scraping, as with deep scraping, the hook scraper is applied with even pressure in a draw stroke. Skew it to the line of pull where necessary to bridge and flatten hummocks made by machine planing or by previous strokes of coarser tools. Run your hand over the scraped surface to detect any ridges or depressions. Scrape them out.

Best — Steel is sheared cleanly off the cutting edge and drawn on to the backing. No "feather" remains.

The "look" of a fine-scraper's edge —

Filing the Edge

What kind of file to use? The Nicholson Company, which makes files for every purpose, at one time made a file especially for hook scrapers. It was a fine-toothed flat file with no teeth on its edge. The lower part of the file was smoothed and rounded to be its own handle. I have not seen one of these in years, so nowadays I use a standard fine-toothed "flat" or "mill" file, preferably a new one with sharp teeth. Experiment with round and saw files when altering scraper blades to fit mullions or mouldings. As with all areas of hand-tool operation, a few minutes of intelligent sharpening earns large dividends in good mileage thereafter. Why struggle with a heavy sander?

Hook scraper —

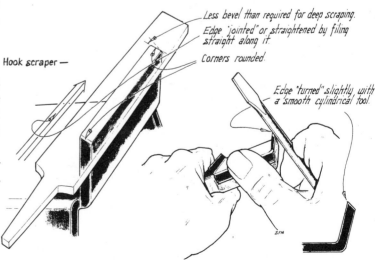

Less bevel than required for deep scraping. Edge "jointed" or straightened by filing straight along it.

Corners rounded.

Edge "turned" slightly with a smooth cylindrical tool.

Rough and deep scraping — with a toothed or serrated hook scraper

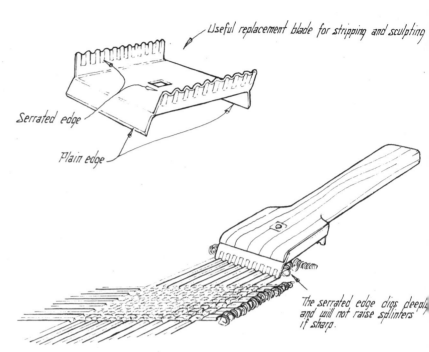

Useful replacement blade for stripping and sculpting

Serrated edge

Plain edge

Serrated Scrapers

Serrations in the scraper's edge allow the tool to be pushed deeper than it normally would go. Notches filed into the edge of a straight scraper do almost the same service as serrations and can be made and deepened with the corner of your flat file. Whether straight-bladed, serrated, or given homemade teeth, a hook scraper is sharpened in the same way: by filing the bevel into or along the cutting edge, never with strokes directed off the cutting edge. Your scraper may stay sharp for only a foot-square area in stripping paint, so when the tool's "eagerness" gives out, give it six to ten heavy strokes with a new flat file and continue the work. There's no dust to this work. Just paint chips or rolls of goo. You'll be amazed at the weight of the paint chips that you sweep up.

The serrated edge digs deeply and will not raise splinters if sharp.

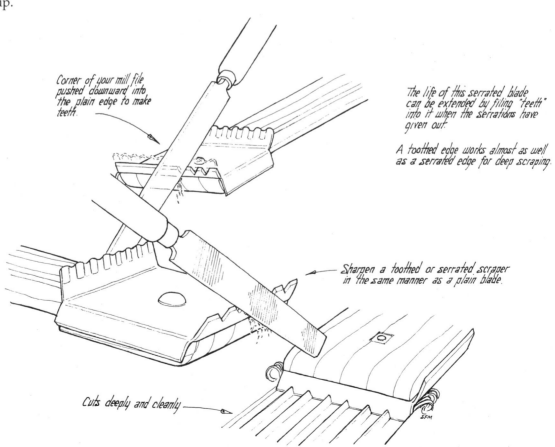

Corner of your mill file pushed downward into the plain edge to make teeth.

The life of this serrated blade can be extended by filing "teeth" into it when the serrations have given out.

A toothed edge works almost as well as a serrated edge for deep scraping.

Sharpen a toothed or serrated scraper in the same manner as a plain blade.

Cuts deeply and cleanly

SFM

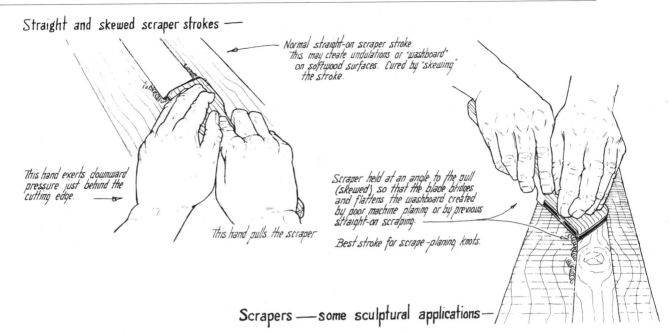

Straight and skewed scraper strokes —

Normal straight-on scraper stroke. This may create undulations or "washboard" on softwood surfaces. Cured by "skewing" the stroke.

This hand exerts downward pressure just behind the cutting edge. →

This hand pulls the scraper

Scraper held at an angle to the pull (skewed) so that the blade bridges and flattens the washboard created by poor machine planing or by previous straight-on scraping.

Best stroke for scrape-planing knots.

Scrapers —some sculptural applications—

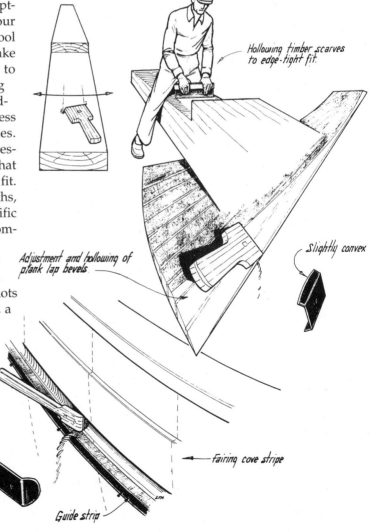

Hollowing timber scarves to edge-tight fit.

Slightly convex

Adjustment and hollowing of plank lap bevels.

Fairing cove stripe

Guide strip

Sculpting Wood with a Scraper

While stripping paint is a surface operation, sculpting involves modeling the wood beneath. Here, your sharp scrapers get into real stride as the finishing tool to burnish surfaces and remove chisel marks; to make slight adjustments to the bevel of a keel rabbet; to smooth, flatten, and slightly hollow the changing gain of a dory lap; or to improve any carved wooden surface with successive strokes that remove less wood than the finest setting of your hand planes. Clearly, the scraper employed to gentle the expression of a carved wooden face is not the same one that you'd use to fay backbone timbers to a light-tight fit. Here's where you make your own, creating widths, blade shapes, and handles suited to carry a specific scraper tip into areas not easily reached by the commercial models.

The serrated or toothed deep scraper is a great instrument for flattening or sculpting raw wood, particularly where unruly grain areas surround knots or hollows otherwise difficult to plane. If sharp, a serrated scraper can be applied along, across, or diagonally to the grain without raising splinters. It cuts cleanly through its own corduroy swath, leaving pinnacles of bad grain or ossified knotwood easily sheared at their roots by follow-up strokes of a straight-bladed scraper.

Hardwoods scrape easily. Softwoods take a little more care. Skewing a scraper blade to the direction of pull allows it to bridge and flatten any hummocks that may have developed. Deep scraping is often the best solution for hollowing fayed surfaces to edge-tight fits, or for fine-sculpting any wooden shape that is curved.

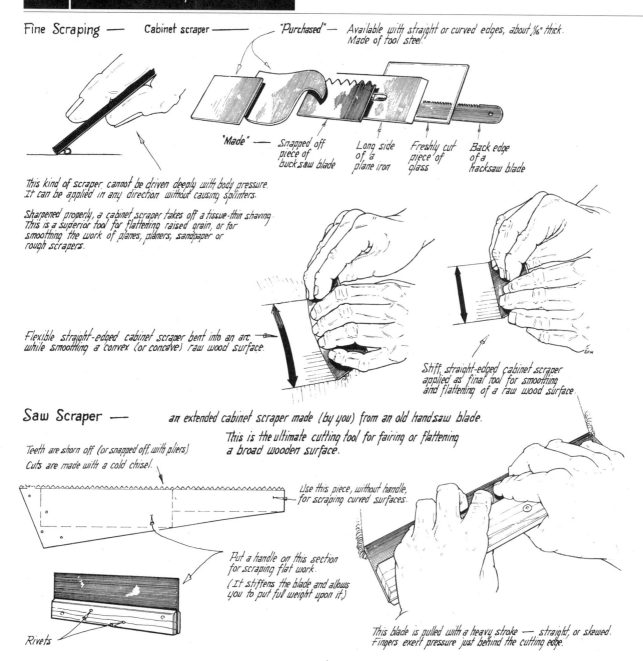

Fine Scraping — Cabinet scraper — "Purchased" — Available with straight or curved edges, about 1/16" thick. Made of tool steel.

"Made" — Snapped off piece of bucksaw blade   Long side of a plane iron   Freshly cut piece of glass   Back edge of a hacksaw blade

This kind of scraper cannot be driven deeply with body pressure. It can be applied in any direction without causing splinters.

Sharpened properly, a cabinet scraper takes off a tissue-thin shaving. This is a superior tool for flattening raised grain, or for smoothing the work of planes, planers, sandpaper or rough scrapers.

Flexible straight-edged cabinet scraper bent into an arc while smoothing a convex (or concave) raw wood surface.

Stiff, straight-edged cabinet scraper applied as final tool for smoothing and flattening of a raw wood surface.

Saw Scraper — an extended cabinet scraper made (by you) from an old handsaw blade.

This is the ultimate cutting tool for fairing or flattening a broad wooden surface.

Teeth are shorn off (or snapped off, with pliers). Cuts are made with a cold chisel.

Use this piece, without handle, for scraping curved surfaces.

Put a handle on this section for scraping flat work. (It stiffens the blade and allows you to put full weight upon it.)

Rivets

This blade is pulled with a heavy stroke — straight, or skewed. Fingers exert pressure just behind the cutting edge.

Fine Scraping

Fine scrapers are the final cutting tools used on a wooden surface to flatten it, or to bring it to a fair curve, and to polish it. Belt sanders do the work of fine scrapers in most production shops today, but the operator loses the ability to hand-feel the worked surface for lumps or hollows or the fairness of an overall curve. And he'll need a respirator.

Fine scraping remains the best way to fair a wooden hull to a glassy sheen prior to hand sanding and paint. It is also the best way to flatten and burnish your dining-room table top for a mirror finish. A fine scraper produces gossamer-thin shavings, and no face mask is needed.

Cabinet scrapers, the smaller variety, can be found in hardware stores. These scrapers are plates of thin tool steel, usually rectangular, that can be sharpened on all edges, some of which may be curved along their length. Some edges may be beveled. A sharp-cornered square edge is the classic form for a fine scraper. (The edge of a pane of window glass, freshly cut, also makes a fairly good fine scraper.)

The broader the surface being fine-scraped, the broader your fine scraper should be. You may need to make this tool for yourself.

The shipwright's saw scraper is a larger, homemade edition of the cabinet scraper and is made from a squared portion of a sacrificed handsaw. Unless bowed into a curve for scraping cylindrical surfaces such as spars, this large scraper is usually given a wooden grip or railing along its top to keep it stiff and to allow the exertion of full body weight upon it. It's ideal for broad surfaces.

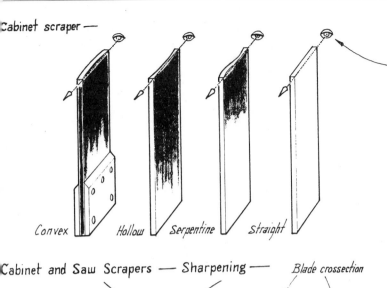

Cabinet scraper —

Learn to sight along a cabinet scraper's edge to detect non-straightness.

Hollows or humps will leave their impression on a scraped surface.

Remedy by re-jointing the length of its cutting edge with a sharp flat file.

Convex   Hollow   Serpentine   Straight

Cabinet and Saw Scrapers — Sharpening —

Blade crossection

Set up a vise close to the work site

Filed (this edge is serviceable)

Turned (better edge)

Sharpen with lengthwise strokes of a mill file (your newest) held squarely to the cutting edge.

burnished top

wire edge

Filed again (one heavy stroke) for maximum "grab".

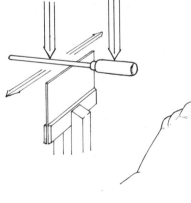

Turn the edge with a burnishing tool so that the steel mushrooms outward slightly on both sides of the blade.
Use heavy strokes, two-handed, back and forth, with the burnisher held squarely across.

Then give one more heavy lengthwise stroke with the file to flatten the burnished top and to thin the protruding wire edges on both sides.

Sharpening Cabinet Scrapers

Sharpen steel cabinet scrapers edge-upward in a vise. The squared edge is sharpened by planing it with heavy strokes of your sharpest flat file laid lengthwise on the cutting edge, held squarely to it, and pushed along its whole length. Only a few strokes should be necessary to produce a flat, square top to the edge of the scraper, with corners biting-sharp on both sides. This "jointing" of the scraper with a sharp mill file may be enough treatment to give good scraping results.

However, the scraper edge(s) can be improved for finer scraping by uniformly drawing out the scraper's edge with long strokes of a burnishing tool so that the edge mushrooms out on both sides into a wire-thin cutting edge. If you don't own a burnishing tool (a hard, polished steel tongue, shaped like a letter opener), you can do a creditable burnishing job with any hard steel tool that is polished and narrow. I often use the polished, flat side of a ¼-inch chisel blade for this purpose. Or a scrap diesel injector.

Use both hands when burnishing. Lay the burnishing tool across and squarely to the edge of the scraper and push or pull it along the whole length of the scraper edge with heavy force downward. In a few such strokes, the whole length of the scraper edge will begin to curl outward on both sides.

Try the tool on wood. One side may be sharper than the other. No matter. Correct it on the next sharpening. Keep your vise set up close to the job. You'll be jointing and burnishing frequently to keep the "eagerness" in your blade. The sharpening is a bit of a knack, but it's easily learned.

Looking Good Again

A REFINISHING STORY

——— by Maynard Bray   Photographs by Benjamin Mendlowitz ———

About the boat: White Cap is one of the so-called 12 ½-foot (waterline) class built by the Herreshoff Manufacturing Company of Bristol, Rhode Island. She is gaff rigged, and her overall length is about 16 feet. The class was designed by Nathanael G. Herreshoff, and the first boats, which were for use on Buzzards Bay, were introduced in 1914. White Cap dates from 1929 and carries HMCo hull number 1107. It was with the cooperation of her new owner, Mr. H.W. Detert of Norway, Maine, that these photographs were possible.

The scene is Riverside Boat Company in Newcastle, Maine; the time is January 12, 1981; the temperature is 12 degrees at 12 noon. Paul Bryant, who runs the yard, is beginning to sand the Herreshoff 12½-footer White Cap, which is scheduled for a thorough refurbishing. He's doing this outdoors where at the end of the working day the temperature will have dropped to 7 degrees.

Working with the weather, and in spite of it when he has to, is something Paul has grown up with. The yard was started by his father, and Paul has worked there since he was in the sixth grade. With only two other men besides Paul, the yard maintains about 70 of the 90-odd boats it stores and does as good a job of it as you're likely to see anywhere. With few exceptions the boats are stored *outside under canvas covers during the winter, and the smaller ones are cycled through one of the two heated shops a few at a time until the weather breaks and the others can be worked on outside.*

Riverside faces conditions similar to many do-it-yourself owners: outside storage, limited time for each job, a schedule to meet, and the return of the same boat season after season. There's much to be learned from their experience.

Power Sanding

Heavy-duty disc-type machines, held flat and kept moving, are used whenever possible, because they're the fastest way to fair and smooth a surface.

For fairing and shaping, and for stripping off paint and varnish, the coarser grits of a very abrasive heavy paper called "greenbak" (like that used in floor-sanding edgers) on a firm pad in a medium-speed (5,000 rpm) grinder work best. A slower machine can be used, but it takes longer.

The finer sanding for smoothing up painted surfaces and feathering off flaked paint is best done with a low-speed (2,000 rpm) disc-type sander/polisher with a soft foam pad. A higher speed machine heats up the paint, making it so gummy that it clogs up the grit of the finer papers. Neither a vibrator nor a belt sander are used much, since they don't do as good a job and are slower working.

The two machines favored by Paul are the Black & Decker model 4046 grinder (4,800 rpm) with a very firm phenolic pad and 7-inch Norton "Bear" brand "greenbak" metalite abrasive discs (grits 16 to 80), and the Rockwell model 661 (2,000 rpm) with a Norton 8SR-K sanding-pad kit and 8-inch-diameter aluminum-oxide production-paper sanding discs (grits 36 to 220). Norton No. 10 disc adhesive, a type of contact cement, holds the discs to the foam pad.

The initial hull sanding and fairing, which included the bottom, took about five hours and consumed about 25 discs from 36 to 120 grit. Generally the topsides were sanded with 100 and 120 grit, the boottop (which was taken more or less down to the wood for rescribing) with 80 and 100, and the bottom with 36.

1

Getting rid of old paint and varnish and fairing off *White Cap*'s transom is a snap with this grinder. The coarse 36-grit disc makes a quick job of it, and the firm pad enables one to build up more pressure for grinding off troublesome spots, aids in fairing the surface, and leaves crisp corners at the plank ends. Some further smoothing with 50, 60, and 80 grits is then done before changing machines.

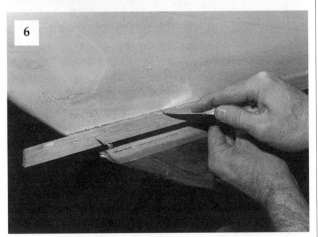

2

The rest of the transom smoothing is done with a foam pad on the low-speed machine, starting with 80 grit and going to 100 and 120. Care must be taken at the sharp corners to avoid rounding them over. The entire process of stripping and sanding this transom took only about half an hour, and when it was finished there were absolutely no sanding marks and the surface was ready for refinishing. A dutchman, however, was later fitted in way of the upper rudder gudgeon, where the wood had gone bad.

3

A foam-backed disc is the most effective way to smooth up a hull for painting. Used with 60-, 80-, or 100-grit paper, it does a beautiful job of knocking down the high spots and feathering out the transition between painted and unpainted surfaces. Provided the paper is sharp, that is. It's a waste of time to use dull discs; they only polish the surface, without fairing or feathering it. When feathering by hand, a coarse grit, say 60, will do the work faster and better — just as with the machine. Final sanding (power or hand) at this stage will be with 120-grit paper.

Scribing the Waterline

4

A crisply painted level waterline goes a long way toward making a paint job look right. There are a number of ways to mark it so it's level, but one of the simplest and most direct was employed on *White Cap*. (Her existing line, like the waterlines on so many older boats, was neither straight nor decisively marked.) First off, the boat is leveled athwartships and two straightedges running in that direction are set up — one forward and one aft, as shown in the photograph. These, of course, must also be made level. From there on it's a case of one person "sighting in" on the imaginary plane between the two straightedges while another person adjusts the pencil until it corresponds with that plane. Gordon and Jason are doing that in the photo, making marks on the hull about a foot apart.

5

The individual marks are then connected with a continuous pencil line by means of a stiff batten held on edge; that is, held square with the waterplane. This batten is hand held as shown and need not be very long.

6

A full-length batten, flexible enough to conform to the marked line when temporarily nailed against the hull, is placed so its top edge is on that line.

7

Scribing tools can be adapted from worn-out hacksaw blades or files, or whatever else is handy and can be used to cut a good scribe line — one that is sharp enough to look good and deep enough to last for a few years. Scribe lines are a great aid in painting the waterline or boottop, but they all fill up with paint eventually and have to be battened off and cleaned out occasionally. The tool shown here was made from a piece of $\frac{1}{16}$-inch brass, filed so it will scrape out a shaving when pulled along the batten.

8

For each width of boottop, a set of these sliding wooden pointers has been made up, a $1\frac{1}{4}$-inch-wide pair being used here. The assembly is kept level (by means of the spirit level built into the try-square), while the lower pointer is placed in the scribe line representing the waterline, and the top pointer is slid into contact with the hull and marked with a pencil where it touches. From there on the process of getting a scribed line at the top of the boottop is exactly the same as for the waterline. No seam compound has yet been applied to the topsides, so the open hull seams are much in evidence.

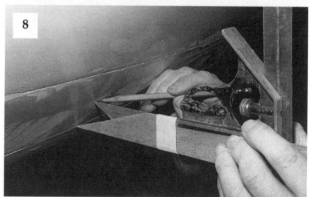

Stripping the Brightwork

Using only scrapers, always kept sharp with a file, most of the varnish is stripped off. (A single application of chemical paint remover on the coamings speeded up the work a bit by softening the surface coats.) All the wood is oak, and it was weathered and stained in places. Careful scraping gets rid of most of the discoloration; bleach has been found ineffective and is not used at all. Almost all the scrapers have at least a slight crown to their blades, so sufficient pressure can be brought to bear on a flat surface and peel off a good shaving. Grinding and filing can shape the blades to fit almost any surface. A fair amount of strength is needed for good control, however; otherwise the tool is inclined to chatter, or the corners of the blade, even if filed off a bit, tend to dig in.

It is often easier to remove all the metal fittings than it is to scrape, sand, and varnish around them. *White Cap*'s were all taken off before any scraping began. The entire stripping and scraping job on this boat took about four hours.

9

If you've never wooded down a round spar by dry scraping, by all means try it. It's the quickest method by far, and you don't need a great deal of strength. Just keep the scraper sharp by frequent filing (use a flat mill file). The small and convenient wooden handle is yard built — only the hardened

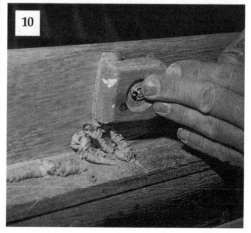

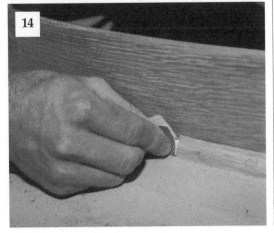

steel blade came from the store. It was simply screwed to the handle.

10

A fairly wide and slightly crowned blade is best for flat surfaces. Here, with the varnish all removed, the weathered wood is scraped away to expose the oak's real beauty. The big-handled commercial scraper is okay here, where two-handed force is needed.

11

A small scraper, guided by the left hand and drawn along with the right, does a fine job of getting into the corner between the sheerstrake and the covering board, and cleaning out all the old varnish and discoloration. Some of the other scrapers and the ever-present sharpening file are lying on the deck, along with a putty knife. A chisel or sharpened putty knife is sometimes useful in getting into corners where a scraper won't fit.

12

A convex scraper mates well with the concave shape of the Herreshoff molded sheerstrake. A deft touch is needed, but it's not difficult to develop such a "feel" after a bit of practice.

Sanding the Brightwork

Sanding is the most tiring of all jobs, and more than a man-day of hand-sanding alone was done on this boat — and that just on brightwork. Coarse 40- and 60-grit paper makes the work go faster, but it's still a big task to recover from a period of neglect (this is *White Cap*'s first year at Riverside). Sanding is done with the grain, and a backing block is used on uneven surfaces to make them fair. Six sheets of 40 grit, a couple of 50, one of 60, and two of 80 were used before the brightwork was ready for final sanding with 100 grit and refinishing. The feathering of peeling brightwork that has not been stripped is best done with coarse (about 60 grit) paper, after which the scratches can be sanded out by going "through the numbers" to 120 grit.

13

The basic sanding technique is back and forth with the grain of the piece being sanded. A sanding block sometimes helps cut down the high places or even cut away the scraper marks, but much of the work is done with the folded piece of paper itself. Gloves keep the skin from being abraded.

14

Torn into small pieces, the sandpaper fits into tight places.

15

The sheerstrake is sanded fair with the aid of this drum made from a short length of plastic drain pipe around which a sheet of sandpaper has been taped.

16

The rest of the sheerstrake is done barehanded in order to feel any unfairness.

17

A sanding block held like this evens out the edge of the newly installed covering board. Loose or blackened bungs in the sheerstrake and coaming were popped out and renewed, and the new ones were glued in with quick-setting epoxy. Great care must be taken during all hand sanding to keep from rounding off any corners that should stay crisp.

18

A strip of sandpaper wrapped around a putty knife gets into tight comers.

19

Moisture leaking in behind unbedded woodwork or joints is the greatest cause of lifted and discolored varnishwork. Rebedding is an effective solution, and that's what is being done here with these trim pieces. The opened joint between the top of the stern knee and the transom will be filled with a fitted wedge, since a warped transom plank prevents the joint from being drawn up tightly by refastening.

Filling and Surfacing

White Cap's hull has dried out and her seams, particularly topside, have opened up. She'll swell again after a time overboard, so a soft, non-drying seam compound that will squeeze out is called for. Paul chose Interlux No. 31 and is planning to resand and repaint the hull again in mid-season once the seams have come together. In the future such excessive drying out will be prevented by a good buildup of paint and by keeping the boat out of the hot sun or heated sheds while ashore (except for a brief annual visit to the marginally heated paint shop). Trowel cement, Interlux No. 93, is used on nicks and scrapes; in subsequent years it will be used in the topside seams also as long as they haven't opened up.

20

A wide, flexible putty knife assures an even application of seam compound and trowel cement (no sanding is planned afterwards), and masking tape keeps the compound from getting into the grain of the yet-to-be-varnished sheerstrake. A good vacuuming and priming are needed before the seams are

filled with compound and before the hull planking is faced up with trowel cement; neither substance sticks well over dust or bare wood.

21

Paul uses a combination filler and stain as a base for all brightwork. He used Interlux No. 1643, a natural color, on this oak and thins it out to a brushing consistency with turpentine, brushing liquid (Interlux No. 333), or special thinner (Interlux No. 216), depending on the drying conditions. The excess is rubbed off after a few minutes and the remainder is allowed to dry overnight just as is a fresh coat of paint or varnish. The filler/stain's purpose is twofold: it fills the open grain and enables a glass-like varnish job, and the protection of the surface that goes with it, with fewer coats, and it gives a more uniform appearance to the wood — some of which is old, some new, and some a bit weather stained.

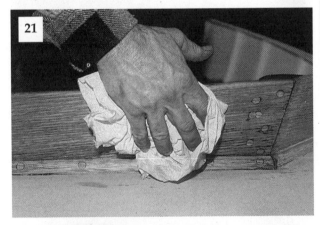

Buildup

From this point on it's a case of building up enough coats of varnish and topside paint to give good protection and appearance. This amounts to three coats of topside paint over the first thinned-down coat (for best adhesion Paul used Interlux No. 220 semigloss right over the bare wood and for the subsequent coats as well) and five coats of varnish (Interlux No. 90) — the first coat cut about 25 percent with turpentine. Sanding is needed between all coats; 120 grit is used with a fairly light touch on both the varnish and the paint. Each sanding is followed by vacuuming and wiping down with a tack rag to eliminate dust, and each new coat of paint is preceded by facing up with either trowel cement or seam compound, as appropriate, in order to have the hull virtually flawless when the buildup is complete. Trowel cement, if used after the buildup (i.e., just before the final painting) will cause flatting out of the gloss by "flashing through" the finish coats.

Final Sanding

22

This consists of hand sanding the varnish with 150-grit paper and machine sanding the paint with 220. As always, the varnish should be sanded insofar as possible with the grain of the wood, and care must be taken to go very lightly, if at all, on the sharp corners, as on the toerail, for example. Once the buildup is complete, Paul never sands the sharp corners, feeling that they are vulnerable to wear in service and need all the varnish they can get. Yet inside corners, such as those at the base of the coaming, often don't get enough sanding, so for good adhesion, it's important to be thorough there.

Final Cleaning

23

Dust and dirt are the enemies of high-gloss finishes, and are most commonly produced by a dirty surface to begin with, dust in the air, which settles on the surface while it is still wet, dirt in the paint or varnish, and dirt in the brush. A thorough vacuuming — even on parts of the boat that aren't being worked on — and subsequent dusting off with a painter's tack rag (paint stores and auto body shops have them) will take care of any dust on the surface itself. But a clean shop that has been well swept down and vacuumed out beforehand is a must also. (If you're working outside, then get the boat far away from sources of dust, such as busy dirt roads, and do your work on a day when there is little or no wind.) Paul religiously strains all his paint and varnish before use; he is very careful to keep his brushes cleaned out so that paint won't dry on their bristles, and stores them where they won't get dusty. His consistently dust-free jobs make all this extra fussing worthwhile.

Final Varnishing

Since it's easier to cut paint into varnish than the other way around, the final coats of varnish are done before the final painting. Paul has found it best to apply the last two coats of varnish without any sanding between them. The resulting thick film holds its shine through the season without the need to "freshen up" in midsummer.

Interlux No. 90 varnish, always strained before use, is what Riverside uses. Rarely are additives used, only a bit of Interlux No. 333 to keep the varnish from setting up too fast in unusually good drying conditions, or some turpentine to thin it in cold weather.

A very thorough vacuuming and wipe down (with a painter's tack rag) precedes all the varnishing, but they're particularly important before the final coats.

The 1½-inch brush used on this job by Jason Burns, one of Paul's crew, is of badger hair, and those fine bristles will spread about as uniform a coat as it's possible to get. That's the whole secret to good varnishing: getting a coat that nowhere is thick enough to sag or run yet is sufficiently heavy everywhere to protect the surface and make it shine. Varnish has to be "flowed on," as the books all say, but flowed on evenly. Considerable brushing with the right technique is needed to achieve this end no matter what kind of varnishing brush is used.

Paul himself never bothers with fancy badger hair brushes. The success of his varnishing depends more on the application techniques, an important one being speed. Go fast so the stuff is all brushed evenly

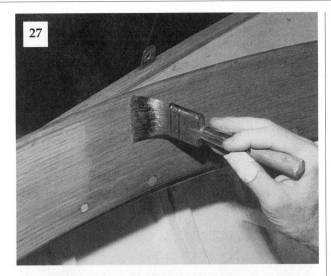

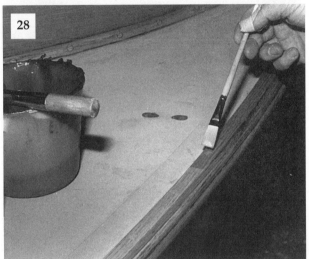

before it starts to set up and there's no need of an expensive brush, Paul advises.

Vertical or near-vertical surfaces are where the runs develop, so the varnish must be brushed out a bit more on them than on horizontal surfaces. Here we show the techniques of applying varnish to the coaming, where inner and outer surfaces must be coated at the same time.

24
Getting enough varnish on the top of the coaming is assured by applying it in this manner.

25
The varnish is then smoothed out with a light stroke along the top edge.

26
Any runs off the top edges must be picked up and blended into the coating now being applied to the sides, as on this outside face, for example. Every brushful of newly laid-on varnish is brushed out until it feels and looks smooth and even. Jason is doing only the vertical side of the coaming, stopping at the covering board, which will be done separately afterwards.

27
Now the same treatment is given to the inside face of the coaming, always stroking back into the already-varnished area with the final smoothing.

28

For better control of the film thickness on top of the toerail, a small brush was used. That brush also comes in handy for varnishing in tight places where the bigger brush won't fit.

29
Frequent sighting for runs, sags, and bare spots while the varnish is still wet enough to make corrections is very necessary. These imperfections show up better, of course, in good light. Note the graving piece or dutchman set into the transom in way of the rudder gudgeon, and the newly painted name — applied just before the final coats.

Final Coats of Paint

Getting a good gloss job is more than simply having a good surface to start with. Good paint, with the right additives to make it flow well, a good brush that will lay on a paint film of uniform thickness in a reasonable amount of time, and the correct technique for laying it on are the other things to consider. In regard to additives, Paul has this to say: "Painting is something that requires adjusting to the prevailing conditions. When painting outside in the wind or on a hot day, or in a shed where a hot-air furnace is running, there is always a need for adding a retarder (Interlux Brushing Liquid No. 333) to the paint. If the weather is cold, some thinning (with Interlux Special Thinner No. 216) is a must to achieve the right viscosity — and if the wind is blowing it will probably need some retarder also." If drying conditions are really poor, certain solvents such as Japan dryer can speed up drying. Good-quality natural-bristle brushes are what Paul generally uses for painting, ones that are big enough to spread paint fast and fine enough to spread it evenly. *White Cap*'s topsides, however, were painted with a 2½-inch synthetic-bristle brush, which Paul admits doesn't stay as firm — and therefore is not as good for cutting in — once it has had some use.

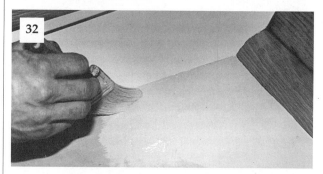

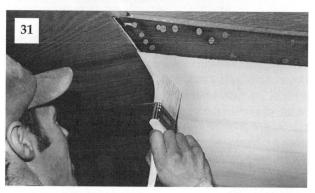

30

One has to keep moving to avoid lap marks and the runs that sometimes go with them (retarder helps here), and at the same time cut in accurately against other colors (such as the sheerstrake on *Whitecap*). Paint put on too thinly (brushed out too much) won't flow enough while drying to develop a good shine, and paint that is too thick (not brushed out enough) is almost certain to sag and run. The objective is to get a job that is between these two extremes while still cutting in accurately and leaving no bare spots. Brushing back into, rather than away from, the fresh paint, as Paul is doing here, tends to give a smoother coat.

31

The fastest and easiest way of cutting in is with a bigger brush than you'd imagine, turned on edge. Small brushes are of little use here; they just don't hold enough paint. When cutting in around the transom, Paul not only uses the brush on edge, but also forces the bristles to separate into two groups, only one of which is actually being used for cutting in. Thus, only the needed amount of paint is being applied to the plank ends, where any excess would be difficult to get rid of.

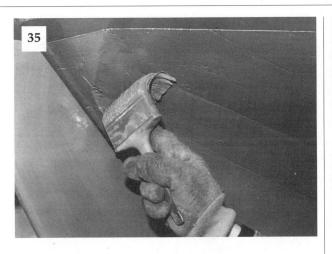

32

This is the proper way to hold a brush when cutting in against other paintwork or varnish. Cutting in or lining off, as it's sometimes called, is done before the adjacent body of paint is applied, care being taken all the while to keep the brush moving in order to maintain a "wet edge" where the next brushful will be worked out.

33

A small brush is the only type for applying paint with good control in tight places like this one. Paul usually has two or three sizes of brush at hand, for example, when painting a deck, and he uses the one most appropriate for the job.

34

With a good scribe line, painting a boottop or waterline is quite easy. Again, the way to do it is with a brush that's big enough and turned on edge. Paint up into the scribe line; don't stop at its lower edge or you'll never have a good-looking job. At the lower edge, the masking tape keeps the red paint from getting spread over the green, but the final line there, as at the top, will be done "with only a sure eye and a steady hand."

35

Bottoms are hidden from view once the boat is overboard and needn't be fussed with as much. A big brush is called for here to get this nasty job done quickly. Cutting in can be done with a slightly smaller brush if you want, and it is done just as for the top of the boottop — that is, the paint is run up into the scribe line, not stopped short of it. Unless the owner requests otherwise, Paul prepares boat bottoms for painting with only a serrated scraper; sandpaper is not used at all. He sticks with oil-based paint, which lends itself to scraping, unlike some of the vinyl bottom paints now on the market.

Completion

How much time did the refurbishing of *White Cap* take while at Riverside? The refinishing of the hull and spars, described in this chapter, consumed about 110 man-hours. Beyond that, about 40 additional man-hours were spent on repair (new toerails, covering boards, seat supports, transom repair, etc.).

Many elements combine to make up Riverside's efficiency, but one of its keys is good organization. As Benjie Mendlowitz, who took all these photographs and who has seen a lot of this type of work going on in other yards, observes, "Each step here is done in its proper order to completion and perfection before and in preparation for the next step. This is probably obvious, but it is the cornerstone of the whole operation. They don't work on 'areas' of the boat; they do all the scraping, then all the sanding, then all the filling, prime everything, varnish everything coat by coat, then paint in the same way." It's doubtful that anyone who isn't doing this type of thing every day and is without the experience of Paul Bryant and his crew at Riverside could get the same results in the same amount of time, but by utilizing these techniques we feel certain that your spring outfitting will go faster and look better.

36

Paint on the hull interior and floorboards, and installation of the newly varnished seats just about completes the job on *White Cap* except for reinstallation of the hardware.

37

Bedding compound, along with the good buildup of varnish over the wood, will keep moisture out from behind fittings — such as the mast partner bale — for a long time to come. While the metal fittings were off, they were cleaned of old paint and varnish and buffed up a bit, both jobs being made easier because the fittings weren't left on the boat. The Herreshoff nameplate, the next item to be put back in place, lies on the deck.

38

Before coming to Riverside, *White Cap* had been reframed and repaired in a mediocre way, and there was considerable time devoted here to making her look

good in spite of this history. She had somehow developed a noticeable hump in the sheer line on both sides forward. New toerails, made higher where they join the stem, and lower in the way of the hump, helped make her sheer look presentable, as did a faired-out and somewhat higher paint line at the bottom of the sheerstrake forward. The new garboards, however, which were apparently installed at the same time, aren't completely fair with the rest of the bottom planking, as can be seen in the photograph.

	Table of Abrasive Grits Used by Riverside Boat Company		
Intended Use	**Aluminum Oxide Paper Sheets** (used for hand-sanding)	**Aluminum Oxide Paper Discs** (used with 2,000 rpm sander and foam pad)	**Greenbak Discs** (used with 5,000 rpm grinder with firm pad)
Removing paint			#16 or #36
Sanding topsides (good condition)	#120 or #150	#120, #150, #180, or #220	
Sanding topsides (flaking)	#50 #60, #80, #100	#60, #80, #100*	
Sanding bottoms (when done)	#50, #60	#40, #50, #60	
Sanding brightwork	#120, #150, #220**	#120, #150, #180, #220**, ***	
Fairing the hull		#80, #100	#36
Canvas deck	#80, #100	#60, #80	

Notes: * This is in preparation for the first of two or three coats of finish paint. Primers or undercoaters are not used since the adhesion to them isn't as good.

** 220 grit is used for one subsequent coat. Two coats, without sanding between them, is the normal way at Riverside with the surface prepared beforehand by 150 grit.

*** Power sanding of brightwork is usually limited to large, flat surfaces, a transom, for example.

The Tally for *White Cap*

Taken directly from Riverside's bill to show the time and materials for each operation.

January 6

Labor — remove foam flotation; remove floorboards; scrape bilge area; remove DOT fasteners; plug all holes. 5 hours
48 oak bungs
Epoxy Ten-Set

January 12

Labor — power sand topsides and bottom; strip off old boottop; strip transom; remove hardware; clean old varnish from hardware; remove rigging from spars for refinishing work. 6½ hours
4 #36 sanding discs - 8"
4 #60 sanding discs - 8"
6 #80 sanding discs - 8"
6 #100 sanding discs - 8"
1 #80 sanding discs - 7"
1 #36 sanding discs - 7"

January 13

Labor — remove remaining hardware from boat; strip all brightwork; start sanding brightwork. 7 hours
3 #40 sandpaper
1 pint No. 199 Varnish Remover
1 2" Throwaway brush

January 14

Labor — sand coamings; refasten and fair out forward sections of sheerstrake; glue down canvas under toerails; remove aft sections of covering boards; sand sheerstrake. 6½ hours
3 #40 sandpaper
1 #80 sandpaper
6 1¼" x 10 bronze screws
6 $^{7}/_{16}$" oak bungs
2 oz. copper tacks

January 15

Labor — finish sanding sheerstrake; replace bungs on sheerstrake, port side; sand transom; start stripping mast hoops; cut out and install pieces around center lift-out section of floorboards. 6 hours
1 #100 sandpaper
4 #80 sandpaper
1 piece oak
6 $^{7}/_{16}$" bungs
½ pint No. 214 bedding compound

January 16

Labor — plot and scribe waterline. Two men, total 3 hours

January 19

Labor — inlet gudgeon in transom and fasten on; strip seats, smooth and apply stain; clean and prime topsides. 5 hours
2 7" sanding discs
6 sheets sandpaper
⅓ pint wood filler stain

1 ¼"x 2 bronze bolt, n/w
1 1¾" x 14 bronze screw
⅔ pint No. 220 white

January 19

Labor — finish all sanding of brightwork; vacuum and stain brightwork. 6 hours
3 sandpaper
Masking tape
½ pint wood filler stain
¼ pint No. 216 special thinner

January 20

Labor — plot and scribe boottop; vacuum entire boat; varnish all brightwork first coat. 6 hours
1 pint No. 90 varnish
Masking tape
Turpentine

January 20

Labor — sand all spars; strip gaff and sand smooth; strip boom crutch; prime gaff. 4 hours
6 sandpaper
2 sandpaper
¼ pint No. 90 varnish

January 20

Labor — sand transom and gaff; vacuum and varnish transom, gaff, molding forward side of coaming, misc. parts. 3 hours
2 sandpaper
⅔ pint No. 90 varnish

January 22

Labor — putty topsides; sand brightwork, including seats and boom crutch; clean up stem fitting. 5 ½ hours
5 sandpaper
½ pint No. 93 trowel cement
½ pint No. 31 seam compound

January 23

Labor — sand knees for seats, gaff, tiller, cockpit floor, bulkhead; strip and sand bracket for cleats; install stem fitting; vacuum entire boat; varnish brightwork. 5 hours
5 1½" bronze screws
3 sandpaper
1 sandpaper
1 pint No. 90 varnish

January 23

Name lettered on transom in gold leaf

January 26

Labor — sand all brightwork; sand topsides; clean all surfaces and paint topsides, seat brackets, ceiling and bilge area. 6½ hours
6 sandpaper
8 sanding discs–8"
1½ pints No. 220 white
1 pint red lead

January 27

Labor — paint bilge area second coat; paint floorboards first coat; paint boottop first coat; strip rudder, smooth and stain. 5½ hours
1 pint red lead
⅓ pint No. 235 vermilion
½ pint buff (special mix)
⅓ pint wood filler stain
2 sandpaper

January 27

Labor — varnish brightwork third coat. 2 ½ hours
1 pint No. 90 varnish

January 28

Labor — paint inside of hull, ceiling, etc.; fasten down cockpit floor and putty all holes; paint topsides and boottop. 4½ hours
1½ pints No. 220 white
⅓ pint No. 235 vermilion
26 1" x 8 bronze screws
Wood dough

January 29

Labor — sand topsides final time; sand brightwork final time on boat, seats, gaff, boom crutch, etc.; vacuum all surfaces and varnish brightwork fourth coat. 7 hours
6 sanding discs – 8"
8 sandpaper
1 tack rag
1 pint No. 90 varnish

January 30

Labor — paint cockpit floor, varnish miscellaneous parts; paint topsides final coat. 3½ hours
½ pint buff (special mix)
¼ pint No. 90 varnish
1¼ pints No. 220 white

February 2

Labor — varnish all brightwork final coat (including all spars, seats, crutch, etc.) 3 hours
1 pint No. 90 varnish
¼ pint No. 333 Brushing liquid
¼ pint turpentine

February 3

Labor — paint foredeck, bridge deck, and floorboards. 2¼ hours
1 pint buff (special mix)
¼ pint turpentine

February 5

Labor — paint boottop final coat; attach hardware; prime bottom. 5 hours
16 $^{7}/_{8}$" x 8 bronze screws
6 2"x $^{10}/_{24}$ brass machine screws, n/w
2 1½" x 14 bronze screws
8 ¼" x ¾ brass machine screws, n/w
2 1"x 9 bronze screws
⅓ pint No. 235 vermilion
1½ pints No. 59 Bottomkote green

Linear Polyurethanes

—— by Doug Templin ——

"**B**ut it has got to breathe!"
"What has to breathe?"
"The wood," my long-time boatbuilder friend exclaimed. "The wood has got to breathe!"

Frustrated, I asked my antagonist how he had been convinced that wood had lungs and needed to breathe. I had been through this sort of discussion hundreds of times during my many years in the paint industry, selling linear polyurethane coatings. I had momentarily forgotten that there are, indeed, many intelligent people who are skilled, knowledgeable, and curious but who, nonetheless, simply cannot imagine applying "plastic" to wood. The common denominator in their collective objections seems to be that plastic coatings impede the wood's need to take in and release moisture. My friend James was a staunch supporter of this theory, and it was clear, before the conversation deteriorated further, that I needed to spend more time making my point to the contrary.

James had just completed a beautiful new boat and had asked for my advice on finishing it, having long appreciated the glossy urethane finish on my 36-foot wooden Angleman Sea Witch ketch, *Sea Mist*. He, like many of the other skeptics I had run into, would think nothing of applying 8 to 10 coats of varnish on his brightwork, or coat after coat of enamel primer and topcoat to achieve a scintillating finish. He would even be more relaxed with the application of epoxy coatings, both inboard and outboard, for protection. All of these coatings isolate the wood from the environment to the degree that the coating films are very impermeable to the transmission of water vapor and/or actual moisture. Yet James and many other builders still differentiate these applications from the newer urethane systems as far as moisture exchange is concerned.

Nicely varnished trim on a wooden boat prevents that wood, for all practical purposes, from having any contact with water vapor or moisture. That is why such trim can maintain its beautiful looks for season after season, as long as the varnish film is maintained. We all know what happens, however, when the film wears too thin or a break occurs — at a loose scarf joint, for example. The water gains entry through end-grain, and very soon the wood becomes moist and discolored. This oft-seen occurrence should quickly illustrate how well even a varnish film obstructs moisture transmission when it is intact.

A urethane film over wood, applied over a substantial buildup of epoxy primer, does the same thing. It helps isolate the wood from its environment, preventing water vapor and moisture from contacting the wood. These new polymers do an even better job of isolation than that performed by traditional finishes, owing to their very dense, chemically cross-linked structure and the very substantial adhesive forces between coats. Compared to enamels and enamel primers, urethane has fewer and smaller spaces between pigment particles, fillers, and resin molecules, in turn offering greater obstruction to the movement of water molecules.

As James could see, my wooden boat looks beautiful with her urethane system; I've done two applications over the course of 10 years. The first was still looking gorgeous and glossy after five years and could have gone longer, but because I'm in the business and *Sea Mist* is a showpiece, I treated her to a second application.

Sea Mist met the criteria for a urethane system — dry wood, tight joints, and no flexing — and her urethane system was properly applied and has been carefully maintained. Though the initial cost was higher than it would be for a traditional yacht enamel finish, the urethane has lasted far, far longer and has always kept its stunning gloss and color. Clear linear polyurethane can armor-guard varnish on a boat's exterior, enhancing the effect of varnish and greatly prolonging its life, and it can be put to good use below decks, too.

What's a Urethane?

Urethane chemistry, with us for awhile now, still represents state-of-the-art technology, since little has come down the pike in the interim to improve much on the more advanced systems.

When first conceived, the early two-component urethanes were soon found to be durable, chemical and abrasion resistant, color retentive, and long lasting. The coatings were quickly adopted by the aviation market, where corrosion protection was critical, aesthetics were important, and the cost of recoating was high. They proved successful in that market and quickly branched out to the marine field for the same reasons. The automotive, truck, and industrial markets soon followed suit, accepting the higher cost of urethane coatings because of their long life expectancy and durability. Today, we see an endless array of industrial applications.

The chemistry involved in urethane curing is relatively simple. It consists of a reaction between two materials: one we call an isocyanate; the other a polyol. The isocyanate is composed of chemical groups containing a nitrogen, a carbon, and an oxygen atom, unusually bonded to be very chemically reactive. The isocyanate chemistry was developed in Germany by the Bayer Company (the aspirin folks), who subsequently licensed Monsanto in the United States to produce the product to their formulation, later purchasing their interests and creat-

ing a domestic company, Mobay Chemical, which still produces the purest and highest-technology isocyanates available.

A great deal of improvement has occurred over the years, making isocyanates less volatile and much safer to use, with better performance properties. Though the word isocyanate has a nasty twang, it has no relationship to cyanide, the common poison. It is, however, a respiratory irritant. (The solvents used with urethanes, however, are toxic.)

The polyol component of a urethane is usually a high-molecular-weight alcohol containing pigments, flow agents, fillers, and other miscellaneous ingredients, commonly called the color base. The polyol is loaded with reactive hydroxyl (OH) groups, the same hydroxyl that is found in the water molecule (H OH). They are, however, most reactive in the types of polyols used for urethane chemistry, and their greater availability increases the number of reactions that can take place with the isocyanate component, forming a denser cross-link meshwork when the components are mixed.

There are as many polyols as there are coating companies, each having been designed to serve a specific purpose or a fairly narrow marketplace. Some are designed for economy, some for resistance to temperature or chemicals; others are designed for heavy film thickness or corrosion protection; and the ones we use in the marine field are built for high initial gloss and long-term gloss retention.

Marine Urethanes

Let's take a closer look at the urethanes that are designed for marine applications. Some of the differences among them come from the two types of polyols that are used: those containing acrylic resin, and those with a polyester "backbone." It is the resin that provides the structural backbone and helps characterize what the ultimate film will or will not do. The acrylic systems are generally referred to as modified urethanes, while the polyester systems are usually regarded as "pure."

Acrylic-resin-based systems are generally designed for quick drying, a fairly hard surface, and the ability to be buffed. They are more vulnerable to heat and chemicals, but they dominate the auto and transportation industries, where the buffable feature is so important. The acrylic systems are usually not as elastic or abrasion resistant as their polyester counterparts.

Dupont's Imron dominates the acrylic-modified systems available to the transportation industry, and they are certainly the leading such system in the marine field. But in high-corrosion environments and in the southern latitudes, Imron does not seem to demonstrate as much gloss and color retention as the high-quality polyester systems do. Because there are polyester-modified systems with better elasticity, I think Imron is better suited to metal or fiberglass boats than it is to wooden boats. Its use is also limited by the fact that it is not satisfactorily brushable.

The polyester systems are found more frequently in the jet aircraft industry, where high solvent resistance and elasticity are mandatory. The dominant polyester coatings on the market are manufactured by the Sterling Lacquer and Chemical Manufacturing Company (the Sterling System); U.S. Paint (Awlgrip); International Paint Company (Interthane); and Koppers Company (Z-Spar). These systems, all polyester "backboned," are quite different from one another, even though the ultimate performance properties can be considered rather similar. Each has a brushing system that has received fairly wide attention in recent years.

The Right Conditions

Stories about coating systems seem to run the gamut — we've all heard and seen success stories and disasters, all involving the same coating system! Naturally enough, everyone would like to end up with a successful boat finish, and there are some very important preliminary considerations that will help the job turn out well.

Dry Wood—Urethane coatings are only appropriate for wood that is uniformly dry and has reached equilibrium with the environment. There should be no manifestations of excess moisture, such as blistering or bubbling paint. If enamel paint only lasts one season on a boat, wet wood could be the culprit. You won't have success with a urethane finish over such wet wood, either.

Any healthy, properly dried, dimensionally stable wood is an appropriate candidate for polyurethane, although we have the most success with hardwoods. Problems can be experienced with woods such as "pissin' pine," because it continually bleeds sap from its many knots.

No Flexing—If your boat has a hull or deckhouse where there is a good deal of shear movement between planks, you shouldn't use urethanes on those areas. The older the boat, the looser it is likely to be and the more plank movement is to be expected along its seams. This can happen from the stresses imposed by driving in a seaway, or it can simply be caused by moving the boat from very hot to very cold climates, very wet to very dry environments, and vice versa.

Any hull whose seams have worked in the past is sure to do the same whether a urethane or an oil-based coating has been applied, shortening the life expectancy of the finish. When cracks or breaks develop in the coating, the finish begins to lose its "integrity," water gets under the coating, and it is no longer doing its job.

If you want to get maximum life out of a urethane system, you should only apply it to a wooden boat that does not flex — a well-built plank-on-frame boat in top condition, a strip-planked boat with glued seams, a plywood boat, a cold-molded boat, or one that has been sheathed with fiberglass.

Grooved seams, left exposed and sealed with a flexible caulking, offer the best accommodation for the expected occasional shear movement on even the tightest of hulls. Not all boat owners will find grooved seams aesthetically pleasing, however, and once the grooves are cut on the plank edges, they're there for good. But these V-grooves mask incipient tiny seam cracks through the coating, being far less visible than they would be on a hull with flush seams.

Polyseamseal, a single-component, water-soluble latex caulk, is an ideal material to finish off grooved seams. A light bead of this quick-drying caulk is applied along each groove, and a wet fingertip is used to make a smooth, concave bead below flush. The excess is wiped off the already-sanded planks with a damp cloth, leaving a very thin meniscus to cover the seams. Don't sand the seam afterwards; this will tear the bead.

Polyseamseal is also ideal for running small beads along bulkheads and bulwarks, beneath caprails, along trim moldings, or anywhere there is a possibility of joint movement. Creating a small radius in such areas the night before the urethane topcoat is applied allows for the greatest possible flexibility of the film.

Tight Joints—A wooden boat should be closely monitored to be sure all butt joints, scarfs, seams, and cracks are sealed tightly to prevent the entry of water into structural members, where it can work its way along interspaces and within the wood grain. Nothing destroys a finish faster than creeping water, and it's not uncommon for this to be overlooked by the naive wooden boat owner — who will eventually discover troublesome and unsightly blistering and bubbling of the coating film in areas where the moisture comes to the surface. A polymer film is no more resistant to this than an oil-based enamel; in fact, it may be more vulnerable, because entrapped moisture working its way to the surface will not pass through the more impermeable polymer film as readily as it would through a less dense enamel coating. Such moisture tends, therefore, to push the film off the surface, forming a blister.

Safety Considerations

Urethane and epoxy coatings generally have more toxic ingredients in them than traditional enamels do, but you should beware of the enamels, too, since, as the manufacturers make them more sophisticated, they contain primers and thinners with solvents that are every bit as toxic to breathe or get on the skin as those commonly found in urethane systems. Epoxies, as we all know, have many ingredients that can cause dermatological sensitivity and other reactions. They should be kept off the skin, and good respiratory protection should be used — fresh activated-charcoal filters on a tight-fitting mask are a minimum.

The isocyanate component in a urethane system is aerosolized during spray application and can find its way quickly into your lungs. Its progress is slower during brush application, because its high molecular weight keeps the molecules from evaporating so readily. But whether you're brushing or spraying, you will be exposed to the strong, toxic solvents in the system, which evaporate rapidly and head for the lungs. You must protect yourself.

If you're working outside in the fresh air, fresh activated-charcoal filters on a tight-fitting respirator mask will give you protection at a minimum. If you wear a beard, you should know that it's very unlikely that you'll be able to get an airtight fit, and therefore you will not get adequate protection from this kind of respirator mask. If you're working in closed quarters, if you have a beard, or if you want more reliable protection, you should use a positive-pressure fresh-air supply respirator. The respirator and gloves should always be worn when you're mixing, applying, or cleaning up these chemical products. If you can taste or smell the products at any time, your exposure is dangerous and should be corrected. Be sure you read the Material Safety Data Sheets (available from your supplier) for any chemical product you use; don't just read the back of the can!

Why Sterling?

My business, DETCO Marine, manufactures, markets, and distributes adhesives, sealants, and coatings, so I've had experience with a wide variety of products. I've also had time to develop a personal bias, to which I freely admit. The application instructions that follow are geared toward the Sterling Company's products, one of the coating systems which my company handles and with which I've had a great deal of experience. I happen to like the Sterling urethane system, and although I know a case can be argued for the other good urethane systems on the market, I'm going to limit my practical advice to this one system.

I've had experience with both spray and brush applications; in fact, I use both on my boat. I don't recommend a spray application to anyone who hasn't already developed some expertise with spray-painting techniques. But I've found the Sterling brushing system to be unusually user-friendly, and generally the results for anyone experienced in brushing enamel are better than the applicator expected.

The urethane system is a thin, tough, very glossy coating — either colored or clear — that will only look its best if it is applied over a perfectly smooth surface. Even the most minute scratches and hairline scratches will show through this film. So surface preparation is every bit as critical as proper application, and the steps for a colored topcoat are different from those for a clear finish.

For a Colored Application

If a boat's enamel paint is intact and in good condition, it can work very well as an undercoat for the Sterling urethane system and need only be sanded with 180-grit paper, glazed, and primed with U-1000 primer before topcoat application. You should be very discriminating about the existing paint job, however. If the enamel paint is not in good condition, you will have much better results with "wooding" the boat and starting from there.

There are two widely accepted methods of surface preparation, both involving epoxies over bare wood. The first option is to use, for a sheathing, grain-filling function, any good-quality, moisture-resistant unfilled epoxy resin, such as Chem-Tech, Cold Cure, DETCO, System 3, Travaco, or WEST System (in alphabetical order). Two or three coats may be applied with a roller, rough sanded, and cleansed according to the manufacturer's recommendations, to serve as a base for subsequently applied primers.

As an alternative, a product like Sterling U-2555 High Build epoxy primer can be applied directly over the bare wood, in several applications, by brush, roller, or spray (if you have the equipment and expertise), until sufficient coating thickness has been achieved so that the low spots can be brought up to the highs in the sanding process. This primer is mixed 1:1 with the U-2566 catalyst and should be allowed to stand or pre-react after mixing for up to one hour before application. The high-build epoxies are very tough and difficult to sand, but they help strengthen the wood and reduce its vulnerability to dings and scratches later. Do not be duped into using a high-build primer that's easy to sand, because it won't have enough impact resistance. Remember, easy sanding means easy dents; hard sanding gives you the best resilience.

If rolled, the high-build epoxy primer goes on with a noticeable stipple that is difficult to sand flush. Going around the hull several times with spray here is a great timesaver, because the primer levels itself, building the coats more quickly.

Once an effective barrier coating has been applied to the wood — and it is best done with epoxies — some fairing might be in order. If so, a putty can be made up using epoxy resin, phenolic microballoons, and a dash of silica (CAB-O-SIL or equal), and applied with a squeegee. A factory-made low-density fairing compound, such as Sterling U-2706, may also be used.

When the faired surfaces have been board-sanded, smoothed, and all major low spots filled, the broken surface must be loaded with High-Build primer again so that the open cells of the hollow spheres exposed during the sanding process can be filled above flush. After brush, roller, or spray application, and drying, the surface is sanded to the 100- to 150-grit stage.

Epoxy primers contain solvents that assist their flow and, as the system cures, evaporate from the drying film. As the solvents leave the surface, the film shrinks, and will continue to do so until it is completely free of solvents. Do not be too quick therefore, particularly in cold weather, to sand a heavily built-up primer surface, particularly if numerous coats have been applied, before each one has had a chance to thoroughly release the solvent.

Finely filled epoxy putty, such as Interlux Red Hand, may be used to glaze out the remaining wood pores and nominal scratches, and the surface is then taken to a 150- to 180-grit profile.

Lacquer glazes are often used instead of epoxy putty for the very finest in defect filling. They aren't recommended by the coating companies, but they work reasonably well — although they should always be allowed to dry overnight to prevent shrinkage and, ideally, should be spot-primed.

I don't recommend using a polyester putty, such as Bondo, for glazing on a wooden boat. Polyester resin is a water-attractive material, and these putties are very porous with substantial solvent in their makeup; they tend to shrink or swell later with ambient moisture changes.

You're not ready yet. Now it's time for a finish-sanding surfacer. I like using the Sterling U-1000 primer for this, combining it 2:1 with the U-1000C catalyst, thinned appropriately for brush, roller, or spray application. A quick-drying urethane, it is quite elastic, demonstrates excellent adhesion on all substrates, and has beautiful sanding qualities. It should be applied in a smooth film, appropriate for finish sanding to 220-grit.

After finish sanding, a close survey of the film with one's fingertips should reveal no palpable defects — a perfect surface for a perfect finish.

Now you're ready! The color base is mixed 2:1 with the U-2964 brushing catalyst, and, generally, small amounts of the U-2900 accelerator are used to speed drying of the film so that it behaves much like a good enamel. Accelerator also helps prevent blushing of the gloss, something that can occur in exterior applications if moisture falls on the surface before it is sufficiently cured.

After mixing, allow a pre-reaction or induction period of 30 to 45 minutes to provide time for the early formation of polymer structures and to help the film behave more predictably when spread thin.

After this induction period, brushing thinner (U-2965 or variants, depending upon climate conditions) is added at a rate of about 25 percent of the catalyzed mixture. It is important to reduce the paint's viscosity, or it is guaranteed not to flow as desired. Too much thinning, however, will prevent proper coating thickness from developing and will reduce long-term gloss retention.

Use a good-quality brush — not necessarily the most expensive, but a bristle/oxhair combination brush, such as the Corona "Europa," Redtree, Linzer, or even the more expensive Hamiltons, if you wish. Have several on hand, because you'll probably go through quite a few.

Brushes must be thoroughly cleaned immediately after use, then rinsed, wire brushed or combed to remove all traces of cured material, and squeegeed again several times with clean thinner. Usually a brush will not be clean enough to use for topcoat application after two days' use because of cured material in the heel of the brush; at that point relegate it to primer application.

On large surfaces, such as powerboat cabin sides and hulls, we've found that low-nap foam roller sleeves, phenolic-coated to prevent solvent intrusion, are ideal for applying the urethane. The painter or co-applicator creates the initial wet line with the roller by going from top edge to bottom edge in, say, a section about 1 foot to 1 ½ feet wide, wetting the roller moderately and pushing the material into a thin film. The brusher follows immediately behind, tipping the film two or three times in vertical and horizontal directions. Some applicators swear by a final vertical tipping, since fewer sags and runs are thus produced; others follow the more traditional method of sweeping the brush with the sheer on the last pass. I've found that sags are more easily prevented by tipping the last time in a vertical pattern. Thinner may be added as the job progresses, any time the coating feels sluggish, just as one would do with a brushing enamel.

If the system is to be sprayed, the color base is catalyzed 1:1 with the U-1001C spray catalyst, accelerated as necessary, and allowed to pre-react. The mixture is then thinned about 30 percent with the thinner selected for the day's climate conditions.

The first pass over the work for the tack coat should show a nice gloss and should not be "fogged." Just enough coating should be applied so that the film stretches into a nice, reflective surface. (Many other products, when applied this heavily on the first pass, will quickly sag.)

The first pass is allowed to become touch-dry (one-half hour to one hour), and then a wet coat is applied, once again with enough material so that the surface stretches into a nice gloss within a few minutes after application. These two spray passes generally create sufficient coating thickness.

Accent stripes may be applied as soon as the film is hard enough to mask (wait at least overnight, or longer in cooler temperatures). If the film has dried more than 48 hours, areas to be coated should be lightly sanded first.

Cleanup is easy with MEK solvent; remember to wear your gloves and a respirator.

For a Clear Application

We've had lots of experience applying clear linear polyurethane under all sorts of conditions, and my instructions include some important basics, learned from years of experimentation and lots of failures.

Just as with a colored topcoat, we have the same concerns about creating an intact film over dry, non-flexing surfaces. But with a clear coating, we also have to consider the effects of the sun on wood. It is best to apply urethane over a well-built-up coating of varnish. The amber-colored particles and ultraviolet barriers in varnish protect the wood from degradation. By itself, varnish is a relatively soft, scratchable surface that goes dull quite quickly from exposure to sunshine. But the clear urethane is hard, brilliantly glossy, and very scratch resistant. It will protect the varnish and produce an excellent combination of benefits. We have seen this package outlast varnish by a factor of four to five — or more — time and time again, in Florida, Southern California, and in the tropics.

After the varnish has been built to sufficient coating thickness to produce a defect-free surface —

usually eight coats or so — allow the last coat to dry hard, sand to 220 grit, and then apply two to three coats of clear Sterling urethane, preferably one coat a day over successive days. Sand between coats only enough to remove dust spots and minor surface defects; the film is vulnerable to chemical intrusion for at least 48 hours after application, making it unnecessary to do a thorough sanding as long as reapplication occurs within that period. But a very thorough sanding to remove all gloss will be necessary if the film dries for more than two days.

We've had excellent luck applying clear Sterling in this fashion over teak, mahogany, oak, spruce, pine, cedar, rosewood, padouk, ironbark, ash, and many other woods. Below decks, in the absence of ultraviolet exposure, clear Sterling can be applied directly over bare wood and is a great way to "armor-plate" floorboards, lockers, galley surfaces, and any other areas that take a lot of wear and tear, for it is nearly indestructible.

Because there's nothing easier to keep clean than a high-gloss urethane surface, we've tried it — with great success — in the bilges, on the engine, and on brass for an easy-to-clean shiny surface. It has also been found to be a good protective coating over epoxy resin in cold-molded construction, since it reduces sun-induced oxidation and chalking.

Maintenance and Repair

Maintenance of a linear polyurethane coating is easy — simply wash with soap and water from time to time. Stubborn grease, oil, and paint transfers on your topsides from other boats, buoys, and docks can be easily removed with strong solvents without injuring the Sterling film.

Keep a sharp eye out for any cracks or breaches in the coated surface where water could gain access, and repair them immediately. Remember, you don't want moisture to creep under the film.

After a painstaking paint job, the inevitable usually happens — an errant buoy, a side tie by a careless skipper, a wild billfish, or even a blister will cause that "Ferrari fender" look to move from the limelight.

A small scratch or chip can easily be touched up by mixing a small quantity of the color base and catalyst. Allow it to sit after mixing for an hour, so that it thickens up considerably. Then use a small brush to fill the spot. If necessary, repeat the process several times to build the depression up to flush.

Larger scratches can be repaired professionally with spray techniques so that they are hardly visible. After repairs to the area have been made, preferably with epoxy putty, and the area has been masked, a very light spray film of primer can be applied, finish sanded, and the area then topcoated by spray. By not moving the wet line all the way to the masking paper, an unsightly masking line is eliminated. After a few days' drying, the dry spray at the edge of the repaired area can be lightly sanded with 1500 grit, wet or dry, then buffed with a very fine rubbing compound and, lastly, buffed with plexiglass polish for an almost perfect repair.

The boat owner himself can do a spot repair with brush techniques; the result will be as good as the same kind of repair to an enamel paint job, but not as invisible as the professional method just described. I've had the best results by dry-brushing at the perimeter of the repair to bring the newly applied coating as close to flush as possible. If done correctly, such patches are difficult to see from a few feet back.

Now the Bad News, or Is It Good?

Most linear polyurethane coatings cost from around $100 to $120 per catalyzed gallon (1987 prices), while the primers, depending upon quality and type, can cost from $50 to $100 per catalyzed gallon. This boils down to a cost per square foot of around 40 cents for brushing and 60 to 70 cents for spray (the difference is because of overspray — paint that does not land on the surface). Enamels, by contrast, can be purchased at about half that cost if one uses a medium-grade marine enamel, or nearly as much with a high-quality import, such as Epifanes, which sells for just over $100 a gallon.

Given a proper boat, with proper preparation, application, and post-application monitoring, a polyurethane application is certainly capable of enduring three- to five-years' service. Through this period, the coating will be easier to clean and more scratch and abrasion resistant than an enamel coating. It will shed soils, oils, and fuel stains far better, and the colors will stay brighter and more vibrant. The tradeoff for twice the price at the time of application, then, turns into a payoff after the second year, just on the cost of materials alone.

We all know how labor-intensive any haulout and coating project can be, so after the second year, one really saves money on the urethane system. It is little extra work to brush or spray a urethane primer over a solid enamel substrate and then apply the topcoat, than it would be for an enamel system. Starting from scratch, from bare wood, is unquestionably more expensive, but since the boat should have to be painted only once or twice over a 10-year period, it is easy to visualize the savings. Don't be shocked, therefore, by the initial expense of materials without considering the service they are capable of providing.

The combination of wood and urethanes can be a winning one, The result can be absolutely stunning and should far outlast a traditional yacht enamel finish. Now you've heard my argument for putting "plastic" on wood.

Water-Based Clear Coatings

—— by George Fatula ——

How would you like to be able to "varnish" the hatch cover, tiller, and cockpit seats you brought home for the winter — right in your warm cellar — and do it without smelling any solvent fumes or making a mess, clean up with water, and finish the job (eight coats) in one weekend?

All you need is a source for an aliphatic aqueous colloidal dispersion of a urethane polymer engineered to air-dry and be ultraviolet-light (UV) resistant. You can apply it with a foam brush, just as it comes from the can, and a single coat will be dry in an hour or so. You should have no problem applying four to six coats in a single day, without sanding. The same brush can be used for the entire job by storing it in water between coats. Just rinse and blot it dry prior to each use. Spills clean up with water, and there is little or no smell.

A high-gloss clear finish with exceptional hardness, flexibility, and abrasion resistance will be the result of your efforts. You can walk on the finish the day it is applied if the drying conditions are right. If that sounds simpler than working with your present varnish, I encourage you to give one of these new coatings a try.

Testing Three Water-Based Varnishes

With the help of Ninni Lemus, one of my students at Washington County (Maine) Technical College's Marine and Industrial Coatings class, I tried three of the new water-based "varnishes" on the market today: Hydrocote Polyshield, Seaman's Choice Wood Coating, and Landmark's Waterborne Industrial Acrylic Lacquer. We used new teak surfaces as test panels and applied the products right out of the container with foam brushes, following the manufacturers' recommendations. During application, the temperature ranged between 60 and 70 degrees, and the relative humidity between 30 and 50 percent. As the test proceeded, we made subjective evaluations on the ease of application, flow-out, and gloss.

Surface preparation was fairly standard for all three coatings. They are sensitive to surface contamination and less forgiving than conventional varnish if oil or grease is present. Before working with these products, you should pay particular attention to cleaning the surface so that it is free of all residues.

Hydrocote's Polyshield is a water-based polyure-thane coating. It is recommended for both interior and exterior applications and, like the other products we tested, is UV-stabilized. Hydrocote offers both gloss and satin formulations of Polyshield, and there are several additives available that can be used to increase hardness, custom tint, and perform a variety of "manipulations" that are usually of interest only to professional finishers. Hydrocote's well-prepared catalog offers clear explanations for all their products.

As you would suspect from the name, Hydrocote Polyshield is water soluble. It looks "watery" in the can and has a gray-white opaque color that disappears upon drying. It is dry to touch in 30 to 50 minutes when applied by brush and when drying conditions are favorable. It is dry to sand in an hour or two and can be re-coated in three hours. Polyshield has a very mild odor.

The results of our tests with Polyshield were encouraging. Its application differs from that of spar varnish; it doesn't have the same "body" and isn't as difficult to spread. It goes on thinner per coat but can be recoated in less than half the time of spar varnish. Because Polyshield is fast drying, it has a tendency to trap bubbles. Extreme care is necessary when brushing it out, especially at the edges; the flow-out you are used to getting from your favorite varnish just doesn't happen with Polyshield. The finish is clear. It is tough and sands harder than regular spar varnish. If you routinely use a heat gun for varnish removal, you will find that a properly applied coat of one of these water-based polyurethanes will be much more difficult to remove.

Seaman's Choice is also a high-quality water-based urethane finish. This product is aimed specifically at the marine market and already has an impressive performance record in the boating arena. Application characteristics are very similar to Polyshield's. As we began our tests, we had some flow-out problems with this product, and our first applications were too heavy. A surface-tension problem caused the coating to gather in pools, leaving some voids. A call to the company resulted in receiving samples of their new formulation, which flowed out beautifully.

Careful surface preparation is required for optimum results with Seaman's Choice. It dries very fast, so on large surfaces you need to work quickly to keep your "wet edge." Adding small amounts of water to the coating extends the flow-out period nicely. The manufacturer encouraged us to go ahead and apply two or three coats without sanding between coats, and this worked well. I prefer a light sanding or scrubbing with a Scotchbrite pad after each coat, and under normal conditions this can be done within an hour of application. These are thinner coats than a phenolic varnish gives with each application, but the re-coat times allowed us to complete an eight-coat finish in one day. Seaman's Choice provides a tough finish and will stand up to sanding between coats.

The Singh-Ray Corporation, manufacturers of Seaman's Choice, continues to refine this product. Their latest formulation is reported to flow out even better than the one we tested. It's an attractive finish, but I'm looking forward to trying samples of their amber-colored formulation. If it looks anything like my "old" phenolic varnish, I'll use it on my own boat.

Landmark's Waterborne Industrial Acrylic Lacquer did not perform as well as the other two products we tested. In all fairness to Landmark, their product isn't intended to be a high-performance yacht varnish. It is marketed as an industrial finish, with protection being its primary characteristic, but the company is also interested in exploring the marine market. We had some flow-out problems with the coating and found that it tended to produce a rougher surface than the others. There was also a slight purple tint on our panels after 10 coats of the finish.

Advantages and Disadvantages

The availability of these water-based finishes is due,

in part, to the tightening regulations on the percentage of volatile organic compounds (VOCs) allowed in paint. The solvents used in traditional paints and varnishes require special precautions for their use and disposal. When working with traditional finishes in a confined space, organic vapor respiratory protection should be used, with respirators fit-tested to ensure proper protection. Even when ventilation keeps the vapor levels below permissible exposure limits, solvent odor is a problem. Because the percentage of VOCs is decreased in water-based coatings, many of the usual hazards are reduced. But some of these new compounds may pose greater risks than our old solvent-based friends because they seem so benign. Skin exposure and eye contact should be avoided, as with all finishes, and there are situations when proper respiratory protection is needed, even with water-based coatings.

The environmental impact of the products we have grown to depend on over the years is being looked at much more closely now. What do you do with the dirty solvents you generate as you get the boat ready each year? Is it a coincidence that most boat-storage areas support very little vegetation? And what about the ozone layer?

Our expectations for finishes may have to change as the regulatory process tightens controls on the manufacturers of coatings and application equipment. Some coatings are already unavailable (remember Micron 33?), others are being replaced with new formulations. Paint companies are trying to meet regulations and please us at the same time — and we are not easily pleased. Perhaps we should begin to adjust our expectations and accept new, not necessarily lower, standards of performance or different standards of appearance from the coatings we now use.

I like the warm look of eight coats of quality phenolic varnish on the oak coaming of my catboat. On a good day in Perry, Maine (45 degrees north latitude) in late May, I might even be able to apply two coats. The next day, if drying conditions are favorable, I can carefully sand with 220-grit paper and repeat the process. A complete varnish job in this part of the world might take an entire week if the weather cooperates, longer if it doesn't, but it is a labor of love and I appreciate the finish every day of the season.

A colorless high-tech coating is something I am not used to yet, but it could prove to be an acceptable alternative. The simplicity of application and the speed with which it can be accomplished are very attractive. However, I don't really want to give up the golden color I have grown accustomed to. But the Singh-Ray Corporation assures me that virtually any tint can be engineered into their Seaman's Choice coating.

There are many happy boat owners who have already

discovered these water-based finishes. I've seen testimonials indicating no signs of finish deterioration after as many as 18 months' exposure in the Florida sun. No loss of gloss, no lifting, no cracking, no dead varnish — it is difficult to believe, but my own preliminary tests have been positive, too. Our (subjective) shop tests judged these finishes to be harder, more abrasion resistant, and easier to work with than solvent-based varnishes. The lab test data supplied by the manufacturers indicated outstanding physical properties.

Of particular importance to me is the tolerance these finishes have for humidity during application. If there's anything you have to be particularly careful of, it is surface contamination with oil. But these finishes are compatible with cured solvent-based coatings and can be applied directly over them after sanding and cleaning the surface properly.

One of the things I am most interested in about new coatings is their safety. I am anxious to use safer products. Carcinogenic chemicals should become a concern of the past, especially for nonindustrial use. I am not alone in feeling this way, and the marketing departments of paint companies are paying attention to that. These water-based coatings can be accurately described as nontoxic. With their decreased dependence on volatile organic compounds, they certainly have a lower potential impact on the environment, and flammability concerns are drastically reduced. They are not, however, without hazards. All painters should obtain a copy of the applicable Material Safety Data Sheet whenever they purchase a new product. Read the MSDS carefully and follow the precautions indicated.

These new water-based coatings address some important environmental and safety concerns. They also seem to offer the performance required for the marine environment. Try one of these products on a small varnish project, and see if these coatings of the future are attractive enough to keep your brightwork addiction satisfied.

For more information:
Hydrocote Finishing Products
77 Milltown Rd.
East Brunswick, NJ 08816
908-257-4344

Landmark Coatings, Inc.
1306 Ballentine Blvd.
Norfolk, VA 23504

Seaman's Choice, Inc.
153 Progress Circle
Venice, FL 34292
800-969-3006

Antifouling Paints

―――――― by Aimé Ontario Fraser ――――――

Without antifouling paint, a wooden boat is the ideal environment for all kinds of tiny aquatic creatures to grow on and in. It's amazing, when you stop to think about it, that a couple of coats of paint could so effectively arrest the fecundity of the sea. We need such potent poison to keep our boats clean and healthy, though, that we tend to forget that using poison is like using a two-edged sword. The leading edge protects, but if we brandish the sword excessively, the back edge can hurt us in ways we never anticipated.

Antifouling paint has been keeping boats and ships from becoming part of the local ecosystem for well over a century with no apparent ill effects on the environment. It wasn't until large numbers of pleasure craft coated with very highly efficient and highly toxic paints crowded into relatively shallow harbors that damage was observed.

More than a decade ago, fishermen and marine biologists began to see some disturbing abnormalities in a variety of sea life — most notably oysters, sea snails, salmon, shrimp, and some algaes. Studies found high levels of tributyltin — the active ingredient in the most toxic and highly touted antifouling paints used by recreational boaters — in the affected organisms and the surrounding water.

Experiments both in the U.S. and abroad soon found that as little as 0.9 part of tributyltin (TBT) in one billion parts seawater was acutely toxic to oyster larvae, and that chronic levels as low as 0.02 part per billion retarded growth, caused deformed shells, and resulted in reproductive aberrations.

Water samples taken from around the U.S. in the mid-1980s showed TBT levels well in excess of these amounts in almost every major port, with the highest readings, 1.0 part per billion, coming from San Diego Harbor and Chesapeake Bay. It was noted that the areas of highest concentration of TBT were the harbors with the greatest density of boats, and that the concentrations of TBT were higher in the upper 6 feet of water. The highest TBT levels were found in the spring, when many freshly painted boats were launched. These findings led the EPA to consider restricting the use of TBT. (California and a couple of other states had moved faster and already done so.)

Before imposing any restrictions, the EPA took a careful look at how TBT antifouling paint was used. They found that some 1,000,000 pounds of TBT went into antifouling paint each year, and that about 40 percent of that amount was used on pleasure craft. Of those boats painted with TBT, 79 percent were hauled and recoated more often than the paint required, thereby not making full use of the paint's main advantage — its ability to last for long intervals without hauling and repainting. It seemed that pleasure boaters would likely save money if TBT were restricted, since they would no longer be paying extra for benefits they did not use. Owners of larger pleasure craft, as well as commercial and military users, tended to take full advantage of TBT by hauling and recoating only when the paint was no longer effective.

In the late 1980s, the EPA concluded that since the majority of TBT pollution was in shallow waters frequented largely by pleasure craft, and since the majority of those pleasure craft would get all the protection they required from less exotic paints, restricting TBT paints would not cause a great deal of hardship for their owners. As a result, the use of TBT paints on boats under 82 feet in length is now restricted to aluminum boats (there is as yet no galvanically appropriate alternative). The ruling also classifies TBT as a pesticide, meaning that except for small spray cans labeled for use on aluminum outdrives and such, TBT paints can only be handled and applied by a trained painter certified by the EPA. Furthermore, the ruling specified a lower TBT release rate for the TBT paints that are used.

The EPA restrictions produced a great deal of bad press. Boat owners reacted with shock and confusion. Perhaps they felt guilty when they realized that their recreation had serious environmental consequences, but many jumped to erroneous conclusions about the intent and extent of the regulations and assumed that the selection of effective bottom paints had become seriously limited. They figured that the only good paint had been banned, and that the remaining ones were hopelessly inferior.

Nothing could be further from the truth. While it's true that the EPA keeps tabs on all formulations of antifouling paint by requiring that each product be registered, no paint other than TBT was affected by the ruling. There are still dozens of copper-based antifouling paints to choose from, and they are available in a wide variety of hardnesses, toxicity, and prices.

Copper-based antifouling paints are not quite as effective as those containing TBT, but the trailing edge of the copper sword is dull by comparison to TBT. To have an effect on what the EPA calls non-target marine life, concentrations of copper must be 100 times higher than those of TBT, and when damage does occur, it is not as severe. As paint companies tweak the chemistry of their copper paints, new formulations are being developed to rival TBT in protection and longevity

The Basic Types of Copper Paint

There are five basic formulations (and a sixth currently available from only one company) of copper antifouling paint. They are based on vinyl, epoxies (or modified epoxies), copolymers, rosins, and resin-rosin combinations. The basic chemistry of the paint doesn't play a large role in how effectively it prevents fouling, but it is very important to the coating's hardness and longevity.

Vinyls

The hardest formulations have a tough, vinyl base. Having moderate protection against fouling, they offer a super-hard, smooth finish. Vinyl-based paint is ideal for racing boats, since it can be wet-sanded and burnished with copper wool to an almost polished finish.

Vinyls are conventional leaching-type antifouling paints, meaning that the biocide is mixed into the paint like the chocolate chips in cookie dough. When the boat is first launched after painting, the biocide at the surface of the paint is rapidly released into the water,

creating an unfavorable environment for the growth of fouling organisms. After a while, the biocide at the surface is depleted, but it is steadily replenished by fresh biocide bleeding up through the paint. A leaching antifoulant such as this gradually loses its effectiveness, however, since the biocide must travel farther and farther to reach the surface; eventually, the biocide can no longer make the trip. At that point, the paint ceases to prevent growth even though nowhere near all the biocide has leached out. Viewed under magnification, the surface of leaching-type paint after several months of service looks like a sponge: what began as a smooth paint film has tiny holes where the biocide has bled through.

Vinyl-based paints use very powerful solvents capable of lifting other paints when applied over them, so all the old paint has to be stripped before any vinyl goes on. Other formulations, however, can be applied over a vinyl film after a thorough sanding. Two coats of vinyl are recommended (as for all leaching paints); they will last for a year or so of continuous immersion, depending on conditions, or for an entire season for boats that are wintered ashore. After a few weeks out of the water, the antifouling loses its effectiveness and the bottom must be repainted.

Epoxies

Epoxy-based paints are tough, hard paints (some can even be burnished) that can be purchased in various levels of antifouling protection. They are very abrasion-resistant and work well for boats that are trailered or beached, and are good for any boat that goes fast. Epoxies can remain effective for more than a year when continually immersed, oftentimes longer if they are cleaned periodically. Like vinyl paints, they lose their effectiveness when out of the water, but there's a 60-day grace period before that happens.

Epoxies are compatible with other paints and can be applied over just about anything. The only paints to avoid overcoating with epoxy (or anything else, for that matter) are paints to which some slickening agent, such as graphite or Teflon, has been added, and very soft paints, where adhesion would be questionable.

Rosins

The softest antifouling paints are based on very old formulations made from rosins and oils (from trees) as opposed to the resins (from petrochemicals) in the newer paints. The least costly of antifouling paints, they don't stand up to abrasion very well, and they don't have as much biocide. Still, they are entirely suitable for slow-speed craft in cool waters. These paints also act by leaching, but since the paint is so soft, the action might be better described as sloughing. Actually, much of the paint wears away in the course of a season. This means less paint buildup, but a shorter useful life.

Resin-Rosins

Midway in hardness between resin and rosin paints are those containing some of both, often described as semi-hard. They won't stand up to frequent trailer launchings, but they can handle most of what an average displacement boat will meet. These aren't sexy high-tech paints, but they do what's needed in waters where fouling is moderate. They are probably the best all-around paints for cruising boats that spend the winter out of the water.

Copolymers

The new copolymer formulations designed to replace TBT paints protect from fouling by eroding away — or, as the paint companies prefer to say, ablating. Instead of the mixed biocide bleeding through the surface of the paint, the biocide in copolymers is built into the chemical structure of the paint. Fresh biocide is continually exposed as the motion of the water over the paint slowly wears the surface away. Whereas a leaching paint is always releasing biocide, an ablative paint only does so when the boat is moving. On the down side, this means that a boat that is not often used will not be protected by ablatives, but the up side is that when the boat is hauled, the action stops. A boat can be ashore for any length of time, and a simple scrubbing before relaunching will reactivate the antifouling protection.

Ablatives wear away at the rate of about one coat per year of continuous immersion, so three coats will keep the boat clean in moderately fouling waters for three years. If the boat is hauled each winter, it's possible to go four or five years between paint jobs, a fine thing for a wooden boat, since it means the bottom can always be well protected from the cold, drying winds of winter.

Copolymers are moderately hard, and while they cannot be burnished they can be wet-sanded to give a true racing finish. Brush on an extra coat, and go to it. These paints wear very evenly, much like a bar of soap, so once the bottom is smooth, it will remain so until the paint is gone.

Most companies recommend three or four coats of ablative paint. On wooden hulls, the first one should be thinned 10 to 15 percent and should be a color that contrasts with following coats. If the first coat is blue, for example, and the following coats are red, when traces of red start peeking through the blue, you will know it's time to repaint. Put on three full coats, and then another where the water runs with the most force — near the waterline, the leading edge of the keel, and the leading edge of the rudder.

Water-Based

The sixth type of paint is, at this writing, represented solely by Woolsey's Neptune II. It is, believe it or not, a water-based antifouling paint. The company isn't giving away too many details about this formulation, but they say it is a fairly hard paint, able to withstand trailering and beaching. It offers moderate protection, and experience suggests it will be nearly as long lived as the copolymer ablative paints. Neptune II was developed in anticipation of regulations limiting the amount of solvents in paints, which are considered to be a significant cause of smog. With only one pound of solvents per gallon, Neptune II far exceeds the nation's most stringent guideline of 3.3 pounds per gallon.

Technically, Neptune II is a leaching paint, with the biocide mixed in. It works a little like a sloughing paint, because its chemistry causes it to erode more than the usual leaching paint. As the coating erodes, the biocide trapped near the bottom of the film can readily leach to the surface. However, it acts more like an ablative paint, because the erosion takes a long time and the remaining coat is fairly hard. As a result, you get a multi-season paint that can be reactivated by scrubbing, and which can be removed by a 1,500-psi pressure wash.

Neptune II has been applied over a variety of materials and coatings; there seem to be no compatibility or adhesion problems as long as the surface has been prepared. Applying Neptune II is not particularly difficult compared to conventional paints, but it takes slightly different techniques. The paint is thicker, and that takes some getting used to. The "wet edge" is more difficult to brush out, unless you have a stiff brush or a substantial phenolic-cored roller. On the plus side, the solvent wash is nothing more than a good hose-down; then wait until the hull is just damp so the paint will flow on better.

Choosing the Appropriate Protection

Paint failure below the waterline is far more consequential than it is above, especially for wooden boats. Antifouling may be a mere convenience for owners of fiberglass and metal boats who are concerned with preventing drag, but it is essential on wooden boats to prevent marine borers from entering the keel and planking and eating them from the inside out.

The length of time during which an antifouling paint is effective is based on its formulation, but the degree of fouling it can control is based on the amount of biocide it contains. The more copper the better the paint can handle severe fouling conditions. The degree of protection is related to the formulation only in that some types of paint can accept more biocide than others.

Generally speaking, the warmer the climate, the more severe the fouling, and the more copper required to control it. However, there are other factors, such as salinity, pH, the presence of electrical currents, the amount of sediment, and pollution (both thermal and chemical). There can also be extreme local variations.

Guidelines can only be extremely basic. The right paint depends on the micro-climate at the dock or mooring, the boat's speed, how often the boat is hauled and for how long, the smoothness of finish required, and the depth of the owner's pockets. The best thing is to ask around and see if there is a consensus on what works in your home waters. Still, let's take the trouble here to classify copper antifouling paints by their degree of protection — at least roughly.

The most powerful are the epoxies with copper contents on the order of 90 percent. These include Interlux UltraKote, Pettit Unepoxy Tropic, Woolsey Neptune, and Rule Super KL. All are tough paints that will last a year or two when continually immersed. They are suitable for fast boats and/or tropical waters.

Most companies also have epoxy paints with less biocide for more moderate conditions, something like 50 to 60 percent copper. These are equally tough and long-lived, but they are more suited to southern waters as opposed to tropical waters. The super-hard vinyl paints are in this range of potency.

Ablative paints and Woolsey's water-based Neptune II fall in about this same category, although they are not suitable for high-speed boats, or for boats that spend the majority of their time at the dock. Their main advantage is that they don't need to be reapplied each year, so that a single paint job can last from two to five years.

Next in protection come the resin-rosin paints, which cannot be formulated to carry as much copper as the above paints. These are suitable for cruising boats in temperate climes and mid-range water temperatures. They will last a season. Examples are: Pettit Tropicop, Z-Spar Multitox, Interlux Bottomkote, and Gloucester Commercial.

Finally, we have the rosin bases, which the paint companies usually recommend for general use and by commercial fishermen. These are unsophisticated but effective paints, suitable for slow boats in cool waters, especially when the season is short. Examples are: Gloucester Tar and Wonson, Interlux Red Hand, and Pettit Yacht Copper.

It is true that any boat anywhere can use the top-of-the-line super-toxic tropical paint, but that would be overkill — literally. Remember the two-edged sword. There is no need to use more poison than is necessary to do the job.

Paint Base	Relative Hardness	Suitable Speed Range	Available Fouling Protection	Life Expectancy	Maintenance	Compatibility (always check with manufacturer of new coating)	Other
Vinyl (Conventional)	Very hard (burnishable)	Fast	Mid-range	One year or season	Occasional washing	Apply only to bare wood or other vinyl. Any type may be applied over it.	Offers low drag when burnished
Epoxy (Conventional)	Hard (some are burnishable)	Medium, some for fast	Severe to moderate	One year or season	Occasional washing will extend life	Over any well-sanded paint except slick paints (graphite, Teflon, etc.) or soft paints	
Resin and Rosin (Conventional)	Semi-hard	Slow to medium	Moderate	One year or season	None	Same as above	An economical choice for cruising boats hauled for the winter
Rosin (Sloughing)	Soft	Slow	Low	One short season	None	Can be applied over all paints. Should be removed before applying harder paints to enhance adhesion.	
Copolymer (Ablative)	Hard (can be wet-sanded smooth)	Medium	Upper mid-range	Two to three years in or out of water	Scrub before relaunching	Over any well-sanded paint except slick or soft paints	Boat must be used often to activate protection
Water-Based Neptune II (Conventional, but similar result as ablative)	Moderately hard	Medium	Moderate	Two-plus years in or out of water	Scrub before relaunching	As above	Can be removed w/ 1,500-psi power wash; water cleanup

Quick Steps to Spring Varnishing

—— by Anne and Maynard Bray   Drawings by Kathy Bray ——

Our claim among varnishing gurus isn't great, and, under scrutiny, *Aida*'s varnish would miss out on top honors. But given the relatively little time we spend keeping up her brightwork, she measures up quite well. For the almost three decades we've owned this wonderful Herreshoff-built yawl, no one but us, or occasionally our children, Kathy, Nat, and Sarah, has ever touched a paintbrush or varnish brush to her. Although portions of her brightwork have been stripped down to bare wood and refinished, nothing but annual sanding and varnishing has been done to the cabin sides and coamings for more than 30 years.

What we have to share is how we've managed to keep *Aida* looking presentable without a total refinishing, and how it's possible to enjoy doing the brightwork portion of our annual outfitting and be comfortable with the results.

A short season and inside storage have contributed as much as anything to the ease of maintenance, and we highly recommend this approach when possible. Beyond that, we recoat all the exterior surfaces every year, being convinced, in spite of claims to the contrary, that an old surface simply won't stand up. By streamlining the surface preparation and application of paint and varnish, the task is not unreasonable, and a new-looking boat emerges each spring.

Each year we begin by hand-sanding everything on deck, including the varnished sheerstrakes — paintwork as well as brightwork. This takes a couple of days — short ones, if there are two of us, and long ones, if just one person is doing the job. Sanding and cleanup of the paintwork comes first, so that pigmented dust doesn't get scrubbed into the brightwork as it is being sanded. Touchup of damaged surfaces, if required, comes after the varnish has been sanded, and takes only a few minutes here and there, although spread out over several days. After about four coats of touchup varnish over the bare wood areas, there comes a thorough vacuuming of everything that has been sanded. Shortly afterwards, the tacking and varnishing commences.

Although we do our practical best to avoid dust, holidays, lap marks, and runs, our children invariably point them out to us. But the overall job is still a knockout as long as you don't scrutinize it too closely. There's plenty of shine and, most importantly, the woodwork is protected from the weather. And there's always next year.

Since deck, cabin top, and cockpit sole have already been sanded, their painting takes place a day or two after the varnish has dried, so they can utilize the same pre-varnish cleanup. The boat then gets hauled out of the shed for machine sanding, filling, and painting of the topsides, boottop, and bottom — usually a two-day procedure. (You would be surprised to see how well a single coat of flattened topside paint covers.)

That's our basic fitting-out on *Aida*'s hull. Her two masts, spreaders, and boat hook are sanded and varnished annually, but because the booms are protected by the furled sails, they get varnished every second or third year,

What follows are some thoughts about routine exterior varnishing that we feel can help keep down the cost of annual maintenance. This is not intended to be the ultimate treatise on the art of varnishing, and we realize that there are other approaches that have proven equal to or better than ours. Like the short form of the income tax return, these techniques can be great timesavers as long as they apply. But they apply only if your goal matches ours, which is to keep the cash and labor outlays within manageable limits while protecting the wood with a decent-looking film of varnish. If you're after the ultimate in brightwork, and if you are willing to make a commitment year after year in quest of perfection, you'll probably want to look beyond this. Rebecca Wittman's *Brightwork: The Art of Finishing Wood* (International Marine Publishing Co., Camden, Maine) is an excellent resource on the subject.

Brushes

A single 1 ½-inch or 2-inch brush with fine, natural bristles will be perfectly satisfactory for most work. If you're dealing with very large expanses, a larger brush is better, especially in hot weather when the varnish has to be spread fast so as not to lose its "wet edge." For getting into tight places, it also helps to have a small artist's brush handy.

Badger-hair brushes are best, but simulated badger-hair brushes have worked out just fine and can be purchased for less than $10. Stay away from nylon and other coarse brushes; they leave deeply furrowed brush marks that tend to sag.

Disposable foam brushes work perfectly well on small jobs, but they don't hold enough varnish for efficiency on large ones, and they are difficult to use in tight places. A foam roller is good for quickly applying varnish to very large areas, such as topsides, if it is followed immediately by a foam or bristle brush to smooth out or "tip" the fresh varnish before it begins to set up.

Brush Care

Methods of brush care are a matter of preference, since there are several ways that work. For conve-nience, however, it's difficult to beat wet storage in raw linseed oil. You only have to remember to flush out the brush with turpentine before and after each use, and to keep the bristles fully submerged. Drop a Baggie down over the whole works if you're concerned about dust; then your varnish brush is set for long-term storage.

Dirty brushes give very disappointing results, and there seems to be no way to rid a contaminated brush of foreign particles once it has picked them up. If you have any question about your brush's cleanliness, don't use it for finish coats. Take a new brush and shift the old one over to a less critical use, such as varnish buildup or non-gloss painting. A brand-new brush may shed a few bristles while it is being broken in, so keep an eye open and pull them out before the varnish begins to set up.

Varnish

Personal preference has a good deal to do with what brand of varnish you use. More from habit than from logic, we mostly use Z-Spar 1015. We've also had good luck with McCloskey's Man-O-War varnish. You can read about which varnishes shine the most and which ones last the longest in a number of Consumer Report-type articles. There are differences between brands to be sure, and in harsh, long-season environments, selecting the best one becomes a more important issue than it does in areas where the boats are in the water for only a few months in relatively cool climates.

Although clear linear polyurethane (LP) is often used nowadays because of its durability and shine, it goes on so thinly and, when dry, is so inflexible that its use is best confined to surfaces that are very stable and have been prepared to absolute perfection. LP varnish does not have the gap-bridging properties of old-fashioned phenolic varnish. The LP finishes we've seen turn the wood unnaturally dark and lack the richness that is characteristic of a thick film of phenolic varnish.

You always get a better job with a freshly opened can of varnish, and, unless you're really slapping it on, a pint will usually suffice for a day's work. Purchase your varnish by the pint, therefore, instead of by the quart, even though there's a bit more relative expense.

Sanding

Old-fashioned flint sandpaper, which dulled within a stroke or two, went out with high-buttoned shoes. Garnet paper isn't much better. Tan aluminum-oxide production paper, such as Norton's Adalox, or white silicon-carbide Tri-M-ite paper by 3M is what we mean by "sandpaper."

Unless there's a compelling reason for doing otherwise, sand the entire boat, or at least that portion

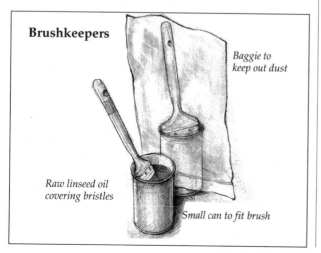

Brushkeepers

Baggie to keep out dust

Raw linseed oil covering bristles

Small can to fit brush

above the rail — including the paintwork — before you start to do any varnishing other than touchup. That way, you'll need just one major cleanup. Wash surfaces that are grimy or greasy so they will be clean before you start to sand; the paper will last much longer. A soap-and-water scrubbing or a washdown with solvent are both acceptable methods. Use whichever gets the job done most efficiently, but bear in mind that normal sanding, by itself, will remove what might be considered "normal" surface contamination and make a washdown unnecessary.

Brightwork is best sanded by hand rather than by machine; since you have more control over the rate of cutting, there's no risk of accidentally leaving swirls or digs, and there's far less noise and dust. In most cases, sandpaper works better if it is backed up with a pad, although the several layers that result from folding a half sheet of sandpaper will stiffen it considerably. We've found that if fine sandpaper is wrapped around a soft but firm pad, such as a piece of 1-inch Styrofoam, the sheets will last longer and cut faster. Use a block of wood or some other hard object to back up coarse paper; otherwise, it is apt to cut unevenly. A half sheet of sandpaper, folded in thirds, is about right for hand-sanding, although the size and shape of the block may have some influence over how you tear and fold the paper.

Sanding takes two forms: coarse and fine work. Coarse paper fairs out the bumps and feathers (tapers) the transition between existing varnish and bare wood, but it leaves scratches. Progressively finer paper gradually eliminates those scratches by knocking off the peaks until they disappear altogether and the surface is nearly glass smooth. "Running through the numbers" from, say, 80-grit (coarse) to 100 and 120 (medium) and finishing with 150- or 180-grit paper is the most effective and efficient way to prepare a rough and unfair bare or partly bare wood surface. But for spreading varnish over an existing finish that is in reasonable condition, a single sanding with 150- or 180-grit paper will usually do the job.

Within reason, the thicker the total film of varnish, the better, so there's no point in sanding away any more of the existing varnish than you have to. The object is to give the old surface some tooth, so the fresh coat will stick to the last one. With 150- or 180-grit paper, you only need to kill the gloss to achieve the necessary "tooth." (Even finer grits are used by those in quest of perfection, but if you sand "with the grain," the scratches made by 150- or 180-grit paper are virtually invisible, and these grits cut much faster and last much longer than the extra-fine ones.)

On outside corners, as on the top corners of a toerail or hatch coaming, you don't need to sand at all. Paul Bryant of Riverside Boat Yard in Newcastle, Maine,

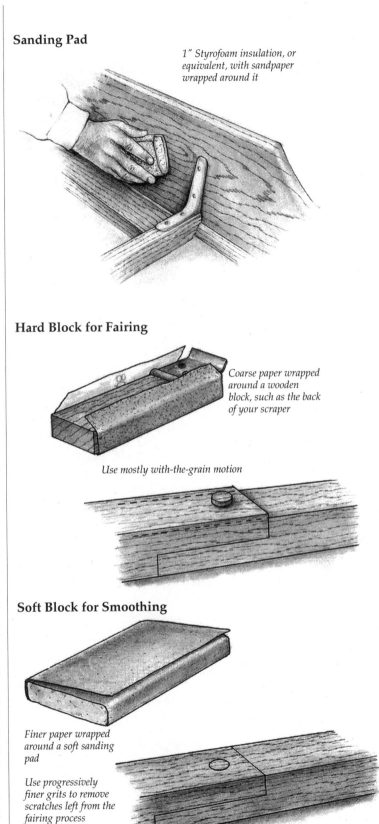

Sanding Pad

1" Styrofoam insulation, or equivalent, with sandpaper wrapped around it

Hard Block for Fairing

Coarse paper wrapped around a wooden block, such as the back of your scraper

Use mostly with-the-grain motion

Soft Block for Smoothing

Finer paper wrapped around a soft sanding pad

Use progressively finer grits to remove scratches left from the fairing process

Sanding Pad

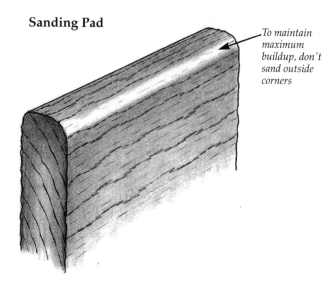

To maintain maximum buildup, don't sand outside corners

Inside Corners

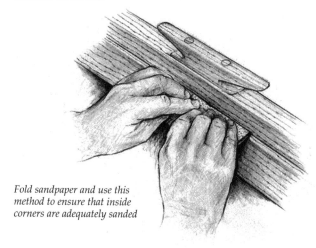

Fold sandpaper and use this method to ensure that inside corners are adequately sanded

Irregular Surfaces

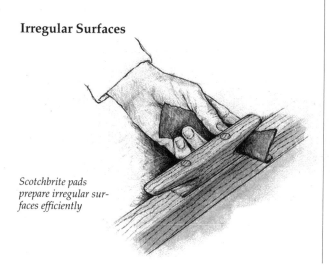

Scotchbrite pads prepare irregular surfaces efficiently

uses this trick for retaining the maximum possible film thickness at the points of heavy wear, and over many years and many boats he's had no problems with lack of adhesion.

Inside corners are another story. They tend to get too much buildup and too little wear. It's too easy to leave them glossy and unsanded, and this invites lifting varnish later. So fold your paper and push it into all the tight places, always attempting to remove just the gloss and as little varnish as possible.

Irregular surfaces, such as trim moldings, wooden cleats, and seat knees, can be sanded faster with Scotchbrite pads, because they conform better to these intricate contours than do folded sheets of sandpaper.

Self-adhesive "Stikit" rolls and molded-for-your-hand rubber sanding blocks have come into use over the last few years. They have won widespread support among hand-sanding aficionados, since they're so convenient and effective. But for limited sanding, the Stikit system may not be worth the considerable investment.

Years ago, we tried wet-sanding our brightwork with wet-or-dry paper. We gave up on the idea after this one experience, even though the paper lasted much longer when lubricated with water. The slurry created by such sanding spread everywhere, the surface had to be wiped dry as we went along (an extra step), and the moisture that got into tight places took forever to dry fully.

Avoiding Dust

While protecting the wood's surface should always be considered the primary reason for applying either varnish or paint, you'll be more satisfied with the results if your final coat dries dust-free. You can control two of the three sources of dust by making sure that there's no dust on the surface that you'll be varnishing and that the brush you're using isn't contaminated with particles. Airborne dust that lands on wet varnish is something else again, and it seems that here a measure of luck is needed for a superb job.

Sweeping or wiping alone won't get rid of the sanding dust you've created in preparing the surface, but it's the obvious way to begin. Washing off what's left makes a mess, and by using water just before varnishing, you risk moisture entrapment — a sure cause of lifting varnish later on. Use a vacuum cleaner or compressed air to clean the crevices and eliminate the dust that is lodged there, so it won't be picked up and spread around by your brush. Vacuuming creates less airborne dust, but compressed air is much faster: use the vacuum if you plan on varnishing immediately afterwards. No matter what method you use, however, you'll need to remove the last few dust specks with a tack rag just before you start laying on the varnish.

Tack rags are the sticky, coated, folded gauze rags that come in individual packages and are sold in auto supply stores as well as marine hardware outlets. Don't even think about a first-class, or even a second-class varnish job without using one.

The need for a clean brush has already been discussed. Even if you think last year's brush is okay, it pays to have a new one on hand in case the first few strokes with the old brush indicate that it is shedding specks of dried varnish or dirt. There never seems to be quite enough time to spread varnish in a leisurely way, and it's very discouraging to have to shut down for a half hour while you hunt down a new brush.

Now for that airborne dust that ruins your beautiful work before it has a chance to dry. Wind is the major culprit, so at least pick a day that's fairly calm when you begin — but there is usually a heat-induced afternoon breeze to worry about. Some days, you just can't win, and you'll have to accept a little dust and think of that job as having provided a good, protective coating over the wood and hope for better luck next time. Indoors, where there's shelter from the wind, is one of the best places to do your varnishing, but an inside location isn't always (or even often) possible for many boats.

The less dust there is to be picked up by the wind, the less of it you'll have to contend with. If your boat is outdoors and you have a choice between gravel or grass beneath it, grass should be the strong favorite. If there's dust on adjacent objects (including yourself), sweep, vacuum, or blow it out of range. Your own boat should be cleaned of all standing dust, not only on about-to-be-varnished surfaces, but also on the deck, cabintop, and other areas where it might blow onto your work.

Applying Varnish

There's a current fetish that says you have to use masking tape anywhere one type of surface finish butts against another. It makes you wonder how boats were ever painted in the pre-tape era, but they were, and the carefully cut-in lines back then had a more natural look than today's taped edges (especially if there are runs under the tape). Taping is of questionable benefit for paint, and it is totally unnecessary for varnishing. In fact, there's better protection if the varnish is deliberately overlapped a little onto the adjacent paintwork. Transitions from varnish to paint usually occur at joints and seams, and this overlapping ensures that these potential moisture entry points get good coverage. Varnish first, then do the painting, including the cutting in (hopefully without benefit of masking tape) afterwards.

If you're about to apply the finish coat, use a freshly opened can of varnish. You'll find there will be less leftover varnish if you purchase pints rather than quarts. Save the partly used cans for buildup and touchup. You can apply varnish directly from the can, if you choose, but it's often more convenient to pour off about half a pint into a small, clean can, and dip into that. A rag tied around the can partway down will catch the drips. Put the cover back on the original container so the varnish left behind doesn't thicken.

Don't believe the old saying that the most important part of the job is preparing the surface; your brushing technique is just as vital. Holidays, runs, sags, and lap marks will negate the most careful preparation. Skill comes with practice in handling your brush, but you might avoid some early pitfalls if you consider the following advice.

The first thing you should realize is that the goal is to apply as heavy a coating as possible without allowing runs and sags to develop. This gives maximum shine and protection. The coating should be uniformly thick as well. All the while, you have to keep moving

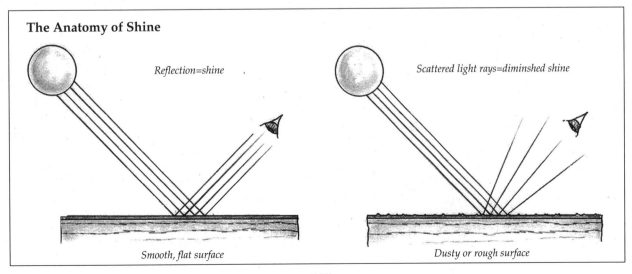

The Anatomy of Shine

Reflection=shine

Scattered light rays=diminshed shine

Smooth, flat surface

Dusty or rough surface

Cutting In: Varnish to Paint

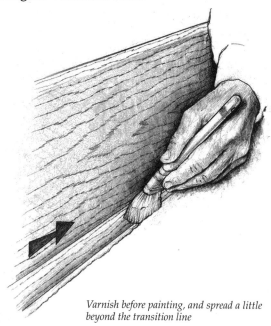

Varnish before painting, and spread a little beyond the transition line

Cutting In: Paint to Varnish

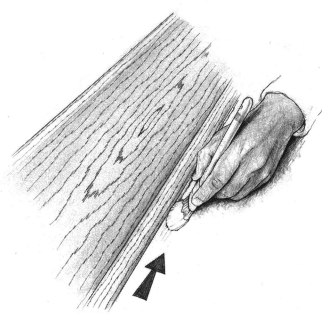

Paint up to the transition with smooth, continuous strokes and considerable pressure on the brush

along fast enough to maintain a "wet edge," so that you're not brushing back into an area that's dried so much that the brush marks won't level out, with each area showing the lap marks that "connect" it to the previous one.

Achieving this is a lot easier than it sounds. Varnish is wonderful stuff to work with because you can "feel" the thickness and uniformity through the handle of the brush by the amount of resistance or drag. If the brush feels as if it's floating on a sea of fresh varnish, the coating is too heavy and should be pushed into a dry area with some heavy strokes before it sets up and starts to sag. If the brush begins to pull hard, it's time to dip into the can for another brushful. In applying varnish, a good sense of feel is as important as good sight.

There are two rather distinct steps in applying varnish, each having its own rate of speed. When you land on the wood with a brushful of varnish, the goal is to move fast and spread the varnish to a reasonably uniform thickness, with brush strokes going every which way. After you feel the brush begin to drag, you smooth out what you've just spread with slower, lighter strokes, generally in the direction of the grain of the wood. Some vertical surfaces may come out best with vertical tipping, even if it's across the grain. During this tipping operation you should begin sighting for holidays and runs, because the varnish will still be fresh and can be pushed from one spot to another fairly easily.

Even though tipping is more deliberate than spreading, don't dally, because as soon as the varnish is spread, it starts to dry, and you'll risk losing the wet edge. If you begin your varnishing on a noncritical part of the boat, chances are good that you'll develop an effective pace by the time you get to the big, flat surfaces.

If possible, avoid varnishing in direct sunlight. Early loss of your wet edge and subsequent blistering may result. If the boat is outside on a warm day and you simply can't move fast enough, the job may require another person swinging another brush. Or, you can add some retarder to the varnish. Which brings us to the next subject.

Additives

Adding retarder extends the drying time, as opposed to adding accelerator, which hastens it. It isn't often that either retarder or accelerator has to be used, because if you're selective about the day for your varnishing, the out-of-the-can consistency and time for setup is usually just right. Varnish is a real joy to apply, in fact, and unless the weather is unusually hot and windy, it's best not to complicate things by stirring in any additives. If you're trying to build up an area, however, and don't want to drag out the job, a little dryer added to varnish will allow you to apply two or three coats in a day instead of the usual single one.

Retarders and accelerators are often sold by the same manufacturers that produce the varnish, and you're probably safest if you stick to the use of matching brands. Living more dangerously, we've never had problems when we've mixed one of our old standbys, Interlux 333 (retarder), or Interlux 216 (accelerator), with Z-Spar 1015 or whatever other oil-based, phenolic varnish we happened to be using.

Repairing Damaged Varnish

If a springtime inspection indicates that varnish has lifted here and there, but, by and large, the brightwork has survived okay, it makes sense to repair the brightwork locally rather than to strip everything down to bare wood. Repairing varnish involves stripping away only the damaged film, and then blending the resulting areas of bare wood into the surrounding unaffected varnish work.

A sharp scraper, carefully controlled, gets rid of damaged varnish most efficiently. Chemical remover can help things along on large areas, in which case the adjoining finish should be protected against spatters by masking. The same scraper can also do a decent job of tapering the stripped area back into the adjacent varnish work. A 1½-inch Red Devil scraper blade screwed to a piece of scrap pine is a wonderfully handy little tool. We've long been grateful to Paul Bryant of the Riverside Boat Yard for passing along this tip.

Sharpening of the scraper blade is done with a few strokes of a mill file. You'll soon become proficient at this, as these scrapers must be sharpened frequently to remain effective. Remember that you're only clawing away bad varnish here, not giving a hardwood tabletop a mirror-like "hand-scraped" finish; there's no need for creating rolled edges on the edge of the blade, or for honing, or for any of the more sophisticated and time-consuming procedures used by cabinetmakers for sharpening their scrapers.

After you've done all you can with a scraper, go for the sandpaper, backing it up with a firm block and using 100-grit paper. Most of your rubbing will be devoted to feathering from bare wood to undisturbed varnish — short strokes with considerable pressure. Shift "through the numbers" until you reach the same grit that you're using for the overall job (150- to 180- grit).

When all damaged areas have received this treatment, take a good look at each one to see if there's an obvious cause for the damage (usually lifted varnish) that can be corrected. If there's a seam or a joint that's allowing moisture to penetrate, and you can make it watertight, you may avoid a recurrence of this problem and save yourself some time next year. Epoxy

The Two Steps of Applying Varnish

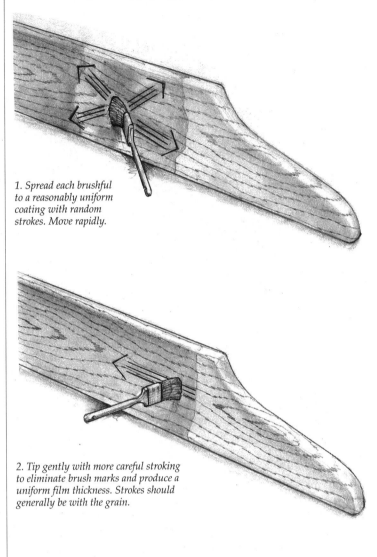

1. Spread each brushful to a reasonably uniform coating with random strokes. Move rapidly.

2. Tip gently with more careful stroking to eliminate brush marks and produce a uniform film thickness. Strokes should generally be with the grain.

Blistering

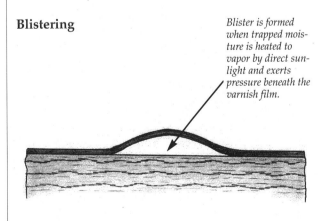

Blister is formed when trapped moisture is heated to vapor by direct sunlight and exerts pressure beneath the varnish film.

Handy Scraper

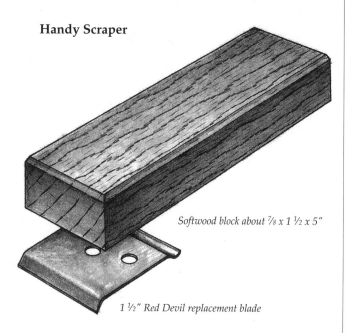

Softwood block about ⅞ x 1 ½ x 5"

1 ½" Red Devil replacement blade

Feathering Damaged Brightwork

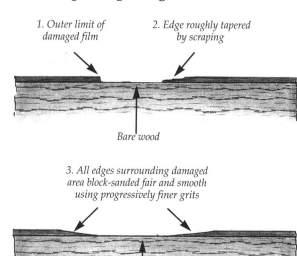

1. *Outer limit of damaged film*

2. *Edge roughly tapered by scraping*

Bare wood

3. *All edges surrounding damaged area block-sanded fair and smooth using progressively finer grits*

Bare wood

mixed with sanding dust (from the same species of wood) makes a secure and wonderful filler that's hardly visible afterwards. For larger areas, graving pieces — also glued in place with epoxy — may work, and here a close color match with the existing wood is worth some attention.

The process of building up the repaired area to the same varnish film thickness as the adjacent finish is called touchup. Before touchup commences, however, you may find that a little stain rubbed into these bare wood areas will make them blend better into the overall tone of the surrounding brightwork than if varnish alone is used. Each situation is different, and you'll have to experiment. With patience and luck, you'll probably get a pretty close match.

Then go for the varnish, thinning the first coat a little so it will penetrate, and applying the subsequent coats full strength. One important caveat: Sanding residue, especially pigmented residue that lingers after sanding adjoining paintwork, must be vacuumed away or otherwise eliminated from the grain of the bare wood before it is stained or varnished; otherwise, it will cloud the resulting finish, no matter how carefully that finish is applied.

Not having the time or the patience to give the damaged areas sufficient coats of touchup leaves many owners having to repeat the same repair year after year. This is discouraging, so don't walk away from the touchup phase until there are at least four coats of varnish over the bare wood. Then you can give your brightwork its annual overall coating. Sanding between successive coats of touchup can generally be dispensed with, because the adhesion is good between fresh coats. Concern yourself only with keeping a reasonably smooth surface while the buildup is taking place and, of course, a final sanding with 150- or 180-grit paper just before applying the overall final coat.

Care

Keep varnished surfaces clean. A chamois (genuine or synthetic) works best, used with fresh water. If you can get to the boat before the morning dew dries, you'll find that the dirt and salt crystals have been softened by the dew and will wipe off easily. A dockside hose is great for washing down later in the day, if you're lucky enough to have access to such a luxury; otherwise, keep a bucket of fresh water at hand as you move along on deck with your chamois. Although in most harbors thorough cleaning isn't required every day, as in the age of liveaboard professionals and coal-burning machinery, it should be done often enough to keep dirt from being ground into the varnished surface and abrading the film, and to eliminate salt crystals, which are known to shorten the life of any high-gloss finish.

Shielding your brightwork from the weather goes

a long way toward lengthening its life. If possible, shade it from the sun with awnings or protective covers. Exposing varnish to freezing dew or rain is lethal! On old boats where the joints and seams of the wood underneath the brightwork tend to be loose or leak due to dried-out bedding compound, the traces of moisture that invariably become trapped beneath the varnish are the culprits. This little bit of moisture, perhaps undetectable to the eye, expands every time the temperature drops below freezing and turns to ice. Gradually, but relentlessly, cycle after cycle, the varnish is pushed away, and the next thing you know a blister appears. The single most important precaution you can take, then, to keep your varnish intact is to keep it dry during freezing weather, especially during as many of the dramatic freeze/thaw swings of fall and spring as possible.

Although a worthwhile undertaking, mid-season touchup is often overlooked. But if you're more conscientious than most of us, you'll find that those foam throwaway brushes make the task much less formidable. You'll get your reward when next spring comes around. The wood will have retained its natural color under your quickly executed touchups, and there will be no weathered or blackened wood to scrape away.

Frequency of Recoating

A once-a-year varnish job generally lasts for the three- to five-month boating season here in Maine. Boats with longer seasons or operating in more severe climates may need revarnishing every few months. There will be an accepted recoating interval among the owners of well-maintained boats in your area, and also some local application techniques that should be learned and adhered to. It will pay to become a part of the brightwork grapevine wherever you live. Remember, however, that the most reliable advice may not come from folks who have a newly acquired boat that looks fine now, but rather from people who have gotten to know their boats and have kept them presentable over a number of years in your particular part of the world.

Stripping Varnish

While a complete guide to the removal of an old brightwork finish is beyond the scope of this chapter, you should know that bare wood is too sensitive to be left exposed outside for any length of time. The hot sun will shrink and cup it, dampness will swell it, and standing moisture, even in the form of dew, will stain it. A single afternoon's sun shining down on a freshly stripped hatch can easily pop its glued seams and begin to cup the individual pieces from which it is made. Pieces of smaller cross-section with

Building Up Damaged Brightwork

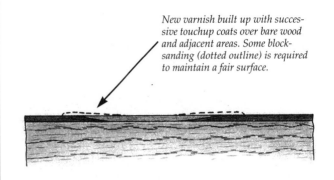

New varnish built up with successive touchup coats over bare wood and adjacent areas. Some block-sanding (dotted outline) is required to maintain a fair surface.

Keeping Out Moisture

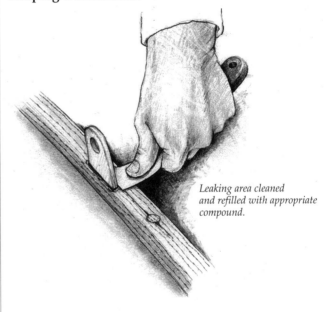

Leaking area cleaned and refilled with appropriate compound.

Freeze Damage

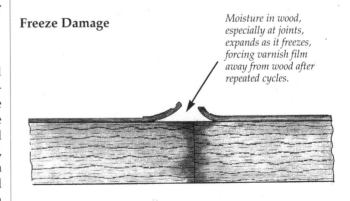

Moisture in wood, especially at joints, expands as it freezes, forcing varnish film away from wood after repeated cycles.

Fillers

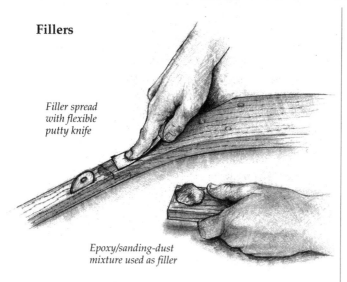

Filler spread with flexible putty knife

Epoxy/sanding-dust mixture used as filler

Mid-Season Touchup

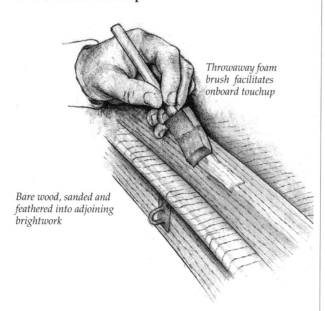

Throwaway foam brush facilitates onboard touchup

Bare wood, sanded and feathered into adjoining brightwork

Bare Wood Exposure Damage

less flat surface are not as vulnerable, but they will still be stained by water. So, do your stripping under a shelter, or get a protective sealer on the bare wood before nightfall.

Sealers

If you've spent all day stripping brightwork and it's too late for varnish to dry before the dew falls, a fast-drying sealer can help. Acrylic sealer is watery and volatile and will provide short-term protection from moisture. It also has another use, if you're really in a hurry, and that is to raise the wood grain — which it always does anyway — so you can sand off the resulting fuzz and make the first coat of real varnish a little more effective. You'll get to a glossy finish in about one less coat by using sealer, but the down side is that in the long run the finish may not adhere quite as well as it would with a first coat of slower-drying, thinned-down varnish.

Fillers

As mentioned previously, sanding dust from the same species of wood as the brightwork, mixed with clear epoxy resin, is one of the very best fillers there is. Although it sticks well and blends in, slow drying makes it impractical at certain times. In such instances, fast-drying wood dough may be the answer. Wood dough is a hardware store-type product sold under a variety of trade names and is available in several shades formulated to match the common wood types. It is much like old-fashioned Plastic Wood, but in your choice of colors. Within minutes after application of a not-too-thick-layer, a wood-dough repair is ready for sanding and coating.

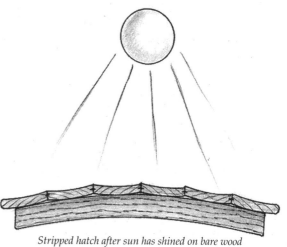

Original hatch protected by varnish

Stripped hatch after sun has shined on bare wood

Woods for Varnishing

Some woods lend themselves better than others to varnish. Varnished teak is a knockout; it's difficult to understand why anyone would choose to let this beautiful wood remain bare and turn a weather-beaten gray. The penetrating oils commonly used on teak result in only a marginal improvement, not at all in the same league as teak glowing through a good coating of varnish. "The word," long accepted among boat owners, is that it is difficult to keep varnish stuck to teak because of the oily nature of this wood. To a degree that may be true, but there are too many success stories — boats that go year after year with teak brightwork — to dismiss the idea as impractical.

Mahogany probably comes in second to teak as a favorite wood for varnished trim. Honduras and Mexican mahogany take on a lovely hue with nothing more than varnish applied, but Philippine mahogany does not. Filler-stain, rubbed into Philippine mahogany grain before the varnish is applied, provides the best results. Use your choice of brown-toned or red-toned stain; it's a matter of taste, and either one will provide a richness and uniformity that this wood, by itself, does not have.

New oak and ash take on a light golden color under varnish and are nearly as striking as teak. Either species equals Honduras mahogany in varnished beauty. But let a trace of moisture get into the grain and the wood quickly goes black. You can try bleach to remove water stains from oak and ash, but the results will make you realize that scraping away the discolored wood is the only reliable approach. This, of course, can be carried out only so many times before the reduced thickness of whatever piece you're scraping becomes a problem. The message of the varnished oak and ash story is this: Varnish is great on new work, nearly impossible to keep looking good over the long haul, and, down the road, paint may be the best practical solution. Locust, although not as widely used for trim, falls in the same category.

White pine may have to be changed from varnish to paint even sooner than oak or ash, since the staining strikes deeper into the grain and the wood is too soft to lend itself to scraping. The spruces are the same, including Sitka, of which wooden spars are made.

Parting Thoughts

If you come to appreciate the minor battle scars, wear marks, and unblended touchup that age and normal use bring to any fine object, then you can ease off on the fillers, stains, and much of the fussing that otherwise might accompany your annual varnishing task. Perhaps we should even celebrate this patina, since it can't be duplicated in new work, any more than a contemporary reproduction can be made to look like a 200-year-old tavern table. Patina indicates that your boat has successfully survived the passage of time. Be proud of it, not ashamed. There's really no compelling reason to make your older boat look like a new one. This is not to recommend slovenliness, only to point out that you don't need to fret about obscuring all traces of natural wear. This standard isn't lower than a blemish-free one — just different.

Hot-Weather Varnishing

_____ by Ian Bruce _____

I have had many years of experience on charter yachts in the Mediterranean and the Caribbean, where most varnishing is, of necessity, done in very hot weather and can be diabolically difficult. Many of the beautiful, old classic yachts — the Fifes, the Camper and Nicholsons, and the Abeking and Rasmussens — have very extensive areas of brightwork.

The larger the area you are trying to varnish, the more difficult it is to maintain a wet edge in hot weather. Contributing to the problem is the fact that the best varnishes — those that have the best gloss-retention characteristics and durability — are also the most difficult to use, particularly in hot weather.

Another factor that makes varnishing and the maintenance of varnish such a challenging occupation in the charter business is that many of these boats work a double season: the Mediterranean in summer and the Caribbean in winter, or the Caribbean in winter and the East Coast of the United States in summer. Some boats remain in the Caribbean year-round — 12 months of blazing sunlight. Prolonged ultraviolet radiation dramatically shortens the life span of a clear coating.

A number of factors affect varnishing in hot weather. Air temperature is the most obvious one, causing the varnish to dry so quickly that the brush marks do not have time to level out. Other factors are humidity, the temperature of the wood surface, the area of the varnish, the time of day, the type of varnish, the additives used, and the type of brush. Even the preparation of the wood is of some importance.

Stripping

Should you, or should you not, strip your varnish down to bare wood when it becomes somewhat cloudy and darkened?

It is fairly common in New England, and no doubt elsewhere, to sand old varnish heavily, removing all but the first coats, before revarnishing. This removes the old age-darkened and cloudy layers and leaves a smooth base for further fresh coats. This practice is highly recommended by some experts.

This method is, without a doubt, less work than stripping the varnish to bare wood, and is appropriate under certain circumstances. It can be an acceptable procedure — possibly even one to be recommended — for boats that are laid up in winter, have only a short summer season, and seldom receive really intense doses of sunlight. However, it is not a good practice for vessels that spend extended periods in sunny climates. Under those conditions, varnish suffers largely from age darkening, abrasion, and cloudiness due to moisture absorption — factors that do not primarily affect the bond between the wood and the varnish film.

Boats that operate year-round in strong sunlight, however, encounter a fundamentally different problem. Ultraviolet rays cause the surface of the wood underneath the varnish to undergo a chemical change, which separates the varnish film from the wood. This takes place long before the varnish has had time to develop any other ailments, such as age-darkening.

Scratches can be coated over and dings patched until the varnish shows signs of separating; then it has to be stripped right down to bare wood. The first sign of separation is the dreaded "white ding," which begins to appear in places where the brightwork has been dented or nicked. The varnish lifts from the wood around the ding, and this shows as a yellow spot. When the bond between the varnish film and the wood is very weak, such a separation can result from a tap so light as to leave the actual coating undamaged. When you take a scraper to the area, you will find that you cannot fair it in properly — the varnish insists on peeling over a larger and larger area. The varnish may still appear to be in perfect condition, but it is difficult to patch and is due for stripping.

Priming

It would be wonderful if there were a clear primer or sealer that would bond strongly enough to the wood to prevent separation, but so far, most sealers appear to be no better at resisting separation than the traditional sealer, which is simply thinned varnish.

The first two coats of varnish should be thinned 50 percent, and the third coat should be thinned 25 percent. You may thin the varnish with turpentine or paint thinner; or if you are varnishing spruce, ash, or oak, there is some advantage in thinning the sealer coats with linseed oil. These woods, especially spruce, are very prone to blackening, and linseed oil reduces such action; it also helps to prevent water penetration if the varnish film is later damaged.

Commercial sealers are handy, mainly because of their quick-drying properties. Under no circumstances should you apply undiluted varnish as a first coat — particularly in a sunny climate — as separation and lifting will occur substantially sooner.

Some epoxy resin manufacturers claim that epoxy resin is a good sealer to use under varnish, as it clings very tenaciously to wood fibers. This is true; but, unfortunately, epoxy tends to go milky in ultraviolet light. WEST System® resin, used with the slow hardener, is reputed to resist turning milky for longer than most epoxies, but few people relish the idea of stripping the stuff off when the time comes — as it must — to refinish.

Don't be tempted to fill dings or widened seams in brightwork with epoxy glue; the thick resins that seem most suitable for this purpose turn milky in sunlight very quickly.

Sanding

There is nothing special about sanding prior to varnishing in hot weather, except you may need a finer grade of sandpaper. If the drying conditions force you to thin the varnish more than usual, the sanding scratches may show through and reduce the gloss. People who are particularly obsessed with the danger of runs may succeed in applying a coat so thin that the fine scratches left by 220-grit paper will show through.

If you feel the need to use 320 grit, you probably will have to resort to wet-or-dry paper to avoid clogging. Be very careful to wash off the scum so produced, frequently and with plenty of water. In hot, dry weather, this scum is capable of transforming itself into a very tenacious white "paint," which, when it dries, may be so difficult to remove (even with the aid of thinner) that you will be forced to sand off your sanding residue.

Brushing Technique

Brushing technique is very important in hot weather. You have to work very fast to maintain a wet edge. There is no time to take sips from your beer can, no time for topping up your varnish pot or adding more thinner, and no time to lay down your brush and sight carefully along the just-varnished surface looking for "holidays" — you have to keep moving.

Make sure that there are no obstructions in your way; you will not be able to stop work and move that kedge anchor out of your path.

You must have enough varnish in your pot to complete the area you are working on. If your varnish starts to thicken in the pot due to evaporation, you had better call someone else to add more thinner. Forget about holidays. Going back to touch up a holiday in hot weather when the varnish is setting up rapidly will only result in an unsightly mess.

If you have a large area to varnish, it is important to prepare everything in advance so that you can move quickly. You may pride yourself on your "cutting-in" ability, but any attempt to work carefully around fittings will slow you down enough so that you'll lose your wet edge.

Remove as many fittings as practical. This is always a good policy. If you varnish under your fittings and re-bed them, you will avoid those black water stains that are so common around small pieces of hardware. Tape off any fitting that cannot be easily removed.

If you are dealing with extensive flat areas that have moldings and other narrow pieces attached (such as cabin sides or doghouses, hatch framing, etc.), tape these areas off and varnish them separately. When you varnish the moldings, the areas you are dealing with will be so limited that you will have time to cut in without losing a wet edge. Make sure that the adjacent flat areas have at least skinned over — which will happen almost instantaneously in hot weather — as cutting in against a surface where the varnish is still sticky can result in unsightly join marks.

Another way to limit the area you have to deal with is to look for strong glue lines or seams and use them as borders, so you will not have to maintain as broad a wet edge. Again, it is important to make sure that your varnish is well skinned over, thus avoiding join marks when you varnish the adjacent plank. The surface should be touch-dry to a light touch, at the very least.

When varnishing an area that is longer in one direction than the other, arrange your wet edge so it lies across the narrower side; maintaining a short wet edge is always easier. If this means that you have to brush across the grain, do not worry about it. The purpose of varnishing with the grain is to render brush marks less noticeable; you should plan on leaving no brush marks at all.

Varnishing the caprail of a yacht in truly hot weather may prove difficult if there are padeyes, stanchions, chafing strips, and rail-mounted sheet tracks to work around. Remove or tape everything. You may want to varnish the rail outside the sheet track first and do the inside afterwards. This will leave only two very short join marks, less than half the width of the rail. The gymnastics involved in ducking back and forth under the lifelines, around the stanchions, and through the shrouds, in order to view the underside of the rail on both sides, can slow you down considerably.

You may find that you are leaving a trail of sweat along that blisteringly hot deck, and that drops of perspiration are dropping from your labored brow into the varnish. A headband can be useful in this situation.

I am a fairly sacrilegious person by nature, so I have no qualms at all about admitting to the use of foam brushes. In my opinion, they are easily equal to the best badger-hair brushes in most applications. They are cheap and leave no brush marks to speak of. I find that they are so easy to clean that I wash them out and reuse them (my Scottish ancestry may have something to do with that).

However, a foam brush does have one disadvantage. It cannot carry as large a load of varnish as some of the more expensive brushes can, and this may slow you down. Usually this is not crucial unless you are an inexperienced varnisher, but when you are dealing with extensive areas of varnish in very hot weather, speed is of the essence, and you will do better with the best-possible bristle brush.

No brush of the common rectangular shape, no matter what the bristles are made of, can compare with the oval-section brushes widely used in Europe. These brushes have very fine, stiff bristles, which will carry a truly enormous quantity of varnish and will brush that varnish out swiftly and efficiently. Most small-boat owners are unlikely to need such a brush, unless they have a varnished hull. However, anyone who enjoys owning and using exquisitely effective tools might want to purchase one or two of these brushes and maintain them carefully.

When using a brush that carries a large load of varnish, it is best to apply that load to the surface at two or three different spots along the wet edge; this facilitates and speeds the spreading out of the varnish into an even film.

Types of Varnish

Some years ago, the yacht *Fandango* was preparing to leave Camden, Maine, to sail down to the West Indies. A long ocean passage can wreak havoc on varnished surfaces, particularly if severe weather is encountered, so the crew was putting a quick coat of varnish on the rail as added protection. It was November and conditions were not ideal, but the brightwork would receive further coats in the Caribbean, so a good finish was not essential.

Unfortunately, a few snowflakes started to fall. A passerby, fascinated by this sight, asked if a special type of varnish was being used.

"Snow varnish," a disgusted crew member replied.

I do not know whether the passerby accepted this statement, but of course snow varnish does not exist. Unfortunately, neither does hot-weather varnish.

Some varnishes are less difficult to apply in hot weather than others, but it seems to be an inescapable fact that the very best varnishes — those that produce and retain the best gloss — are just those varnishes that are most difficult to use in hot weather.

Epifanes, a Dutch varnish, is the best I have ever encountered, but to use it in hot weather requires considerable finesse. Captain's Varnish is very popular in the United States and is somewhat easier to apply in hot weather; only varnish buffs will detect the slightly inferior gloss it provides.

To my knowledge, the easiest varnish to use is Benjamin Moore's 440 varnish. It can be applied successfully under the most adverse conditions, often without requiring thinning. I would not go quite so far as to claim that it can be applied with a toilet brush, but it is definitely a good varnish for the inexperienced. There is, of course, a catch:

The gloss is not very good. However, it will protect your wood (which is all that most people want), is cheap, and contains an ultraviolet filter.

Most spar varnishes now contain an ultraviolet filter, and while this does not make application easier, it does help to prevent the cured film from lifting due to degradation from exposure to ultraviolet light.

Additives

A varnish job is most durable if at least five coats of undiluted varnish are applied over the sealer coats. The varnish should be applied thinly enough to avoid runs. Unfortunately, it is seldom possible to apply undiluted varnish in hot weather. The expert varnisher will look at the sky, sniff the weather, and add the absolute minimum amount of thinner to his varnish pot.

Very few people use the thinners recommended by the varnish manufacturers. Ordinary paint thinner or turpentine works very well, and some people even swear by kerosene. These seem to be at least as good as the manufacturer-recommended thinners and are a lot cheaper. (I did try the official thinner recommended on the can — once. One teaspoon of it in a quart of varnish thinned the varnish to the consistency of water and eradicated every vestige of gloss. When used to wipe down fresh varnish after sanding, this thinner stripped the top coat right off.)

If you find that you cannot apply your varnish successfully without thinning it to an excessive degree, try adding a little Penetrol. This will help to prevent the varnish from dragging and, being a fairly thick liquid, will not alter the consistency of the varnish very much.

Penetrol is a very controversial additive, as it has a tendency to reduce gloss. A while ago, I read an angry letter published in a boating magazine. The author had tried Penetrol on the recommendation of someone else, and his paint had dried completely without gloss. It is probable that he followed the directions on the back of the Penetrol can. These directions suggest adding one quart of Penetrol to four quarts of paint, which will extend the quantity to five quarts. I would not advise doing this under any circumstances if you are after a high-gloss finish.

One teaspoon of Penetrol in a cup of varnish is more than adequate. It should be used in conjunction with thinner, and only after thinner alone has proved inadequate. Too much Penetrol will soon reduce the gloss of the best varnish, until it is inferior to that of a cheaper and more tractable varnish. Rather than risking that, it is simpler and more economical to purchase a cheaper varnish, such as Benjamin Moore's 440 varnish. Moore's will probably brush better in hot weather and produce a better gloss than higher-quality Epifanes that has been thinned with too much Penetrol. (Penetrol is excellent, however, in a number of other applications that are outside the scope of this discussion.)

Suggestions

Surfaces that are in direct sunlight get much hotter than surfaces in the shade, regardless of air temperature. It is a good idea to rig an awning over any area you intend to varnish.

The best time to varnish is in the early morning. Do your sanding the day before, and don't wait for the sun to evaporate the morning dew, as the temperature may be up in the 80s by then. Sponge and chamois all dew-covered surfaces until they seem dry, then allow at least an hour for the last dampness to evaporate. If you don't wait long enough, you may find your varnish beginning to blow bubbles as traces of moisture turn into vapor under the varnish. I have seen these cute little spherical bubbles reach a diameter of ⅜". Though they can be just as iridescent and beautiful as any soap bubble, they are not really what you are after in a varnish job. (The better-quality varnishes produce the prettiest bubbles — something to do with the elasticity of the film, I believe.)

You can also hose your brightwork down to cool it before varnishing — but again, make sure it is bone dry before you varnish.

Keep your varnish supplies in a cool place. An effective trick is to place your varnish pot in a bucket of ice to keep it cool while you work. Cooled, or chilled, varnish produces a thicker coating.

Another hazard of varnishing in a hot climate is unexpected rain squalls or thunderstorms. In Florida, as summer approaches, the high humidity can prevent your varnish from drying just long enough for it to get doused by the afternoon thunderstorm. In the Caribbean, rain squalls can appear without warning, pour down rain for an hour, then vanish just as quickly as they came. Even if your varnish has skinned over, the coating of water it receives may retard further evaporation of the thinner, resulting in a finish that appears to be dry but is rubbery underneath. Such a finish will pucker up and tear if you lean on it hard with your bare hand, and you will be forced to strip that coat right off and revarnish.

There is, however, something you can do to prevent this, but for it to be effective your varnish will have to have skinned over well before the rain fell. In hot weather it usually has. Holding a chamois cloth with one corner in each hand, drag it over the skinned-over varnish, being very careful to apply no hand pressure whatsoever. Continue to do this, wringing out the chamois frequently, until the surface is free of rainwater. This will allow the varnish to continue to cure normally.

Preventing Deterioration Due to Sunlight

Many people use a chamois cloth to wipe the dew off their brightwork every morning, believing that the little globules of dew act as magnifying glasses and burn the varnish. I find the magnification theory difficult to believe. Many people also wash the salt off their varnish after a sail for the same reason, believing that the salt crystals act as magnifying glasses. Washing off the salt definitely helps to preserve the varnish, but probably because the salt particles are abrasive, not because of their optical qualities.

The best way to prevent your varnish from jumping ship because it can't stand the heat is to do away with varnished surfaces above decks. But this would be too much of a sacrifice for many people. The next best solution is to have only the vertical surfaces finished bright. Vertical surfaces receive direct sunlight only during the morning and evening, when the ultraviolet levels are much lower. Sliding hatches, which are pure horizontal surfaces, really take a beating from the sun — especially the fore hatch, which, unlike the companionway hatch, is seldom shaded by an awning.

Varnish is best preserved in a hot climate by continually adding another coat. A thick layer of varnish screens out more ultraviolet rays than a thin layer does. There is no need to worry about excessive buildup; your first "white ding" will appear before that becomes a problem.

Yes, it's more work to keep up varnish in those parts of the world where the tradewinds rustle in the palm trees, the sea is blue, and the maidens go topless. Some people give up, and take their boats to the coast of Maine or Alaska, where the varnish lasts longer (though the maidens are well-wrapped). But others are willing to do the extra work, to have their varnish shine where the sun shines.

Two-Can Finishes, or One?

—————— by Nicholas K. Mango ——————

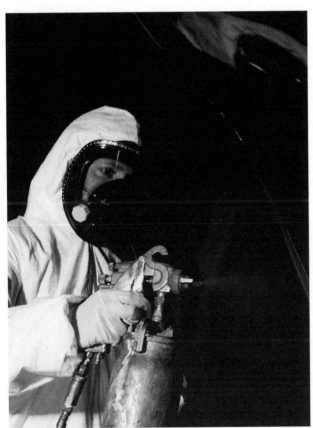

Two-part varnishes can provide a labor cost savings of up to 45 percent because multiple coats can be applied in a single day. The health risks can be minimized by careful preparation.

When people see the varnished runabout that my wife Liz and I restored, they often remark, "That sure is a beautiful boat...must take a lot of work to keep the varnish looking like that." The truth is that it can take more work than they could ever imagine. Varnishing can easily become the greatest consumer of time and money than anything else for a wooden boat owner. Not wishing to spend more of either than necessary, I am always looking for new technology that can reduce the varnishing chores.

For owners who are willing to accept a water-clear coating, and for dry wood components that don't expand and contract, two-part varnishes offer substantial maintenance and cost savings over single-part varnishes. The two-part varnishes can save up to 45 percent of the labor costs of application, more than offsetting their higher material costs. However, the real payback comes in increased coating life, which is at least twice and, with diligent maintenance, may be as much as six times as long as traditional varnish.

To research the advantages of two-part varnishes over traditional single-part products, I spoke with five manufacturers that make both types. (These manufacturers are listed, along with their products, in Table 1.) I did not ask them to contrast their products with those of their competitors; it would be impossible to resolve the conflicting claims. Instead, I asked them to contrast their own two-part varnishes with their best one-part varnish. Their comments turned out to be remarkably consistent, and they provide a concise explanation of the differences between the single- and two-part products. To augment this survey, I traveled to Italy and Monaco to gather information from professionals who have been using two-part varnishes for many years. I compared my experience in refinishing my own boat, a 22-foot Riva Ariston, with traditional varnish, to that of the Riva shop, which uses a two-part varnish.

Characteristics

Every manufacturer stated without hesitation that their two-part varnishes offered superior material properties to even their best one-part products. The two-part products are essentially impervious to solvents, including toluene, acetone, gasoline, and MEK. Single-part products will melt at the touch of any of these substances, and even from the application of common household cleaners like Fantastik. Almost the only solvent that will soften the two-part varnishes is methylene chloride, which is actually fortunate since this chemical is a common paint- and varnish-stripping compound.

A second advantage of two-part varnishes is that they are extremely abrasion resistant, more so than any one-part product. Once cured, the surface is so hard that it will dull common sandpaper very quickly (so, don't plan on removing two-part varnishes by sanding!). This hardness makes two-part varnishes excellent for high-wear areas, such as decks and sailboat toerails where the water abrasion from one ocean delivery can remove an entire coating of conventional varnish.

Finally, and most importantly, the manufacturers state that all the two-part varnishes have vastly superior ultraviolet light (UV)-resisting characteristics. This is critical, since breakdown from the sun's UV is traditionally the major cause of varnish failure. The two-part polyurethane varnishes are sunlight-stable compounds, whereas conventional varnishes are continually broken down under sunlight. Therefore, two-part varnishes do not fail by conventional UV-induced cracking and crazing. Rather, they usually fail at the bond with the wood.

Life/Longevity

Because of the superior characteristics of two-part varnishes, all of the manufacturers stated that their two-part products will outlast their best single-part products by a factor of two to four. This is the most persuasive reason to consider two-part varnishes. A longer-lived varnish job saves not only the expense and time of the actual varnish work, but also the

Table 1. Listing of Varnishes

Manufacturer	Name	Parts	Type	Color	Application Method
Detco	Sterling	2	Polyester-polyurethane	Water-clear	Brush/Spray
	Crystal	1	Tung oil-phenolic	Amber	Brush/Spray
Epifanes	Two-Part Clear	2	Polyester-polyurethane	Water-clear	Brush/Spray
	Clear Gloss	1	Tung oil-alkyd-urethane	Amber	Brush/Spray
International	Interthane Plus	2	Polyester-polyurethane	Water-clear	Brush/Roller
	Clipper Clear #95	1	Polyurethane	Slightly amber	Brush/Spray
Stoppani	Glasstop UV (Note 5)	2	Aliphatic-polyurethane	Slightly amber	Spray
	910 (Notes 4, 5)	2	Aliphatic-polyurethane	Water-clear	Brush/Spray
	Stoppani Gloss UV	1	Polyurethane	Amber	Brush/Spray
U.S. Paint	AwlBrite	2	Acrylic-polyurethane	Water-clear	Brush/Roller
	AwlSpar	1	Tung oil-phenolic	Amber	Brush/Roller

*NOTES
1. Prices converted per U.S. quart.
2. The area covered by a U.S. quart, one film thickness.
3. Time that the surface remains chemically active. This determines the interval a top coat can be applied without sanding.

tedious preparation. Refinishing our Riva Ariston requires nearly 200 hours for disassembly, stripping, sanding, staining, and reassembly. This does not include the varnishing time, which requires nearly another 200 hours.

I can personally offer the following confirmation of these longevity claims. Our Riva is varnished with one of the premium one-part products listed in Table 1. If the brightwork is left uncovered, I know (from painful experience) that the varnish will show signs of crazing in one season of New England saltwater boating (four months' continuous exposure). This crazing is bad enough to require major sanding and revarnishing to correct.

Another Riva I examined — one that Monaco Boat Service (one of the Riva family's restoration firms) had coated with two-part varnish eight years ago — had also been exposed to New England saltwater conditions. Last fall, after seven seasons (21 months of continuous exposure), the varnish on the decks was beginning to haze and had worn through in two small places, but otherwise was in good shape. The varnish on the hull sides, not exposed to direct sunlight, was still in very good condition. The condition of the two-part varnish on this boat was better than

that of our one-part coating after six times the exposure! This is consistent with what the managing director of the Monaco Boat Service told me. He advised that by adding one coat of two-part varnish every three years to a boat kept uncovered in the Mediterranean, the varnish will stay looking perfect indefinitely.

Application

With the exception of International's Interthane Plus, all of the two-part products can be applied two to four coats per day at room temperature. Two-part varnish hardens primarily by catalytic reaction instead of solvent evaporation, and the surface remains chemically active for 8 to 36 hours. During this interval, no sanding is required between coats. This is a tremendous timesaver over traditional one-part varnishes, which require sanding — and the associated vacuuming, tacking, and wiping — to provide adhesion between coats. In theory, with two-part products, buildup can occur indefinitely at two to four coats a day, although some users — including Riva — wait for a full cure and sand once every three coats before proceeding. (The one-part phenolic varnishes, like Detco's Crystal and U.S. Paint's AwlSpar, may dry

Dry Film Thickness	Coverage (Note 2)	Coats per 8-hr day	Recoat Time	Min. # Coats	Price (Note 1)
.0015-.0025"	75-100 sq ft	2-3	24 (Note 3)	6-9	$88
.002"	75-100 sq ft	2	24 (Note 3)	7-8	$28
.002"	114-126 sq ft	2	8 (Note 3)	3	$70
.002"	142 sq ft	1	none	6-7	$27
.002"	165 sq ft	1	none	6	$49
.0025"	125 sq ft	1	none	3	$27
.0016"	102-132 sq ft	2-3	16-24 (Note 3)	2 (Note 6)	$43
.0016"	82-102 sq ft	3-4	8-10 (Note 3)	7 (Note 6)	$35
.0012"	82-102 sq ft	1	none	6	$33
.0007-.0012"	125 sq ft	2-3	24 (Note 3)	10-12	$47
.001-.0015"	150-210 sq ft	2	24 (Note 3)	8-10	$22

4. Product 910 is an undercoat for Glasstop UV; it is not meant for exterior use.
5. Stoppani makes a compatible two-part stain for 910 and Glasstop.
6. Stoppani Glasstop and 910 are used together as a system. There are nine total coats.

Table 2. Application Comparison of Traditional vs. Two-Part Varnish

Riva's Spray Varnish Procedure
*Extrapolated to a 22' Riva Ariston
(Stoppani two-part varnish)

Task	Workdays	Labor(hrs)	Coats
Apply filler stain Stoppani two-part #2527	1	8	
Spray three thinned coats 1.5 hrs between coats Rest three days	0.5	4	3
Sand Spray three coats 1.5 hrs between coats Rest three days	1.5	8 4	6
Sand Spray three coats 1.5 hrs between coats Rest one year for wood to age	1.5	8 4	9
Sand Spray three coats 1.5 hrs between coats Rest three days	1.5	8 4	12
Sand Spray three coats 1.5 hrs between coats Rest three days	1.5	8 4	15
Sand Spray two coats 1.5 hrs between coats Rest three days	1.5	8 4	17
Sand Spray two coats 1.5 hrsbetween coats	1.5	12 3	19
Sand Spray one coat	1.5	12 1.5	20
TOTALS	12	100.5	20

Total film thickness	0.032"
Labor cost (if $40/hr)	$4,020
Est. material cost	$1,077
Est. total cost	$5,097

Author's Spray Varnish Procedure
Used on 22' Riva Ariston
(Premium tung oil varnish)

Task	Workdays	Labor	Coats
Apply filler stain (oil based)	1	8	
Spray first coat (thinned); 1 day rest between coats	1	1	1
Prep, spray one coat	1	9	2
Prep, spray one coat	1	9	3
Prep, spray one coat	1	9	4
Prep, spray one coat	1	9	5
Prep, spray one coat	1	9	6
Prep, spray one coat	1	9	7
Prep, spray one coat	1	9	8
Prep, spray one coat	1	9	9
Prep, spray one coat	1	9	10
Prep, spray one coat	1	9	11
Prep, spray one coat	1	9	12
Prep, spray one coat	1	9	13
Prep, spray one coat	1	9	14
Prep, spray one coat	1	9	15
Prep, spray one coat	1	9	16
Prep, spray one coat	1	9	17
Prep, spray one coat	1	9	18
Prep, spray one coat	1	16	19
Prep, spray one coat	1	16	20
TOTALS	21	194	20

Total film thickness	0.030"
Labor cost (if $40/hr)	$8,120
Est. material cost	$816
The author's est. total cost	$8,936

*Labor times for the Riva procedure are estimates based on actual figures for the 28 'Aquarama rapidly enough under ideal conditions to allow two coats per day.)

Table 2 shows a comparison of time and labor costs of a two-part versus a one-part varnish job. The left-hand column reflects the varnish procedure used by Riva to spray-varnish the 28-foot Aquarama. To allow a direct comparison, I have adjusted the labor times that would result if this procedure were used on the smaller 22-foot Ariston. The right-hand column reflects my records and all-too-painful memory of the spray process we used with traditional varnish on our own Ariston. The individual tasks from my refinishing experience are boring and repetitive; they consist of two days of staining and sealing, followed by 20 sessions of sanding, tacking, wiping, and coating; sanding, tacking, wiping, and coating; sanding, tacking, wiping, and coating.... Each of these sessions required nine worker-hours and produced only one coat. During buildup, the Riva process involves an eight-worker-hour session of sanding and cleanup, followed by four hours to spray three successive coats. The average time, then, to spray three coats, is 27 hours for the one-part process and 12 hours for the two-part process.

The total film thicknesses of the processes in Table 2 are the same. The material cost for the two-part varnish is 25 percent more. However, the labor savings produced by the two-part procedure cut the total time in half: 100.5 versus 194 worker-hours. Based on an estimated rate of $40 per hour for labor, the cost savings are almost 45percent! Riva does not cut corners to achieve these results; their process produces an excellent finish.

Because two-part varnishes fail at the varnish/wood interface, not in the coating, all require different surface preparation than the traditional products. To enhance the bond to the surface as much as possible, the wood should be finish-sanded with 80-grit paper (it is absolutely critical to sand with the grain when using grit this coarse), and the first few coats should be heavily thinned, up to 50 percent. Conventional staining or filling of the wood is not recommended, since the common filler stains are oil based and are not compatible with the two-part systems. If applied on top of oil-based fillers, the aggressive solvents in the two-part varnish may loosen the attachment of the filler to the wood; the entire coating may then detach and lift. To solve this problem, Stoppani sells a special two-part filler stain expressly designed to work with their two-part varnish products. This is available in red, but they say it can be tinted by adding dabs of their two-part colored paints.

One must be especially wary of humidity when applying two-part varnishes, because they are more susceptible to moisture blush while curing than are traditional varnishes. The two-part varnishes contain isocyanate, which joins the hydroxyl groups in the polymers together to cure the product. However, since the hydroxyl groups also exist in water vapor, the isocyanate will combine with these if there is excess humidity. The result is a hazy look to the varnish. Apply your varnish early in the day to avoid condensation, and do not varnish indoors on rainy days.

The number of coats recommended varies with the thickness of a coat of the dry varnish film; the products with thicker films generally need fewer coats. The average minimum total coating thickness recommended is .0116 inch two-part with a range of .006 inch to .015 inch. The average number of coats recommended is seven, with a wide range of three to twelve coats depending on the product. It is advantageous to add more than the recommended number of coats. The Riva film finishes at .032 inch, twice the recommended thickness for the product they use.

Two-part varnishes tend to shrink into the grain as they age. The Italians refer to this as "the wood drinking in the varnish." While this description is charming, the condition is not; it leaves an uneven surface that follows the grain of the wood. To avoid this, manufacturers recommend a rest period after the first few coats to allow a complete cure. This rest period may be 30 days or more. After this period, the now stable surface can be sanded level and additional coats can be applied.

Whether one sprays, rolls, or brushes varnish depends mainly on the task at hand. If you need to varnish only small areas, a brush will win every time. However, be aware that the solvents in the two-part products will destroy all foam brushes I know of. Neither should you expect conventional brushes to survive more than six to ten coats. Rollers must be the epoxy-resistant type. If you need to do a large area, such as an entire boat, then spraying may be the best option.

Spraying may seem unattractive because it is an inherently less material-efficient application technique and requires careful health and safety precautions. The varnish must be thinned more, typically 20 percent, than for brush or roller application. This means the amount of solids applied by the spray, for the same wet film thickness, is less than what would be applied by a brush or roller. In addition, only about 55 percent — maybe up to 70 percent with high-volume, low-pressure guns — of the sprayed material will adhere to the surface. The remainder is overspray, and the result is waste.

Although the wasted material is expensive, saving it may not compensate for the additional labor cost of applying the varnish by roller or brush. I found spray applications to be advantageous for our own Riva Ariston restoration. In our case, we found we could apply a coat of varnish to the entire boat and its miscellaneous parts in less than 45 minutes. I estimate that brushing would have added three to four hours to the time to complete each coat. In our case this would have meant that we could have applied only one coat every other day, extending our varnishing task from 22 days to a staggering 44 days! It appears from the Riva Boatyard example (Table 2) that they feel the labor savings outweigh the material waste for boats under 30 feet.

Some two-part varnishes also can be applied by roller. An alternative that may be attractive to owners doing their own work is to apply the base coats, where finish is less critical, by roller and then level the surface by wet-sanding. The final coats can be applied by spray. This approach gives the excellent surface finish of spraying, but reduces the health and safety problems associated with spraying every coat.

Safety

To learn which safety precautions are necessary when using a material, you should ask the manufacturer for the product's Material Safety Data Sheet (MSDS). This sheet should accompany all hazardous substances. It contains vital safety information on the use of the product, expanding on the information printed on the can. The MSDS should advise you whether the material is flammable, toxic to the skin, poisonous if swallowed, or dangerous if inhaled. It should specify the type of respirator required and its NIOSH/MSHA (National Institute for Occupational Safety and Health/Mine Safety and Health Administration) number.

Contrary to the way people often behave, the application of varnishes, and many other marine materials, can be hazardous. Typically, both single- and two-part varnish products are flammable, may pose an explosion risk, are toxic to the skin and eyes, and are unhealthy to inhale. If you are planning to apply any varnish by roller or brush, proper respiratory protection is essential; this is true whether the varnish is single- or two-part. Varnish manufacturers recommend the use of at least a half-face mask with a good organic vapor (black color) cartridge. Goggles, a Tyvek suit, and neoprene gloves are also a good idea. Before using any hazardous product, you should always consult the manufacturer's technical advisors.

If you are planning to spray, a much higher level of protection is necessary. All the urethane varnishes contain free isocyanates, a deadly material. When spraying, this material is atomized and introduced into the air, increasing the respiratory hazard. According to 3M's technical hotline, by the time you can detect this material by smell, you have already exceeded by 200 times the concentration considered safe by OSHA. The manufacturers that recommend spray applica-

tion of the two-part varnishes specify the use of a NIOSH #TC-19C respirator. This is a full-face, positive-pressure, supplied-air unit that is connected to a breathable-rated compressor or air tank.

Like many people reading this chapter, I look ahead to a lifetime of boat-related work. I personally feel it is best to simply buy a good full-face respirator and use it for all projects with hazardous materials. This type of respirator completely encloses the eyes, nose, and mouth. Using additional interchangeable components, the respirator can be configured for positive pressure, self-contained breathing apparatus, or standard cartridge use. While a full-face respirator at about $150 is expensive, I look at the cost as, literally, a lifetime investment.

Recommended Uses

So, where should you use two-part varnish? Good sites are flat areas or parts with rounded edges that experience extensive sunlight exposure or abrasion. Other good prospects are surfaces that are difficult or expensive to varnish, the ones you don't want to revarnish very often. Examples include sailboat toerails, spars, tillers, decks, and cabintops. Uses on powerboats include caprails, cabin sides, decks, gunwales, thwarts, and transoms. Hot-molded, plywood, or cold-molded boats are excellent prospects, because their hulls are rigid and do not expand and contract much. However, two-part varnishes, just like all topside paints, are not recommended for continuous immersion. If they remain underwater for long periods, water will penetrate and the finish will blister.

Two-part varnishes should not be used where a traditional amber-colored coating is desired. All of the two-part varnishes are water-clear, although Stoppani Glasstop is very slightly amber. Using the varnish over oily woods is also a problem. Wiping with solvent to remove the oil from the wood may work, but it is best to experiment on a test piece and to consult the manufacturer.

The stability of the wood structure is a primary criterion for using two-part varnish. The manufacturers do not recommend using the varnish on the sides of batten-seam-planked boats, such as vintage Chris-Craft or Gar Wood runabouts. The two-part varnishes are very hard, and the expansion and contraction of the planks on these boats will crack the finish at the seams. If you have a very stable double-planked hull, however, two-part varnish may work well.

Because two-part varnishes "shrink" with age, they can develop cracks on objects with sharp edges. Therefore, they are not recommended for raised-panel doors and other items with very sharp corners. Their use on intricate detail may also be inadvisable, for the hardness of the coating makes sanding all of that detail for a refresher coat very difficult work. If the joints in any part of the boat are visibly open, then this part is probably going to move too much for the varnish to hold. In this case, either caulk the opening and varnish each side, or glue it tightly together. Poor joints will not be repaired by two-part varnish; in general, the better the condition of the boat, the better two-part varnish will work.

Can you use two-part varnishes over traditional varnish? The solvents in the two-part products are very aggressive and attack the traditional varnish underneath. This can result in the traditional varnish lifting wholesale from the underlying surface, ruining the entire varnish job. Some professional applicators, however, use this combination deliberately. They apply traditional varnish base coats to obtain an amber color and visual "depth," and then topcoat with two-part varnish to obtain a hard and UV-resistant surface. This is a demanding technique that is probably best left to experts, and it may present a difficult maintenance problem in the event of repairs. I personally recommend the approach used by Riva of simply adding extra coats of two-part varnish to give the finish greater depth.

Conversely, some people recommend placing traditional varnish on top of two-part varnish. This gives a traditional look, but at the price of buying back all the yearly maintenance grief of a traditional varnish. I fail to see the logic behind this approach.

Repair

The manufacturers did not agree on the ease of repair of two-part varnish. Some indicated it was more difficult, others felt it was the same as for traditional varnish. The hardness of the varnish is one reason why repairs may be more difficult. However, this hardness also allows repairs to be sanded and blended in with polishing compound, a technique similar to that used on auto paints. Detco suggests the use of 1,500-grit paper followed by 3M's Finesse-It polishing compound. Since the major cause of failure is not in the coating, but at the wood-coating interface, localized delamination of the coating does not mean that the whole surface is worn out. In most cases, localized repair can be made with good results. Of course, all this has to be taken in perspective. If the coating has already lasted five times longer than a conventional varnish, it is overreacting to become too concerned about learning new techniques for minor repairs.

The author wishes to thank Beniamino Fedrighini of Cantieri Riva and Alex Meneghini of Monaco Boat Service for technical advice in compiling the information in this chapter.

Sources
Stoppani
Yacht Systems, Inc.
P.O. Box 71
Marion, MA 02738
508–748–2266

International Paint
2270 Morris Ave.
Union, NJ 07083
800–468–7589

Detco
P.O. Box 1246
Newport Beach, CA 92663
800–845–0023

Epifanes
1218 S.W. First Ave.
Fort Lauderdale, FL 33315
305–467–8325

US Paint
831 South 21 St.
St. Louis, MO 63103
314–621–0525

A Lasting Finish

PROTECTING YOUR PAINT AND VARNISH

by David L. Jackson

A standing joke in the Pacific Northwest, where I live, is that yacht painters use only wet-or-dry sandpaper, prep in the rain, and then paint when the sun briefly shines. Over the years, we've done things with paint and varnish that would make a paint company chemist's hair stand on end. Like varnishing outside in January — of course, we always try to improve the odds by picking a sunny afternoon and adding a little Japan drier and a little Penetrol. Or painting our schooner, *Sophia Christina*, while underway. A rain squall caught us, but it was thankfully brief, and the schooner reached her boat-show destination looking better than when she'd departed.

Though I'm not a professional painter, I've had plenty of experience and several good teachers. The boats coming through our yard, and our own *Sophia Christina*, have also taught me a lot about what goes into a good paint or varnish finish, and what makes that finish last.

Which Paint?

Nowadays, there are numerous choices in paints. Enamels, epoxies, and polyurethanes each have particular benefits and limitations. Epoxies and polyurethanes work well on fiberglass, steel, aluminum, and cold-molded boats, but for traditional wooden boats, give me enamel! Unlike epoxies or polyurethanes, enamel "breathes" and allows the passage of moisture out through the coating of paint. The yearly cycle of renewing an enamel paint surface lets us take care of small problems before they grow into larger ones. There's nothing like going over a surface with sandpaper to really see what's going on; little scratches and dings show up, along with breaches in the paint's surface that are less obvious from 6 feet away. Enamels are also the easiest paints to repair. Feather out the problem area with sandpaper, undercoat any bare wood, and spot in the enamel.

There is a dark side to gloss. A glossy surface reflects imperfections to a greater degree than semigloss or flat. When time or money is no object, gloss enamel has its place. But the surface must be prepared much more thoroughly than for semigloss if the finish is to look good.

For most of us, semigloss enamel is a good compromise. Semigloss is also a good choice for cabin

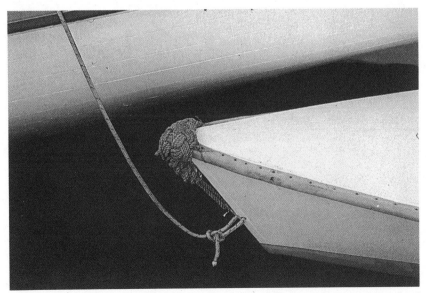

Dinghies and skiffs have a propensity for nuzzling up to their mother ships. The bow "pudding" and gunwale guard on Sophia Christina's *skiff keep the dings and scratches to a minimum on both craft.*

sides and cockpits, where it is significantly less glaring in bright sunlight than a gloss finish would be. The famous brigantine *Varua* has been painted with flat white enamel for the last 48 years. She is an imposing 70 feet on deck, and her flat white topsides give her a no-nonsense air. Of all the choices in paint, flat white enamel is the most forgiving and the easiest to maintain.

Color can play a role in the longevity of a finish. The first few years we had *Sophia Christina* in the water, her bulwark caps were painted medium green. Each summer, the caps would go through daily cycles of heating up during the day and cooling at night. And my beautiful scarf joints — and the paint — were opening right up. I was disconsolate. Finally, I painted the caps white. Guess what? No more problems.

A wooden Sea Sprite ketch in our area received a beautiful linear polyurethane paint job at a local yard. The topsides were the glossiest, purest white you will ever see, and her bulwarks were a deep, glossy green. But within a month, the green paint was peeling back at the plank seams.

Didn't Capt. Nat Herreshoff say that there were only two colors to paint a boat, white or black; and that only a fool would paint a boat black?

Green or black, the point is to avoid using dark colors where they will heat up in the sun. Save that green for the boottop.

Now and then we hear of some crusty old sea captain or master house painter who adds a bit of lamp black or pine tar to his white paint and ends up with the whitest, longest-lasting white. Nobody can figure out if he's a genius or crazy. But perhaps he's a former paint company chemist and knows that the white in paint comes from titanium oxide, a mineral that is mined from the ground, then cleaned, cooked, and bleached to rid it of impurities. Titanium oxide sells for about $1.85 per pound, and a gallon of white paint takes three or four pounds of it. This is one reason why you see very few pure whites on the market; they are too expensive to make.

White, as any painter will tell you, has poor hiding qualities. But the addition of a little lamp black (blue) or iron oxide (yellow) gives the paint more opaqueness and better coverage.

The Varnish/Epoxy Combination

I like to varnish. I even admit it. This is not to say that my varnish work is perfect, or that I always keep ahead of the varnish under my care. But there is something magical about brushing on coat after coat of varnish, each one bringing new depth to the finish and highlighting the subtleties of grain and figure as no other finish can.

I've just been varnishing a set of spars I've made

for a Seattle client. The hollow mast is spruce, and the solid boom and gaff are fir and spruce, respectively. The rest of the fittings are teak, with the exception of the jaws, which are honey locust crooks. I've decided to use an epoxy sealer under the varnish on the spars, both to harden up the relatively soft wood and to seal the end-grain more quickly.

I first heard about using epoxy under varnish from Denise Wilk, a finisher who has kept *Dorade* and *Courageous* in beautiful shape for years. The principle is simple: Use epoxy for the first three coats, then follow with four or more coats of varnish to build the finish and protect the epoxy from ultraviolet degradation. In practice, it's a bit more difficult. Epoxy doesn't flow like varnish. Nor will it sand as easily as varnish. With patience, however, you can use epoxy to fill large and small cracks, splits, end-grain, and crevices, leaving a smooth, hard surface that will hold varnish better than varnish itself.

Patience is the key word here. To fill end-grain or cracks, you have to allow the epoxy to soak in. It's a process that takes time. Whenever possible, I work with gravity, applying a bead of epoxy to the crack, then doing something else for 10 minutes until the epoxy settles in and I can add some more. I keep working the epoxy in and let it settle until the crack is full, usually within the hour.

Clean and careful work is vitally important with epoxy. The final finish must be considered from the very start. Drips or runs (or epoxy on adjoining surfaces) are easily cleaned up with alcohol before the epoxy hardens. But once the epoxy sets, the job becomes much more labor intensive.

Varnish, on the other hand, takes a sure, quick hand. Varnish is laid on once and brushed out very little. It cures by the evaporation of its solvents and usually starts to tack within 15 minutes of application. The trick is to carefully lay on enough varnish to cover the first time, avoiding drips, runs, and sags. The latter problems can be worked out of the job if caught soon enough, so good light and constant vigilance are important. I continually look down the spar, moving the light to catch drips and runs as well as "holidays." A light sanding between coats is useful, mostly to provide contrast between the light sanded finish and the fresh varnish. But on the early coats, I sometimes skip sanding in order to get a higher build with fewer coats, especially if I am recoating within 24 hours.

On this set new of spars, we're using varnish without epoxy for the teak and locust pieces. Epoxy takes longer than varnish to set up sufficiently to sand back, and it cannot give as smooth a finish. I felt that the spars deserved the extra time, but the 26 other pieces in teak and locust did not. They are being varnished separately and are coated on all sides to protect the wood, even on surfaces that will be bedded. (An unsealed wood surface will leach the oil out of bedding compound, drying it out so that it fails.)

After five coats of varnish, all the parts will be lightly sanded and bedded, and screwed into their respective places. They have been previously fitted and temporarily fastened in place so that all the fastening holes have been drilled. Once the excess bedding compound is cleaned off the spars, they will receive two more coats of varnish. The finish is now fussier, since each fitting becomes a perfect place for a run or drip to start. Once the varnishing is done, in the best of all possible worlds, the spars should be left hanging in the shop for two weeks to harden up and fully cure, giving them a tougher finish less likely to be scratched in moving and setting up.

Here are some things to consider when varnishing. Use a paint strainer to filter the varnish into a separate container. This not only filters the varnish, but also allows you to close up the varnish can soon after opening and prevents contamination of the unused varnish. Never pour leftover varnish back into the can. (If I have varnish left over and will be varnishing again soon, I just stretch one of my disposable gloves over the container as a temporary cover.) In cold weather, add a little Japan drier to speed the drying time. If you feel the brush drying, or if there is any wind, add a little Penetrol to improve the brushability of the varnish. Finally, always work clean: latex gloves, clean brushes, tack rags, and a clean work area.

Proper Bedding

The first rule in protecting your finish is always to bed anything that is exposed to weather. Use more bedding compound than you think you need, ensuring a good squeeze-out all around. Bedding compound is cheaper than fixing the damage done by leaks. While I am on my soapbox, let me tell you about my favorite bedding compound, Dolfinite 2005, which comes in white, mahogany, or neutral. According to John Gardner, this stuff has been the industry standard for 50 years. It's slightly thicker than it used to be, and the manufacturers have removed pentachlorophenol from the formula, but that is just as well because I always worried about working with something containing the toxic penta. As long as you keep the water out, you don't have to be concerned about fungus.

Dolfinite is not an adhesive, I hear you saying, and you are right — to a point. But the longer I am in business, the more I realize that boats need to be built so that they can be taken apart. I remember having to pull out a breasthook that was bedded in Dolfinite. I removed all the fastenings, grabbed the breasthook firmly, and gave it a pull. Nothing happened. I looked for other fastenings and found none. Finally, I used a thin hardwood wedge and a mallet, gave her a tap, and the breasthook fell out in my hand. Try that with your polyurethanes.

While working as a surveyor, I supervised repairs on a 1972 Alaskan 55. The previous owner had reportedly sunk $180,000 into a new superstructure; soft wood had been replaced, and the superstructure was completely repainted with linear polyurethane. From a distance, it looked beautiful. Unfortunately, the yard hadn't bedded the quarter-round molding sufficiently at the house-to-deck joint. Guess what happened? Water got behind the molding and then behind the paint. That beautiful, expensive paint job started to unravel from the bottom up.

Remove all molding and hardware before you paint or varnish. This enables the paint or varnish to seal beneath them. Then re-bed the moldings and hardware thoroughly to doubly protect your finish from water intrusion. Remember, water is insidious. It is led by gravity, but it can wick under a finish, too. Seams exposed to weather need all the help they can get against the harsh marine environment. A boatbuilder I worked for in Maine years ago told me, "Give me your best work; it will be just good enough." Keep this in mind if you want your finishes to last.

A Repair in Time...

Touch up small problems before they grow and multiply. Part of my normal cruising gear aboard *Sophia Christina* includes a paint locker stocked with brushes, disposable latex gloves, 16-oz paint buckets, paint filters, sandpaper, glazing compounds, a putty knife, undercoater, gloss and semigloss white enamel, boottop and trim paint, varnish, varnish thinner, Penetrol, Japan drier, rags, and tack rags.

This spring, we'll be scraping down *Sophia*'s guards to bare wood, to rebuild the finish. Our other project will be to bring the booms and gaffs to the shop for their biannual paint job. Since they have the protection of sail covers, their paint lasts about two years — but then it's time to give them a careful looking over, anyway.

When too much paint has built up after years of accumulation, remove the finish by scraping, grinding, or using a heat gun. Taking the finish down to bare wood will give you a better look at what's going on underneath, and will also give you a better surface to finish. Any cracking in a finish acts exactly like an open joint in the wood itself. Subsequent coats of paint or vanish cannot bridge or seal the crack, water gets in, and the finish deteriorates further.

In the marine environment, oxides and salt deposits can build up rather quickly on a finish. When repairing paint or varnish that's six months to a year old, I

Sophia's spring lines chafe against the guard as they run toward the dock. Installing some bronze half-oval strips here is on the list of spring projects.

Leather is easily worked and can be used to good advantage as chafing gear. Here it's used to protect the boom crutch, while half-oval strips are used to protect the boom itself.

Tying this jib sheet bullet block to a deadeye lanyard keeps it from flailing about.

first scrub it down with TSP (trisodium phosphate) and warm water, using Scotch Brite pads and wearing rubber gloves. This cleans the surface and scrubs away the top layer of oxidized finish. The next step involves using a sharp scraper and a sharp file to mercilessly remove any flaking, cracking, or abraded paint. Then sandpaper is well laid on to feather the edges of the different layers of paint. Once the surface is prepared, the finish should go on.

Don't wait for days to paint after you sand. A freshly prepared surface will hold the finish better than one that has been allowed to age. If you have to wait, give the work another sanding and dusting before layering on the paint or varnish. Schedule the work and keep to it until all coats are on and you have your desired finish, whether it's two coats of flat white on *Varua*, or a highly developed gloss finish on *Whitefin*.

Protection from Salt and Sun

Salt spray is corrosive. Morning dew contains fine dust particles. Both, over time, can degrade a varnished finish. This is a good reason to wipe the varnish dry first thing in the morning and to thoroughly wash down your vessel at the end of each cruise.

With varnish, those who are truly fastidious always varnish twice a year or have a boathouse and/or full winter covers. The rest of us can resort to waxing our varnish to give it a little extra protection. Just follow the directions on the can of your favorite wax.

Professional finisher Rebecca Wittman once remarked that a full cover can extend the life of varnish markedly, and that over the five- to ten-year period the canvas lasts, the cover will more than pay for itself in the time and money saved finishing and refinishing. Special covers can be made to protect varnished hatches, skylights, masts, caps, or handrails from the degrading effect of ultraviolet light, as well as from the sandblasting effect of wind and rain. My friends Bill and Jane Brodle have a wooden Lapworth 36 with a canvas cover that extends from the cockpit to the foredeck, completely covering the varnished cabin like a sock. Like most of us, Bill and Jane would rather cruise than varnish.

Protection from Chafe

Chafe is obvious and direct. It can come from mainsheets, spring lines, fender lines, etc. Chafe can slowly wear through your finish and — in extreme cases — through the wood itself.

Sophia Christina's mainsheet, when controlled from the cockpit, runs over the varnished locust coaming cap. Early on, we realized that the varnish was being rubbed away at the starboard quarter, and I decided to make up and install a curved piece of bronze half-oval as a chafing strip.

Chocks aboard *Sophia Christina* help organize the mooring lines and protect the surrounding finish from harm. We have three cast-bronze chocks on each side, set in the bulwarks. The forward and after mooring lines, as well as the breast line, leave *Sophia* without rubbing on the paint. The spring lines, however, chafe along the guard as they run diagonally toward the dock. What's needed is the extra protection of bronze half-oval strips outside the guard — in this case, a piece ¾ inch by 20 feet on each side, bedded and screwed every 6 inches or so. That's another project for this spring.

Blocks on deck are another potential problem for the finish. For the jib sheets, we use bullet blocks shackled into fittings at the bulwarks. The very first time we came about under sail, these poor blocks began to flail the deck as if the jib were trying to beat the deck into submission. We quickly got out the seine twine and tied the blocks to to the deadeye lanyards. No more flailing blocks. If you don't have something convenient to tie the blocks to, a rope deck mat will provide protection. Another expedient to keep your blocks upright is a large spring between the deck and the block. Neoprene-shelled blocks are available from South Coast and Nicro Fico and are less abusive to the surrounding deck than any other block I've seen.

Protection from Bumps

On the second day of a sail-training week I was running aboard *Sophia*, the crew was starting to learn all of the sheets, topping lifts, vangs, and halyards needed to run a gaff schooner, and we had gone through the drills: fire, man overboard, and safety. We were coming into the dock in Friday Harbor after a fine sail from our anchorage at Clark Island, passing through the scenic San Juan Islands. Fenders and lines were rigged on deck by the crew for a port-side landing. Dock space was tight, with a big, black seiner aft, 70 feet of open dock, then an expensive-looking 50-foot white motoryacht forward. Everyone on board knew that we would have to squeeze 62 feet of *Sophia* into her berth between. I was concentrating on the busy harbor traffic and the imminent task of docking. I neglected to check the deck. (Well... it was blowing an afternoon gale.) I brought *Sophia* in hard, knowing she'd back to port. I gave her full reverse to bring in the stern and stop her way just short of the white yacht. I was counting on the fenders doing their job of protecting the topsides. When I stepped onto the dock to tie her down, I noticed that the fenders were still on deck. I was furious with myself, and embarrassed, even though *Sophia* had received only a small scratch.

But there are times when fenders by themselves, even when hanging properly over the side of the boat,

Sophia Christina's bowsprit and foredeck receive the protection of ¼-inch bronze plate armor in way of the anchor and chain. Her sampson post (not shown) has a cast-bronze cap to protect the locust end-grain and shed water.

A bronze half-oval strip protects the varnish on the honey locust crook of the cockpit coaming cap.

Fenders are doing their job here at the dock, while a cast-bronze chock protects the finish from the forward mooring line. When this photo was taken, Sophia's bulwark caps were still dark green and having trouble holding their paint. Repainting them white was the solution.

don't provide enough protection, such as when you need to make fast to dock pilings instead of to a float. What you need then is a fender board.

A fender board is easy to make, requiring only a hardwood plank and two lines. Ours is made from a native honey locust plank, 10 feet long, 8 inches wide, and ⅞ inch thick. It is well rounded at the ends and radiused all around, including the holes bored for the mounting lines. Using the fender board is simplicity itself. Put out the fenders, hang the fender board outside the fenders, and come alongside the piling and make fast. No wooden boat should be without one.

Sophia needs some protection from scratches and dings as my children, friends, and clients learn the art of tending the skiff or as they bring the smaller boat alongside after a trip to the beach. (The skiff bow and gunwales also need something more forgiving than hardwood when they come in to contact with *Sophia*'s transom or topsides.) Our skiff has a canvas-covered strip of rubber around her sheer (sold commercially

by the foot) and an elegant rope bow "pudding" (made by rigger Brion Toss) at the bow. I've also seen dinghy gunwales protected by a rope hawser stretched around the sheer, laced or screwed into a cove molding. This seems to work well, too.

Smaller boats have their own needs when it comes to protecting their finishes. A skiff that gets hauled up on the beach needs protection on its bottom. This can be as simple as oak half-rounds at the run of the bilge, and another strip of oak along the bottom of the keel. Or bronze runners can be added to the bottom. These strips should be considered sacrificial; at some point they'll need to be replaced.

You'll undoubtedly run into opinions that differ somewhat from those I have offered. But as you enjoy your boat, remember to notice what's going on with her finish and, in timely fashion, take care of it. The finish is the first line of defense in protecting the wood from the elements. It's easier to maintain a finish than to strip and rebuild it. And it's easier to paint than it is to replace wood.

Mast Protection

by Dan Conner

The two more common methods of wooden mast protection are varnishing and painting, in that order. Both use identical techniques and require spending a few days aloft each year for mast maintenance. Should you own a medium-sized ketch, you could easily spend a week or more each year in a bosun's chair, depending on how many coats of paint or varnish you wanted. To say that is a comfortable way to spend a few days is naive. It is, literally, a pain in the butt. Plenty of articles have been written on safety aloft. What I am concerned with here is trying to be as efficient and comfortable as possible while you get a good coat of protection on your sticks.

Let's consider the mast itself. If the varnish has lost its luster or rich appearance, it is time for a coat. If it is flat and dull, it is past due for a coat. If it has a good percentage of scrapes or dings, it is time for you to make a personal appearance at the masthead.

Preparations

Staying as comfortable as possible will stall fatigue and have a positive effect on your work. First, use a chair with a board in its bottom; a sling type chair will begin to pinch your legs after a few hours. Dehydration can be a problem as you work, because it is a long way to the water fountain. I fill and take a traveling glass with a good tight lid. You will work better if you are sharp and refreshed.

Use drop cloths whenever possible. Near the top, it's the three boats next to you that will need covers,

so think of them. Down near the deck or in still air, it will be your own nice teak decks that you will be dripping varnish on.

It will help things stay clean if you use a pot in a pail. Tie a pail to the bosun's chair at a height easy to reach in and dip out of. Now put your varnish pot inside the pail and place rags around it so it can't rattle about. Dipping and cleaning off your brush will now be done inside the pail and out of the wind. This will reduce the amount of varnish that is blown off your brush.

As you sand down the mast initially, wipe each section free of dust with a rag before moving your position on the mast. This will eliminate "sanding holidays." Make note of any bad or bare spots. Then, after cleaning your way up with a tack rag, touch up the bare spots, sealing the bare wood on the mast as you come down for the day. Always try to seal up what you have sanded bare each day before quitting.

Cleaning, Tacking, and Varnishing

The next day clean your way up the mast with a light solvent. This is an especially important step if the boat has stood in a sea breeze and collected a film of salt overnight. Sand the touch-up spots as you come down. Now tack your way up and varnish your way back down, using the largest brush you can handle. Use the varnish (or paint) straight from the can, or as thick as possible. The finish on the upper sections is not visible from deck, so don't worry about brush strokes or laps. When you get to the lower spreaders, stop and come down. In hot weather the varnish may have thickened, so freshen it up or doctor it as you feel necessary to achieve a nice finish coat from now on. You need to do this, because this stage will carry you all the way down to the deck and the results will be seen.

Use a tack rag and clean your way up to the point where you left off and start varnishing your way back down. I usually do a section by starting just as high as I can reach and work my way down to just above my knees. I allow my knees to bump the mast to steady me. This gives me maximum working range and lessens the risk of having a large wake from a pasing boat bump me back into my own work. If you have a helper with you working the halyard, he must stay right with you during the lower portion of the mast to minimize the laps and to help spot for holidays.

You should get out of the chair as soon as you're down to a point that can be reached from the deck. Your work will be better as soon as you have gained the deck and can move freely without having to hang on. If the lower part of the mast is cluttered with winches and cleats, it is good to have a competent varnisher as a helper here, so you can split work, each working half the mast. Around the bottom, a small brush will be very handy to help get in and around cleats and other fittings.

A problem area on wooden masts is around the sail track. Varnish or paint doesn't seem to want to stick here as well as we would hope, probably due to the difficulty of sanding or cleaning properly. Care must be taken to get a heavy coating here without covering the track itself. You don't want the sail to jam halfway down the mast the next time you go for a sail.

Now, if you have all that down, all you have to worry about is if it's going to rain later, or if it's too windy, or hot, or humid, or if the stars are properly aligned, or all those other variables that make boating an art and not a science.

Arabol

———— by Dean Stephens ————

Since the end of the 1950s, boatbuilding, like everything else, has experienced the magic of chemistry. It has become possible to build a boat from stuff that comes in a can. In the old days, our goops and gunks were mixed in the boatyard from obscure recipes that involved creosote, coal tar, tallow, and white and red lead mixed with linseed oil for paying, luting, bedding, and slushing. We added poisons to bottom paint, and probably poisoned ourselves in the process. All of this has become unacceptable in terms of human health and the environment, but now we're addicted to resins and thiokols and epoxies and silicones. I sometimes wonder how the old-timers managed so well without today's sophisticated chemistry. Some of us in the trade have become specialists with the new products that were developed by chemists. But the product I want to talk about here comes from a cow.

It's known as arabol and is made from milk. Arabol is a latex-type adhesive that has the appearance and odor of Elmer's white glue, but differs from Elmer's in that it contains other ingredients that make it insoluble after curing. It was originally formulated for use as an adhesive for lagging. For those of you not familiar with the term "lagging," it is the insulation covering on exposed steam and hot-water pipes in plants, on board ships, and on basement heating equipment in lots of public buildings. Before arabol, wheat paste was used to hold this insulation in place.

A number of years ago, arabol found its way out of the basement and onto boats. I first saw it on a boat many years ago and talked with a fisherman who had used it to glue down canvas on a hopelessly leaking deck. He praised the results. Over the past 25 years, I've used it myself when replacing old canvas decks that had been laid in white lead, and on new decks and houses that specified a covering of canvas.

Advantages and Disadvantages

There are a number of advantages to choosing arabol instead of paint or white lead for a canvas-covered deck or house. First, it lasts longer. Anyone who has ever had to replace a canvas deck the old-fashioned way knows what a tedious job it is and doesn't relish removing the hardware, bitts, blocks, cleats, moldings, and coamings more than once in a boat's lifetime. Next, arabol is cheap. It can be recoated countless times and built up over the years without peeling, checking, or flaking. When arabol becomes grubby-looking, you can scrub it with soap and water and brush on a new coat.

Arabol wears well and is virtually scuff proof. Nonskid compounds or sand can be either mixed into it or dusted onto a fresh coat while it is curing. When used with a cotton fabric such as duck, canvas, or muslin, arabol shrinks the material and makes it drum-tight. Arabol can be used with fiberglass cloth or even burlap. It can be colored with the tinting colors you get at a paint store. It is safer health-wise than white lead or red lead, and though warnings on the label indicate it contains chemicals that should not be breathed over a prolonged period in a confined, unventilated area, this is easy to control. You can clean up tools and drips and spills with water before the arabol cures (but after curing, it's there to stay). Finally, it is almost impossible to get a bad-looking job with arabol.

There are a couple of disadvantages that the user should know about and accommodate: Arabol is corrosive to iron or galvanized fastenings, and it will turn copper alloys green. Therefore, any metal fastening should be countersunk well below the surface and plugged or puttied so that the arabol does not come into contact with it. Otherwise, corrosion will bleed up through to the surface and show as a permanent stain.

Application

Because arabol creates such a good sealed surface, it should be used on dry wood — any moisture trapped beneath it will stay wet and could cause rot. To reduce the possibilities of rot, I generally brush on a couple of coats of Cuprinol (copper naphthenate) and then prime over the Cuprinol with two coats of a good metal primer or flat oil-based paint.

As with other surface coatings, careful and meticulous preparations are imperative when using arabol. Dings, dents, and cracks telegraph through to the surface, so do your best to get rid of them so you can begin the job with a smooth surface. Where necessary, remove toerails, moldings, trim, and hardware. Seal off your fastenings, and prime, as I've discussed above, if you think it's necessary. Then, on the dry surface, lay out your fabric. If your surface is smooth, you needn't use a heavy fabric. (I used arabol and cotton muslin to re-deck a 28-foot sloop, and it is still in service and looking fine after 25 years.) You needn't be concerned about creases or wrinkles at this point. If seams are necessary, they look best running fore and aft. Use tape or temporary staples to hold the fabric in place.

Wear gloves when you work with arabol; after it begins to cure, it doesn't wash off. It is essential to work rapidly and coat only a foot or two ahead of yourself. I cannot stress enough the importance of limiting your area of progress to no more than 2 ½ square feet at a time. Start by folding back the fabric about 3 feet at the point where you are beginning, and with a wide brush paint on a heavy coat of arabol to a section of deck. Then re-lay the folded material on the wet adhesive and smooth it with a wiping motion, using your gloved hands. Do not spread more adhesive than can be easily covered by the fabric and smoothed out while the adhesive is still wet.

After the fabric has been smoothed into the arabol, it can be easily and neatly trimmed at the edges with a sharp utility knife, while the adhesive is still uncured.

Depending on the density of the fabric, the next coat of arabol may need to be thinned with a little water so that the application penetrates the fabric and saturates it thoroughly. Do not add too much water. By the following day, the surface will be cured and ready for another full coat, this time without thinning.

Since I make the next coat nonskid, at this point I usually mask the covering boards and mask to create a border around the deckhouses, sampson posts, and sometimes around blocks and cleats to keep those areas smooth in appearance. Then I brush on a full, heavy coat of arabol and sprinkle it with a liberal amount of clean, dry beach sand or plasterer's sand. In 24 hours, the excess sand can be swept off, the masking removed, and another full coat of arabol brushed on over the nonskid. You can tint this final coat for a colored deck.

That's it for the arabol part. Now comes the job of reinstalling the trim and hardware. Maybe for the last time?

Arabol can be found in industrial and plumbing supply stores and some marine chandlers. It is now made by National Starch and Chemical Corporation, Finderme Ave., Bridgewater, NJ 08807; (201-685-5000). In past years, it has been packaged under several labels for marine use (such as Thorpe's Easy Deck), but it's still easily available from National Starch, which labels it "made for lagging." It's fine stuff for boats, too.

Maintenance with Meaning

—— An Interview with Giffy Full ——

Giffy Full, perhaps the best-known surveyor of wooden boats on the East Coast, grew up around the boats and yachts of Marblehead Harbor. He was for many years a professional skipper; his first commission was the 65-foot Alden schooner Escapade, *when he was only 19 years old. Since then, he has cared for a lot of boats, built a few, and surveyed an untold number. His advice is based on cold, hard experience.*

Brightwork

WoodenBoat: *Let's talk about maintaining varnished surfaces. Assume a varnish finish is so far gone that it would require wooding down. How do you go about doing it?*

Giffy Full: The trouble is that I'm awfully old-fashioned. Most people really don't know how to use some of these good hand tools anymore. If I were doing a really nice boat, she'd never be scraped with anything but a cabinet scraper with a rolled edge.

WB: *Do you roll the edge to take the old varnish off, or do you just roll it when you're scraping the wood after the varnish has been removed?*

GF: Both. I roll it all the way. The edge lasts longer, too, and a lot of times when you get used to a scraper, you can wipe it a couple of times with a burnisher and keep the edge going. It takes quite a

Well organized, as is his custom, Giffy carries his painting and refinishing tools in a beautifully varnished box with an inlaid top and a removable tray (shown in the foreground). The brushes are normally kept dust-free inside individual plastic bags. Other items carried in the box include an assortment of scrapers, and a burnisher and a file for sharpening them, putty knives and sanding blocks of different sizes, seam reefing hooks, and a waterline scriber.

bit of practice to learn how to sharpen one of the things, and you can get cut doing it, too. But a properly sharpened cabinet scraper is really the only way to do a nice job. When I used to maintain a lot of yachts, I made up a whole box of different-shaped scrapers. I remember one winter I got a bug in my head that the main cabin beams of a yacht I was skippering would look nice scraped down and varnished. I scraped a lot of paint off all those beams with paint remover and several specially shaped cabinet scrapers.

WB: *Tell us about bleaching and staining.*

GF: Well, some things have changed. There are some new two-part bleaches out now that I think are much better than oxalic acid, which you have to mix yourself and which turns the wood pinkish if you mix it too strong.

WB: *Do you do the finish sanding before or after bleaching?*

GF: You want to bleach first, just after stripping the woodwork.

WB: *But if you sand after bleaching, won't you sand right through the bleached wood?*

GF: You're only bleaching to get out the black spots around joints and bungs. You're not bleaching to change the color of the wood, and you want to destroy as little as possible of the wood's natural color.

WB: *Do you ever spot-bleach?*
GF: No, you've got to bleach the whole surface. I saw one guy spot it like that, and I even warned him not to do it, but he wouldn't listen. When the boat came out, she looked like a leopard. Every square inch of the piece has to be bleached, or else it's going to come out all different colors. Sometimes you do have to concentrate on weathered areas by going back and wetting out a place more than once.

WB: *If you hit a weathered area — the worst case would probably be blackened oak — where water has reached it, do you scrape out as much of it as you can?*
GF: You've got to take off at least a shaving, because after a few years of exposure, that 1/32 inch or so on top is sort of dead. What I'd probably do in a situation like that is bleach those bad places first, and then bleach the whole works. Then sand after bleaching with a sanding block — a good white-pine sanding block for flat surfaces. I remember when the *Canterbury Belle* was being built, a guy by the name of Jimmy McFarland from South Bristol joined her off. When he was through planing her, he traversed her with nothing more than coarse sandpaper over a piece of 2 by 3 board. She didn't have a ripple in her anywhere when he was through. If you don't get a good, flat surface on her, you can't get a good finish on her either. You take a poor piece of finish work, and you can put all the stain or varnish you want on her, but it'll show right up.

For places that aren't flat, you want to use sponge-rubber pads. Not a hard-rubber block, like those commercial sanding blocks that you stick the sandpaper in the ends of; that's a bunch of crap. You need those Ensolite pads, which are more flexible, and fold half a sheet of sandpaper around them. They work beautifully, especially on a rail cap. It's important to do your scraping and sanding with the grain of the wood. Sometimes even at professional yards you'll see poor finishes caused by cross scraping, especially from careless work around portholes and fittings.

But scraping and bleaching brings up something interesting. Few people realize how strong the sun is. I remember a steering wheel that I stripped years ago. I had to bleach it, and I probably used a little too much oxalic acid, because when I varnished it, it had a pink hue. The owner was pretty upset, and I told him just to put it back aboard the boat and leave it for two or three weeks. He thought I was crazy, but I said I'd do it all over for nothing if the

sun didn't bring back the wood's natural color. Sure enough, in a couple of weeks, all the pink was gone right out of it.

Same with new teak. If you varnish a brand-new teak deckhouse or trunk cabin on a yacht, the wood is dark-looking as hell, but after it's out in the sun for a month, it turns a beautiful golden color. Look at some varnished transoms where the name has been changed. You can see the original name bleached right into the stern. Behind the old lettering, the wood did not fade since the sun did not get to it. To get rid of an old name, you have to do a lot of bleaching on the stern of a boat, and usually you wind up having to put on a light stain to be completely effective.

WB: *Do you use stains for the rest of the brightwork?*
GF: I don't like stains. In fact on my own boat I replaced the trim moldings with teak so I wouldn't have to stain them. It depends on the kind of wood you're using. If you're using Philippine mahogany, you'll usually have to stain it, unless it really has good natural color. You shouldn't have to stain Honduras mahogany at all.

WB: *What would be best if a fellow were going to stain? One of the paste filler-stains?*
GF: Pastes work well. There are liquid stains, too, but they don't fill the grain at the same time.

WB: *What are your recommendations for putties and seam fillers for varnish work?*
GF: That's a difficult question. The materials that will cover up a joint or seam won't seal it, and those that will seal it are really difficult to varnish over. We used to make our own sealers from white lead years ago, but nowadays we seem to use mostly prepared products. People don't know how to mix colors from scratch anymore, or how to color putty to fill a seam. There are the mahogany bedding compounds, but they're no good for filler as they're too flexible. You can take straight putty and color that. Trowel cement can also be colored, but it's too brittle for joints. If it were up to me, I'd take straight putty and color it, mixing my own colors with tubes of tinting oil. The best way to do that is to take a little of the mix with your finger and spread it on a piece of glass; then turn the glass over to look at it. If you have the time, it's fun to mix your own colors.

WB: *When you are varnishing, what do you put on for a first coat over bare wood if you're not using a stain?*
GF: I use Clear Sealer 1026, which is made by International Paint. Petit and other companies make sealers like that, too.

WB: *What grit sandpaper do you use after the sealer?*
GF: You don't need anything coarser than 150-grit. As soon as you get a coat of varnish on the surface, 180-grit is about right. All you want to do is knock the gloss off the surface for the next coat of varnish.

WB: *What type of varnish do you like to use?*
GF: I've had good luck with Interlux 98, which contains phenolic resin. I don't know what that is, but I do know that my boat, *Caribou*, was overboard and uncovered all last winter, and the varnish lifted only in one place. That was where the water ran down from her pilothouse windows and somehow got under the half-round rail. I don't think I have enough bedding under the rail.

The other varnish that's really good is Z-Spar Captain's Varnish 1015. Nobody sells Vitalux around here anymore. I used to have very good luck with that varnish, but a lot of yards got into trouble with bad batches. Sometimes when varnish dries flat, without gloss, a "bad batch" is thought to be the cause, when it really isn't that at all. Most people know that varnish applied too late in the day will go flat from the dew. But I've also learned that kerosene fumes will flatten varnish. When I bought *Caribou*, I stripped the brightwork in her cabin one winter. I had one of these Aladdin kerosene heaters going to keep things warm, and after carefully putting on a good coat of varnish one day and expecting to see it dry and shiny the next, I found it was

Giffy finds through experience that flat-plate cabinet scrapers are best by far when it comes to stripping down old paint or varnish. The steel from old bandsaw or hacksaw blades is good if you make your own scrapers from scratch, or you can buy rectangular cabinet scraper blades at almost any hardware store and grind them to suit whatever shape fits the job at hand. Wooden holders, of which four are shown here, are easily made, and make the scrapers easier to hold and control. Those ever-ready sharpening tools — the mill file and the burnisher — are shown here as well.

flatter than hell the next morning. I had to do the job all over again, and this time I used an electric heater. The varnish came out beautifully.

Dust in varnish is also a problem. I've learned after many years of being around boatyards that most of the workers are not very fussy. I never put *Canterbury Belle*'s final coat on in the yard. I'd get her all sanded, put her overboard, and then I'd wash her and tack her down. I would give her a gorgeous varnish job out there on the mooring, away from all the dust and dirt. There's a big difference between living here in Marblehead and living in Maine, believe it or not. I can go out on my boat right now, and find her streaked down her topsides, and dirty on her housetop from industrial soot; but I could leave her in East Boothbay for months and there wouldn't be any dirt on her.

WB: *Do you add anything to varnish?*

GF: Never. The only thing I've ever added to varnish in my life was turpentine as a thinner for the first coat, and that was years ago before we had sealers.

WB: *What else do you do about dust before you varnish?*
GF: There are no tricks that will work if you're in a dirty boatyard. I remember one year I had just put the finish coat on a boat. She had nice caprails, and I had her all covered over with a big dust cloth tied off clear. We wet the ground down, and I washed her and chamoised her and tack-ragged her and wiped her down with white gasoline. I got a nice coat on her and then came in the next morning to find that a God-damned cat had walked the whole length of those caprails, even right up around the bow. I damn near died! That's why I now wait to get a boat out on a mooring before varnishing. You can do all the build-up in the yard, but the finish coat is the one that counts. Another thing to remember is to always paint your housetops last, because it's twice as easy to cut paint against varnish than it is to cut varnish around paint.

WB: *Do you use store-bought tack rags, or do you make your own?*
GF: I buy them. They didn't know what tack rags were in this part of the world until I brought some back from someplace down south. Nobody ever used tack rags on boats 25 or 30 years ago. Then I found some at an automobile place here and bought a box — pretty soon everybody was using them. The funny thing about it is that even now most people don't know how to use a tack rag and end up wasting a lot of it. It comes folded like a handkerchief. They'll use one side, then the other — but you can open the rag up much bigger and keep turning it over. I've seen more guys around boatyards that will just use one side, then the other, and then throw the rag away.

The best thing to do is to have the boat totally prepared, and just wash her with a hose and a clean sponge, no soap, and if it's a good warm, sunny day, by nine that boat's dry enough to start right in varnishing.

WB: *Do you tack all of the surfaces to be varnished one at a time, or do it as you go along?*
GF: I tack it all down once, then do it again bit by bit as I go along. I can remember putting a mid-season coat of varnish on a boat here when it was

unbelievably hot. You could put your hands on her rails, and they were so hot you could raise a blister. We went along ahead of the varnisher and washed her down with water to cool her rails down.

WB: *What type of brushes do you favor for varnishing and painting?*
GF: The best brushes I've seen yet are those by Hamilton. I had a pair of them years ago, and I still have one of them today. There's not much of it left, though. Now I've invested in a set.

WB: *When you say a "set," what sizes do you mean?*
GF: I bought three sizes of the oval type. I don't care for flat brushes. I use the ovals for everything — varnish, paint, everything. The 3½-inch Hamilton brush is too big for average use. The 1-, 2-, and 2½-inch sizes are perfect. And I keep two sizes going right along with me when I'm varnishing.

WB: *How do you take care of your brushes?*
GF: I always keep my varnish brushes in raw linseed oil, cleaned out first. I don't use turpentine, though. I used to keep paint brushes hanging in buckets filled with linseed oil, too, but for the last several years I've just cleaned them in No. 2 fuel oil — not kerosene, but household heating oil or diesel oil. I shake them out lightly and put them in a plastic bag. They stay nice and soft and dust free. I wouldn't clean anything in gasoline. It's dangerous stuff. I know a fellow who lost his house completely from washing out brushes in gasoline, and he got badly burned doing it, too. He'd just painted the last coat on his brand-new house and washed the brushes out in gasoline. He shook them out in the field, then figured he'd better burn off the gas in case someone came by smoking, so he stood back and threw a match into the grass and — Boom! — off she went. When he walked back near the house to pick up the can of gasoline, the fumes from the fire followed him right back and the can went off all over him.

WB: *How many coats of varnish do you apply to build up a surface?*
GF: Less than five coats over bare wood and you're wasting your time, because by July, here, a poor build-up will develop bare spots. Actually, no matter what has been done in the spring, there isn't a single boat that shouldn't have another coat of varnish in the summer.

You'd be amazed how many jobs I've seen where people spend $3,000 to have the brightwork refinished in the spring, but they won't put a coat of varnish on in the middle of July, so by the fall the finish is half gone. Once the wood underneath starts to weather,

you've lost it — except for teak, that is.

Now, there are things you can do to teak that you can't do to any other wood in touching up. All you have to do is take wet-and-dry sandpaper to it, dry it, and then hit it with one coat of boiled linseed oil with a touch of Japan drier in it. Then you can build it back up with varnish to a good finish. I've had some boats that got water in the joints of the rail; the water freezes in the winter, pushing the varnish right off. You just need to knock off the loose stuff, then the wet-and-dry sandpaper will feather it off perfectly. You might start off with 100-grit, then maybe go to 120, and of course finish-sand it afterwards. The linseed oil, used next, evens up the color. If the patched-in area sets out in the sun for two weeks after varnishing, you won't be able to find it.

But that won't work on mahogany, because the color changes too much. All you can do is screw around with it. The production fiberglass boats are using teak trim, but to me the builders are not getting the most from it, because they're using it in name only; there's no finishing. They just run the teak through one of those big belt gang sanders, and give it a coat of mustache wax, and the boat's all ready for delivery. They're saving labor, but the appearance suffers.

WB: *When you get up to about the third or fourth coat of varnish you're apt to get an orange-peel appearance. Do you have to hit that with a coarser grit to get the finish looking even?*
GF: Sandpaper backed up by Ensolite rubber pads will knock it down. I use them for both varnish and paint. I was working in Florida where they were using rubber pads, and I didn't have to work with one of them 15 minutes before I could see that sandpaper cuts twice as well when wrapped around a rubber pad as it does when you just use your fingers. Old-fashioned sponge-rubber kneeling pads have about the right firmness if Ensolite isn't available.

WB: *Let's say you have a boat whose varnish is in good condition and you're just maintaining her. How do you start out in the spring?*
GF: If the boat's varnish were really in good shape, and all I had to do was reseal her, I'd sand with 120-grit, then 180, and maybe finish off with 220. A final sanding with 220-grit will give you a real nice finish. That's pretty fine; you could almost use that for toilet paper. Then I would give it one finish coat. There would be so many layers on her — all in good shape — that one coat is all she would need.

A boat can go for years without having her brightwork stripped as long as you sand off as much as you put on each year and give her attention when she needs it. Teak brightwork could go maybe ten years without being stripped. Same thing with mahogany.

But mahogany does turn black where water gets into the joints. With some of the better bedding compounds that we have today, though, you could put a boat together with mahogany, and you shouldn't get water in the joints. If you seal the end-grain joints with one of the epoxy glues or 3M 5200 sealer, it would be a long time before they'd ever get water in them.

WB: *Would you go over the brightwork again in the summer?*
GF: Yes, and any varnish work I sand is always with at least two grits. If the boat is going to stay out all winter, I'd do her a third time in the fall. But, you've got to realize that maintenance was basically what my job was all about as a professional skipper. The better the boat was kept, the easier my job was overall. But an owner without a paid hand still has to get a mid-season varnish job.

There's a man here who has a nice yawl, and he's had her stripped and refinished more times than you can shake a stick at. He just won't have her hauled in the middle of the summer to have a coat of varnish put on her topsides, which would be cheaper by far. Many think it's a big, expensive job, but it isn't. Varnish is easy to sand down and apply. It doesn't compare with paint at all.

An idea well worth copying is Giffy's favorite sanding block, which is a piece of kneeling-pad rubber cut to fit a half sheet of sandpaper. It is flexible enough to conform to contoured surfaces like the one shown here, yet has enough firmness to bring almost all the sandpaper's surface into play.

WB: *Is varnish breakdown more than a problem of the finish wearing — in other words, are there problems with brittleness of the finish?*
GF: One thing that kills varnish more than anything else is salt. When your varnish gets covered with salt spray, you have to wipe it off if you want it to last. You don't have to be at a marina with a freshwater hose, either — that's not good for her — just get up early in the morning after a nice dew and take a chamois and wipe her off, or do it some other time with a bucket and a sponge. But get the salt to hell off the brightwork. Salt is what kills varnish, and it's what keeps boatyards busy.

WB: *But let's say you get isolated varnish failure and you want to touch up. How do you blend a touched-up area to the rest of the piece without leaving lap marks?*
GF: You have to varnish the whole thing; the whole toerail, or waterway, or whatever.

WB: *When do you sand the rest of it? When you're feathering-in the first time around?*
GF: Yes. And you have to feather-in after each coat

where it overlaps, or you will get a build-up. You know the funny part about it is that talking about varnishing makes it sound like a great, big job. There's really nothing to it. People always make these jobs out to be a lot more than they are.

Paintwork

WB: *Now let's discuss paint. Your last job as a skipper was on the* Vanitie. *What was an annual paint job for her like?*
GF: Because she was black, she usually needed a complete prime coat each year. But she was well sanded a couple of times beforehand — first with 100-grit and then with 120 with the idea of taking off as much paint as would be put back on. Between the prime and finish coats she'd need only a light sanding with either 150- or 180- grit to get her ready for the final gloss job.

WB: *Do you add anything to your final coat of paint to make it flow better or to help it keep a "wet edge"?*
GF: Penetrol is good stuff to use. Sometimes you have to use brushing liquids like Interlux 333, because when you're doing a gloss boat you'd be surprised how a draft of air can move through a building and make paint bite up. On a good-sized boat, you'll need two or three painters working at once to keep this from happening. Yes, I put Penetrol in paint sometimes to make it flow better.

WB: *How about touching up paint, or repairing damaged and peeling areas?*
GF: Feather it away using that wet-and-dry business — same as with varnish work — and then build it up again. Around a seam, of course, it's more difficult. Any flat or unfair place can be faced out and block sanded, which fixes it so nobody will know it's there. For a facing compound, I like International white trowel cement, not the fast-drying stuff, because it bunches up too much, but the old stuff. And you've got to have the right tool to spread it with. In any average hardware store you could pick out a dozen putty knives, and not one of them will be worth anything. A good putty knife has to be lively.

WB: *If you've feathered a place right down to bare wood, do you prime the wood before you trowel?*
GF: You prime it with flat white paint and let it dry.

WB: *What do you think of so-called sanding surfacers or*

hi-build undercoaters in place of regular flat white paint?
GF: I think there's probably nothing wrong with them at all, except that they're a little messy to work with. They're so chalky that you end up sanding off half of what you put on. On the first coat, you probably want to cut [thin] it a little bit, anyhow, so it will sink in.

WB: *What type of bedding compounds do you use?*
GF: The best thing going is 3M's 5200. It's so easy to use, but you've really got to think out the jobs you're going to do with it. If it's something that has to come apart in a few years, forget it. I'm going to haul my leaking peapod out and put her in the cellar, let her dry out for a week or so, then I'm going to reef out her seams and put a thread of cotton in them and 3M 5200 on top of that. It's good stuff.

WB: *Do you use a cabinet scraper to remove paint as you do varnish?*
GF: Yup, and what you use to sand with depends on what you want out of the job. Sometimes an electric sander will do, but an auto-body file works nice, too; it's nothing but a sanding board with a handle on it.

WB: *How about building up over bare wood for a gloss job?*
GF: I start with, and stay with, flat white. You can put the finish coat right on over the flat. Sometimes people will use a finish paint for the last two coats. But you can go from flat to gloss without a semigloss in between, and it will look just fine.

WB: *Any tricks to lining off?*
GF: Cutting in a waterline or boottop often gives trouble. Usually you'll have trouble if there's not a small saw cut or scribed line to paint to. All wooden boats should have a good scratch in them, and every four to six years you have to re-scratch it as it gets filled up with paint. You can do that either with the bent-over tang of a file that has been ground sharp, or with a dovetail saw. Then if you use a fairly wide brush that will hold quite a bit of paint, you can run right along the edge of the scribed line. It's too bad to see people using masking tape for lining off. It's really not hard to paint a boottop. People just get nervous.

I do my own lettering every year, and it doesn't come out bad, either. I'm nervous at the start, but after l0 or 15 minutes I'm okay. It just takes practice and the right brush and the right paint. I've seen lots of people doing little lettering jobs, and 99 percent of them are working with the wrong brush. You've got to have a good lettering brush. The most difficult part is painting around the outline of the letters.

Professional letterers always amaze me. They can work anywhere and always get good results. I had a new boat once — no lettering at all on her — and had this guy come over to put her name on both bows. The water was rough, and the boat was jumping up and down next to a float. All the painter said was, "Well, I guess I'll have to try it." With that boat pitching and rolling all over the place, he did the most beautiful job! He was so relaxed.

WB: *On maintaining and painting inside the boat — anything special?*
GF: I'd just wash her out real good with a hose every couple of years. I did that job on the *Maruffa*, that big ketch in Southwest Harbor. Her bilges were so bad that we took the garboards off to clean them. We sprayed them with a degreaser called "Gunk." The best way to handle a boat that's real bad, however, is to use a steam cleaner adjusted to make hot water instead of steam. With steam you can't see what you're doing. You can use cold water if you haven't got hot, but it takes longer and you need to scrub more.

WB: *How would you paint over freshly laid deck canvas?*
GF: I would paint it the old-fashioned way; that is, wet it down and paint the first coat right on top of the wet canvas. I use ordinary flat paint for build-up and then gloss for the finish coat, just because I like something that's easy to clean. It's not very good to walk on, though — too slippery.

WB: *Would you say that about three coats of flat, a coat of gloss, and then a coat of gloss every year would do it?*
GF: Sure. I don't want to put too much paint on it, so I sand it right back with 100-grit paper on one of those heavy Rockwell sanders and give it one coat with the gloss. Finer grit isn't needed for canvas decks.

WB: *Why the buildup with flat?*
GF: Well, I want to fill in the weave of the canvas. A lot of people don't want to. That's just a matter of personal taste. Gloss will last, but it won't fill weave at all.

WB: *What if you want the deck to retain the nonskid feature?*
GF: The best thing to do would be to mix your own paint. Take flat and mix it half and half with semi-gloss, just enough to give it a sheen so that it doesn't smudge and get dirty.

WB: *What if you run into canvas decks that are full of cracks?*

GF: You'd be surprised how many of them you could save. I was in a yacht once that had been well maintained, but they put too much paint on her housetop, and it was beginning to crack. I couldn't believe that this boat, which was only eight or nine years old, would need new canvas on her housetop, so I just took a dull cabinet scraper and paint remover and shoved the paint right off. Stripped her right back to the canvas. I never let the paint get built up like that again — sanded it down each time with good, coarse paper. The trick is to sand off as much as you put on. When she was 18 years old, that same housetop looked just like new. A lot of canvas-covered decks and housetops could be saved if the paint were stripped off, but people don't do that. Once the paint cracks and buckles, water gets in, and then in three or four years the canvas is gone, and that's it.

WB: *How about patching canvas?*
GF: The guy who knows a lot more about canvas patching than I do is John Jacques, down at Dutch Wharf Boat Yard in Branford, Connecticut. He's done a lot of canvas patching and does a good job. He uses airplane tape and cement. The tape, which is thin and very strong, is stuck on top of the canvas with a high-grade lacquer. Afterwards it gets troweled out. Does a beautiful job.

Another way to make a patch is with a strip of canvas slid under the crack and smeared over with epoxy. It doesn't look too bad. You can go to some extra trouble to feather and face it so that it won't be seen at all. The advantage of the aircraft tape is that it's thinner than a canvas patch

WB: *What do you think of nonskid canvas decks?*
GF: Well, I don't like nonskid, because it just doesn't clean up well. I'd rather fall and crack my head. I realize a nonskid deck is safer, but it's just one of those things that doesn't set well with me. One of the pleasures of using my own boat is getting up in the morning and cleaning up for a half hour or so. I can't stand something you can't clean up. If you do use a nonskid surfacing agent, the secret is to put on two coats. Put the nonskid in the first coat and use just plain paint in the second one. What this does is give enough grit sticking through the surface so you don't slip, but yet you can clean it up. Red MacAllister from Cranberry Isle taught me that.

WB: *What's your theory for laying canvas over a wooden deck? There seem to be a number of workable ways.*
GF: One old method is just to lay the canvas dry. Of course, you have to sand down the surface, fill all the holes so you have a nice, smooth surface, paint

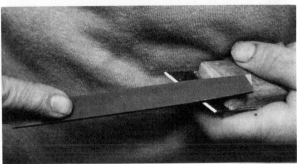

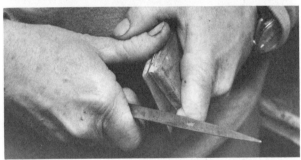

The three basic steps in sharpening a cabinet scraper are shown here. The first two involve the use of a flat mill file. The old edge is filed off from the unbeveled side. The scraper blade is resharpened by filing until its edge won't reflect light and feels sharp to the touch. A burnisher of hardened steel takes over for the third operation, which is to roll over the sharpened edge. While there are more-elaborate ways to sharpen one of these tools, most take much more time and require the use of whetstones and a bench vise. Giffy's method is simple and quick, and is perfectly adequate for the work asked of it.

on a couple of coats of flat white paint and let it dry. The theory here is that the boat can work independently beneath the canvas. If the canvas is bedded down, or cemented, some places will become real tight, and others won't. Then it's going to crack and let go.

WB: *How do you handle joints in canvas where you can't make it in one piece and have to butt two pieces together?*
GF: I've always made it in one piece. I did a housetop on a boat that was all of 40 feet long and 12 feet wide, and there was no seam in the canvas. We got it on special order. If you have to use more than one piece, the best thing to do would be to stitch the pieces together. Of course, you could double the

cloth over and make an interlocking seam shown in a number of books, but that involves visible tacks along the edge, so I think it's much better to stitch them together as one piece before the canvas is laid.

There's always a problem when you come up against a trunk cabin. There's not much you can do there except put a scotia molding on it, being careful to back out that molding to make room for the canvas and bedding compound behind it. You have to have it tight on the top and bottom edges.

WB: *How would you treat a plain teak deck that doesn't have varnish on it?*
GF: If cost were a consideration, I'd probably put Deks Olje on it. I'd probably do something like that just because of the expense of keeping teak.

WB: *What grit sandpaper would you use on a teak deck?*
GF: I'd use 80-grit wet to smooth up a very coarse deck.

WB: *Have you ever used Penta-Var?*
GF: Oh yes. In fact, I think I was the very first guy that ever brought Penta-Var here. I got it from Seattle. It's like a teak oil — thinner than Deks Olje. It penetrates and also acts as a sealer. I'm really old-fashioned, though. If I were doing a really nice yacht, I'd want the teak decks scrubbed without any finish on them at all. I would use Scotchbrite pads to scrub them with and any kind of water, salt or fresh, along with Joy or some other detergent. Bleach is bad for the wood, though, I think.

WB: *Have you had any experience with pine decks, like those used on the big Herreshoff schooners, for example?*
GF: They were scrubbed each morning with seawater before the brightwork was chamoised off. We used to start at six in the morning. When I was on *Valkyrie*, about 1947, her pine deck had all kinds of hollows in it where it had been scrubbed so much. Pine decks were usually scrubbed with salt water and either bronze wool or just a deck scrubbing brush. People lose sight of what yachting used to be like. For instance, 40 years ago, there used to be a lot of Q-boats and P-boats around here, and they all had year-round skippers on them. Boy, if you walked on deck with anything but your stocking feet, they'd kill you. They were beautifully built and kept up like a million bucks.

I know few people today who can afford paid hands aboard their yachts, and that's not the point, anyway. The fact is, you get out of your boat exactly what you put into her. Those hours of work give far more hours of pleasure. If you put nothing in, you're likely to get nothing out.